WHEN MEN & MOUNTAINS MEET

H. W. TILMAN

Cane suspension bridge, Sikkim type, bamboo footrail, no circular supports

WHEN MEN & MOUNTAINS MEET

H. W. TILMAN

TILMAN

First published 1946 by Cambridge University Press
This edition published 2016 by Tilman Books
www.tilmanbooks.com
a joint venture by
Lodestar Books www.lodestarbooks.com
and Vertebrate Publishing www.v-publishing.co.uk

Original text copyright © Simon Heyworth Davis 1946
Additional material copyright © the contributors 2016

Cover design by Jane Beagley
Vertebrate Graphics Ltd. www.v-graphics.co.uk

Lodestar Books has asserted their right
to be identified as the Editor of this Work

Series editor Dick Wynne
Series researcher Bob Comlay

The publisher has made reasonable effort to locate
the holders of copyright in the illustrations in this book,
and will be pleased to hear from them regarding
correct attribution in future editions

All rights reserved

A CIP catalogue record for this book
is available from the British Library

ISBN 978-1-909461-22-2

Typeset in Baskerville from Storm Type Foundry
Printed and bound by Pulsio, Bulgaria
All papers used by Tilman Books are sourced responsibly

Contents

	Foreword – *Simon Yates*	9
	Preface	11
	PART ONE: PEACETIME	
I	The Assam Himalaya	15
II	The Approach	22
III	Our Troubles Begin	33
IV	Base Camp and Fever	48
V	Retreat	57
VI	The Zemu Gap—Failure	69
VII	The Zemu Gap—Success	85
	PART TWO: WARTIME	
VIII	Three Climbs in Wartime	105
IX	Albania	135
X	The Italians Collapse, The Germans Arrive	151
XI	Winter	166
XII	The Tide Turns	176
XIII	Arrival in North Italy	187
XIV	With the Gramsci Brigade	197
XV	The Nino Nannetti Division	210
XVI	The Belluno Division	226
XVII	At Zone H.Q.—The Liberation of Belluno	240

Photographs

Cane suspension bridge, Sikkim type	2
Sherchokpa porters	26
Mönba porters	26
Houses in Rahung	29
Rahung	29
Suspension bridge, Assam type	31
Tembang Monastery	34
Along ridge leading to Poshing La	37
Tembang porters (Mönba)	39
Tembang porter taking snuff	39
Tembang porter on track to Poshing La	42
Crossing the Tse La	44
Base Camp at shepherds' hut in Gorjo Chu	44
Gori Chen from the south side of Gorjo Chu	46
Looking up the Gorjo Chu towards 'Corner' Camp	51
Gori Chen from above Lap	54
The performing 'yak' at the Rupa 'tamasha'	63
Mani wall and chorten, Sikkim	70
The ex-Lama from Yoksam monastery	73
Sikkimese—a lama on the right	73
A Lepcha from Sikkim	76
Head of Tongshyong Glacier	79
Looking down the Tongshyong Glacier	82
Sherpas moving down Tongshyong	82
Camp by the boulder in the Parek Chu	87
Pandim from the north-east	90
Zemu Gap from across Tongshyong Glacier	95
Lower ice fall and Zemu Gap beyond	98
Ruins of Hatra	113
Hatra: Entrance to Temple of the Sun	113
Inside Temple of the Sun	115
Inside Temple of the Sun	115
Rock carvings in the grotto, Tak i Bostan	118

Rock carvings in the grotto, Tak i Bostan	118
Rock carvings: Chosroes in armour mounted	121
The pool and spring, Tak i Bostan	121
On the summit ridge, Bisitun	124
Bisitun summit ridge	124
Old Turkish pack bridge, south Albania	139
House in Shepr used as headquarters	145
Typical hill country, southern Albania	145
Partisan leaders outside H.Q., Shepr	147
Two Albanian partisans	147
Hakmarrje, or Vengeance Battalion	148
Albanian girl partisans	148
Some L.N.C. leaders	155
Shefket Pezi and author in Permet	155
Dolomite scenery	230
Belluno Zone H.Q.	243
Two partisans in Belluno	243
Outside the Prefettura Belluno	246
Outside the Prefettura Belluno	246
Belluno Piazza and the Palace of the Prefettura	251
Belluno Prefettura	251

Maps

1	Sketch map to illustrate Assam Himalaya	14
2	Sketch map of Sikkim: Zemu Gap and Lachsi journeys	68
3	General map of Albania	137
4	Sketch map to illustrate south Albania	152
5	Sketch map of northern Italy to illustrate Belluno area	186

Foreword

Simon Yates

THERE ARE FEW PEOPLE who truly deserve the title 'legendary', but Harold William Tilman certainly does, being both one of the greatest mountaineer-explorers of his time and arguably the best expedition writer ever. However, these two accolades barely scratch the surface of Tilman's very busy life.

Bill Tilman started his adult life by serving as an artillery officer on the Western Front in the First World War, while still a teenager. After the war, he went to Kenya and set up his own flax and coffee plantation—hacked by hand from the forest. There he met fellow plantation owner Eric Shipton and they made the first ascents of the twin summits of Mount Kenya, as one of their opening acts in what would become one of the most celebrated partnerships in the history of mountaineering. When he came to leave Africa, rather than catch the train to Mombasa to board a ship home, he cycled 3000 miles to the West African coast and embarked there; at the time there were barely any roads.

From 1934 through to 1950, Tilman made a series of expeditions to the Himalaya for which, as a mountaineer, he is best known. These included two trips to Mount Everest, and the most notable of his climbing achievements, the first ascent of Nanda Devi in 1936, which remained the highest peak climbed until the French ascent of Annapurna in 1950. In 1937, Tilman's first book *Snow on the Equator* was published, and would be followed by six other mountain-travel books that detail this period. He travelled the length and breadth of the Himalayan chain during this time, as much interested in the exploration of new mountain terrain as in bagging peaks. Tilman and Shipton were also admired for the style of their expeditions, trying to go as lightweight as possible and living off what was available locally. In an era that was characterised by large expeditions with an even larger logistical supply chain, this was very innovative and not adopted as the norm until decades later.

Tilman's mountaineering explorations were rather rudely interrupted by the Second World War and as a reserve officer he soon found himself back in uniform—this time as a middle-aged man. He served in France, Iraq, the Western Desert and then, in the latter part of the war, with partisans in Albania and Northern Italy. *When Men & Mountains Meet* documents his wartime experiences as well as a rather disastrous trip to Assam before the war began. Although the mountaineering achievements in this volume are negligible, this is my favourite Tilman book. Why? I feel that in the wartime section of the book we learn more about Tilman's character as he is plunged into circumstances that are not of his own choosing. What shines through is his stoic sense of duty—to his country, the cause of freedom, and the people under his command; and what is also very apparent is his incredible bravery.

In 1950, Tilman decided that his best days as a mountaineer were over, and turned his focus instead to sailing and mountain exploration, which continued until his death in 1977. He documented this period in a further eight sailing-mountaineering books, which became as cherished by sailors as his previous books were by mountaineers. Tilman was lost at sea in the South Atlantic as an eighty-year-old under circumstances that were never explained. In many ways, it was a fitting end to the man and the life he lived.

In an age obsessed with celebrity, where every banal action is recorded on social media, Tilman comes along as a welcome antidote—his lifetime of extraordinary adventure and achievement recorded in sparse prose, laced with gentle irony, dry humour and timely quotation. Some people of this age might argue that he comes across as reserved, or even stiff-upper-lipped, but those willing or able to tune into his way of expression will soon realise that this is not so. Tilman was a man who lived his long and productive life with humanity, and told his remarkable story with humility.

I hope you enjoy *When Men & Mountains Meet*.

Simon Yates
July 2015

Preface

IN NEARLY HALF THIS BOOK—namely, the chapters dealing with Albania and Italy—there is no mountaineering, but the mountains are there nevertheless. It was fitting, and in accord with tradition, that those who cherished the spark of freedom and finally fanned it to a blaze should have lived for the most part in the mountains of those mountainous countries. In order to forestall an obvious criticism I should like to point out that it is this part only of the book which prompted and, in my opinion, justified the choice of Blake's lines from which the title is taken.

My grateful thanks are due to Dr R. J. Perring of Ryton for his great help in revising the first draft. I am also indebted to H. Swire's book, *Albania: The Rise of a Kingdom*, for some facts about that country.

H.W. T.
December 1945

PART ONE

Peacetime

Map 1: Sketch map to illustrate Assam Himalaya

CHAPTER I

THE ASSAM HIMALAYA

◆

THE TOTAL LENGTH OF THE GREAT Himalayan chain from Nanga Parbat in the west to Namcha Barwa in the east is some 1500 miles. Of this the Assam Himalaya, as defined by Burrard and Hayden in their standard work, *Sketch of the Geography and Geology of the Himalaya*, occupy about 450 miles. These, however, include the Himalaya north of Bhutan; if we consider only that part of the chain between Assam and Tibet the length is about 250 miles.

Of all the Himalaya these are the least known, and it is not difficult to understand the reason. From the Assam-Bhutan frontier for a distance of 250 miles eastwards to the Brahmaputra valley there is only one way over the Himalaya to Tibet, or even as far as the main range, and the existence of this route was not even suspected until the opening years of the present century. Between the last tea gardens and rice fields of Assam and the crest of the Himalaya is a wide belt of heavily forested foothills inhabited for the most part by savage tribes—Miji Akas, Silung Abors, Daflas. The reputation of these tribes, the difficult country, and an extremely heavy rainfall, discouraged closer inquiry until it was gradually realised that between the Bhutan-Assam frontier and the Bhareli river, a distance of some forty miles, the country was not occupied by violent men inimical to strangers, but by peaceful tribes allied to the Bhutanese called Mönba, Sherchokpa, and others. Through the interest and exploration of various Political Officers from Assam, this corridor, known as Mönyul, was slowly opened up. Through it have passed travellers like Col. F. M. Bailey and Major H. T. Morshead in 1913 and Kingdon-Ward in 1935 and 1938.

The journey of Bailey and Morshead in 1913 was extremely interesting, for it cleared up one of the outstanding problems of Asiatic exploration. It was only in 1912 that the discovery of Namcha Barwa by Morshead and the determination of its height as 25,445 ft. had surprised the geographers, who had thought that there could be no peaks above 20,000 ft. north of Assam. A year later Morshead and Bailey discovered the great gorge between Namcha Barwa and Gyala Peri, 23,460 ft., by which the Tsangpo forces its way through the Himalaya to become the Dihang and later the Brahmaputra of Assam. The question of where the Tsangpo flowed after leaving Tibet was the most interesting problem of Asiatic exploration in the last decades of the nineteenth century. Several well-known 'pundits', native explorers and surveyors employed by the Survey of India, had been engaged on its solution. Three of the most famous were Nain Singh, A.K., and Kinthup. In 1884 Kinthup was dispatched from India to Tibet with orders to cast marked logs of wood into the waters of the Tsangpo in the hope that they might be recovered in the Brahmaputra later on. This rather fond hope came to nothing.

It is interesting to note that the discovery of a great peak, or rather two great peaks with only fourteen miles between them, at the point where the Tsangpo breaks through to the plains, confirmed a conjecture of Burrard and Hayden who, in the first edition of their book, 1907, wrote: 'The Sutlej in issuing from Tibet pierces the border range of mountains within four and a half miles of Leo Pargial, the highest peak of its region; the Indus when turning the great Himalayan range passes within fourteen miles of Nanga Parbat, the highest point of the Punjab Himalaya; the Hunza river cuts through the Kailas range within nine miles of Rakaposhi, the supreme point of the range. It will form an interesting problem for investigation whether the Brahmaputra of Tibet has cut its passage across the Himalaya near a point of maximum elevation.'

In their journey in 1913 Bailey and Morshead entered Tibet from Assam by following the course of the Dihang until they were stopped by the gorge east of Namcha Barwa. By a detour to the north they rejoined the river, the Tsangpo as it is called in Tibet, and followed it down past Namcha Barwa to a point less than thirty miles from the place at which they had left it. After this they moved west along the Tibetan side of the Himalaya and returned to Assam by the Mönyul corridor route.

In 1935 and again in 1938 Kingdon-Ward travelled extensively in Mönyul and on the Tibetan side of the Assam Himalaya bringing back many new plants and seeds and much new geographical knowledge.

In 1934 and 1936 Messrs Ludlow and Sherriff, starting from Bhutan, travelled through Mönyul into south-eastern Tibet, also collecting plants and seeds.

The position then in 1939 was, that of the mountains themselves little or nothing was known except that the major peaks, that is, those over 20,000 ft., had been fixed trigonometrically from the plains of Assam. Even the Assam-Tibet frontier had not been defined. It was assumed that it followed the crest line of the main range until in 1912 it was discovered that Mönyul, which is south of the Himalaya, was being administered by Tibetans. In 1913, by some arrangement between the Governments concerned, all the districts south of the Himalaya were ceded to India, but nothing was done to administer the ceded territory, which remained, until 1939 at least, to all intents Tibetan.

Just to the east of the Mönyul corridor, or 'Tibetan Enclave' as it might be called, lies a group of some dozen peaks over 20,000 ft. Only four bear names, which are all Tibetan in origin: Gori Chen 21,450 ft., Kangdu 23,260 ft., Chiumo 22,760 ft., and Nayegi Kansang 23,120 ft. These were the mountains which I hoped to explore, and some of which I hoped to climb. Nothing is known of them and nothing has been written about them, for unlike many other parts of the Himalaya they have no place in the religious history of India. No temples or shrines adorn the banks of their rivers, no pilgrims visit them, no traditions enrich them.

I like to think I can see as far through a brick wall as most people, and in the latter part of 1938 it seemed clear to me, as to many others, that war was inevitable. This affected my plans for 1939. Shipton was returning to the Karakoram to continue the work which we had begun in 1937, and I should very much have liked to join him. But we should be extremely isolated, almost beyond recall in fact, and Shipton's plans necessitated staying out the following winter. I was not so abandoned yet as to consider being beyond recall an advantage. Moreover, the War Office, after twenty years of deep thought, had just remembered they had a Reserve of Officers, of which I was one, and had announced a scheme for their training. I decided therefore that by August 1939 I must be home. This ruled out the Karakoram, and my choice fell upon the Assam Himalaya as being the most accessible and the least known region for exploration.

This would be my sixth visit to the Himalaya, and though occasionally I had qualms about such indulgence, I had so far managed to stifle them without any severe struggle. The appetite grows as it is fed. Like the desire for drink or drugs, the craving for mountains is not easily overcome, but a mountaineering debauch, such as six months in the Himalaya, is followed by no remorse. Should such a feeling arise then one may echo Omar's *cri de cœur*,

> Indeed, indeed, Repentance oft before
> I swore—but was I sober when I swore?

Having once tasted the pleasure of living in high solitary places with a few like spirits, European or Sherpa, I could not give it up. The prospect of what is euphemistically termed 'settling down', like mud to the bottom of a pond, might perhaps be faced when it became inevitable, but not yet awhile. Time enough for that when the hardships common to mountain travel—the carrying of heavy loads, the early morning starts, living or starving on the country—were no longer courted or at any rate suffered gladly.

Having fixed upon the Assam Himalaya as my objective, I had to decide how to get there and what to do there. Obviously the greatest prize for a mountaineer was Namcha Barwa, and a very useful job could be done making a reconnaissance with a view to climbing it another year. It would be necessary to get permission to enter Tibet, but even if one were not allowed to go to Namcha Barwa, the best approach to the Gori Chen group, my second string, was from the Tibetan side. Indeed, when these tentative plans were made on the way back from Everest in July 1938 I was not aware of any other way.

Passport difficulties are not confined to what we call the civilised world. For some of the lesser known parts of Asia entrance is even more troublesome; Tibet is a case in point. Most of the stock of good will of the Tibetan Government as well as the patience of the Indian Government in evoking it is used up by the Mount Everest expeditions. A favoured few can sometimes get in by using the direct-approach method, and one or two omit all formalities and just go in, presenting the Tibetans with a *fait accompli*. The difficulty about this is that if the Tibetan authorities resent this intrusion, the invader is easily checkmated by the local headman who will be told to refuse his unwelcome guest all means of transport. Exceptions have been made. On the way back from Mount Everest in July 1938 I met at Tangu in north Sikkim a party of German scientists led by a Dr Schaefer. They were officially working in Sikkim, but by a direct approach to a high official from Lhasa, who happened then to be just on the other side of the border, they were invited into Tibet where they spent several months. Strange stories of their behaviour were current when I came across them again in a train in India the following July. They must have got home just in time.

For the necessary permission I applied to Mr B.J. Gould (now Sir Basil Gould), British Resident in Sikkim. He had recently been to Lhasa on an official visit and was as well liked by the Tibetans as by the numerous British mountaineers whom he had helped so often. He had been instrumental in obtaining permission for the last two Mount Everest attempts. At that time he was at Yatung in the Chumbi valley, for which place I started immediately on reaching Gangtok, the capital of Sikkim. It is a two-day march with a rise of 2000 ft. to the Natu La (14,000 ft.). Having finished my business I returned to Gangtok in one day, as I was pressed for time, taking fifteen and a half hours for the forty-three miles including halts. I mention this to show that though men coming off Mount Everest are usually in very poor condition, often with dilated hearts, recovery does not take long.

Mr Gould was not very hopeful about either permission for my own journey or for another Mount Everest attempt. Apparently some emphasis had been laid on the fact that 1938 was to be the last time we should ask, and a dispute over the Tibet-Assam boundary (Mönyul as mentioned above) was in progress.

This setback made it essential to visit Shillong, the pleasant hill capital of Assam, 5000 ft. up, where Sir Robert Reid, then the Governor, afforded all possible help. In northern Assam the frontier tracts are what are called Excluded Areas. The one with which I was concerned was the Balipara Frontier Tract which is administered by a Political Officer drawn from the Assam Police who is directly responsible to the Governor. The tract is divided by an 'Inner Line' into administered and unadministered territory, of which the latter is by far the larger portion. The administered territory corresponds roughly to the short strip of plain between the Brahmaputra and the foothills; the unadministered comprises all that from the foothills to the Tibetan border which is supposed to follow the MacMahon line of 1914. The tribes to the north of the Inner Line, Daflas, Akas and Miris, are primitive people with no desire to respond to the soothing influences of civilisation. They receive subsidies contingent on their good behaviour, and for many years they have given us no trouble. Occasionally the Political Officer has to visit them (with a strong escort) to settle disputes, generally by mild persuasion, sometimes by force. The hill tribes are allowed to cross the Inner Line for peaceful purposes, trade or work, but no plainsmen may cross it without a special permit. Few, of course, wish to. As Mr Churchill once remarked when questioned about the efficacy of anti-shark measures in the Pacific, that 'H.M. Government was entirely opposed to sharks', so the tribesmen of those parts are entirely opposed to strangers.

The H.Q. of the Political Officer for the Balipara Frontier Tract was at Charduar, twenty miles north of the Brahmaputra. Permission to cross the Inner Line and to proceed to the Gori Chen area on the Tibetan border was readily obtained, and the Political Officer promised assistance in finding the necessary porters for the first stage of the journey.

All therefore was set for the 1939 campaign; it remained to decide what form this should take. Should it be mountaineering alone, or should I try to bring back something more substantial than a feeling of 'something attempted, something done' by collecting enough data for the making of a map? Would this necessarily add to the conviction, of which I was already assured, that the time had been well spent? Hitherto I had played no very active part in the more technical side of the three expeditions in which map-making had been the main object; in fact, I had on occasion regarded these activities rather as a benign but not too patient uncle might regard his nephews playing trains on the table on which he was shortly expecting his lunch.

Of course, as Lord Conway said, 'in all high mountain climbing there is an element of exploration'; and since the Gori Chen group was as yet unvisited this element would be considerable. But nowadays the explorer who brings his modest offering to the temple of science (may its worshippers increase) in the form of a dirty, illegible sketch, or an incoherent verbal description, is thought a little uncouth. Shipton's whole-hearted conversion to the side of the big battalions was of long standing; and I might have to forgo my admiring sympathy with Mummery, one of my heroes, who in the preface to his *Climbs in the Alps and Caucasus* expressed himself thus: 'I fear no contributions to science, or topography, or learning of any sort are to be found sandwiched in between the story of crags or seracs, of driving storm or perfect weather. To tell the truth, I have only the vaguest idea about theodolites, and as for plane tables, their very name is an abomination. To those who think with me, who regard mountaineering as unmixed play, these pages are alone addressed.' If you can call mountaineering an act of violence, which I think you can, then Mummery's forcibly expressed philosophy is greatly strengthened by a dictum of G. K. Chesterton (another of my heroes), who was admittedly no mountaineer, but who certainly had the root of the matter in him when he wrote: 'Almost any act of violence can be forgiven on this strict condition—that it is of no use at all to anybody. If the aggressor (or mountaineer) gets anything out of it, then it is quite unpardonable. It is damned by the least hint of utility or profit.'

This time I had to reckon with another factor which forbade my taking such a detached view as formerly about the 'scientific' side of an expedition. In the absence of a suitable companion I proposed going alone with a few Sherpa porters. Who they would be I could not tell, so that I might easily find when I arrived that I was unable to do as much climbing as I had hoped. Moreover, without a companion to act as stimulant or counter-irritant it would be an advantage to have something to occupy the mind in the many hours sometimes necessarily spent in camp. On a long expedition the active mind becomes dull, the dull becomes cataleptic. I decided, therefore, to modify my high principles and attempt a modest survey with one of Mummery's abominations, a plane table—but not too much zeal.

CHAPTER II

THE APPROACH

◆

I REACHED DARJEELING on 5 April 1939 to collect my Sherpas. Owing to the many expeditions in the field that year, all of which had bespoken their porters early, good men were hard to come by. There were two German parties, an American party bound for K2, a Polish party going to Nanda Devi East (which they climbed), and Shipton's Karakoram party. Under the Hitler regime German mountaineers were extremely active in the Himalaya. They spent a lot of time and money and lost many climbers and porters, sometimes through bad luck, more often, perhaps, through bad judgment. To lose porters is a heinous offence, and, in my opinion, their use of an aeroplane for dropping stores to their camps on Nanga Parbat deserved a place in the same category.

Our centre of operations was a long way from the starting point. The route led through villages where porters were an unknown quantity, into a region where we could obtain nothing once we had arrived. I therefore had to cut to a minimum the number of mouths to be fed. I took three of the few porters available: Wangdi Norbu, an oldish but very capable and experienced man, who had been to Kamet with Smythe and also to Mount Everest in 1933; Nukku Sherpa, a young and very active porter, who had been with us in the Karakoram in 1937 and to Mount Everest in 1936 and 1938; Thundu, a dark horse, with no major expeditions to his credit, but recommended by the other two.

In 1939 the Himalayan Club instituted a system of grading porters. The graded men were to be called 'Tigers', a name which is not very suitable but one which has stuck owing to having been used of the 1924 Mount Everest porters who went highest. Certainly there are two qualities which the Sherpa shares with the tiger, strength and courage, but he is not a fighting man like his compatriot the Ghurka. The chosen men, the choice being based on the recommendation of leaders of expeditions, had a badge of a tiger's head and were entitled to eight annas a day more than other porters for work above the snowline. In 1939 there were a dozen of them, of whom Wangdi was one.

Travelling by rail from Silliguri on the eastern Bengal line we reached Rangapara on the north side of the Brahmaputra Valley on 8 April where we were met by Capt. Lightfoot, the Political Officer, and taken to Charduar by car. Charduar is a small post on the Inner Line consisting only of the Political Officer's bungalow and a few native houses and shops. A detachment of the Assam Rifles is stationed at Lokra on the Bhareli river two miles away, but the nearest place of any importance is Tezpur on the Brahmaputra, twenty-one miles away by an earth road. The banks of the great river for thirty miles back are flat and covered with tea gardens and rice fields. It is less than 400 ft. above sea-level here; the climate, except in the short winter season, is hot and steamy, and the rainfall about 100 in. Beyond the last tea garden to the north is the beginning of the dense forest running up into the hills. Presumably the forest at one time extended farther south until cleared to make room for tea gardens; for it is upon the 'red bank', which was old forest land, that most of the gardens are planted. Very few, and those inferior, are found on the grass land near the Brahmaputra where the soil is alluvial, light and sandy.

For the next two days we packed our stuff into suitable loads, bought rice and some oddments in Tezpur, and collected 600 silver rupees for paying the local porters. One evening we went down to the Bhareli river to fish. It was a magnificent stretch of water whose sources I hoped soon to see far to the north in the glaciers of Gori Chen. Across the river was the Forest Reserve, the home of elephant and rhinoceros. In the north lay the heavily forested foothills, the territory of the Miji Aka who, according to Lightfoot, had not yet entirely given up raiding the plains for slaves.

On the wireless came news of the Italian invasion of Albania and the mobilisation of the Italian fleet. I felt I ought to be going the other way, but I hardened my heart and arranged to leave on the 11th. Lightfoot promised to send a runner if war started.

Two bullock carts left early with our fifteen loads for the camping ground, known as Tiger Flat, at the edge of the plains and the beginning of the foothills, twenty-five miles away. There we were to pick up twenty-five men of Lightfoot's porter corps, Nepalese, whom he was good enough to lend. The extra ten were for carrying food for the others because the country over which we had to travel for the first five marches is uninhabited at this season. We left after lunch in a car which took us as far as the Belsiri river which was unbridged. Farewells were said, we took to our feet, and once more turned our backs on the civilised world.

At five o'clock we reached Tiger Flat, a clearing on the edge of the forest. Close by there was another European in camp, a Game Warden. The camp was evidently semi-permanent. Sweet peas were growing outside a grass hut, three elephants (tame ones) were tethered hard by, and the Game Warden himself was standing by the bank of a small river feeding the fish which were apparently also tame. Over a drink the local picture was painted for me by my host who seemed as tough a denizen of the forest as the elephant and rhino, whose welfare was his care. From him I received a nicely balanced mixture of hope and fear. Mosquitoes were the first forest denizens about which I sought information. As soon as we had reached Charduar I had begun administering prophylactic doses of quinine to the three Sherpas and myself. Quinine, though a sovereign remedy, could not compare as a prophylactic with the modern drug mepacrine. We had only a bottle of 100 quinine tablets with us, as I assumed we should not be in malarious country for more than two nights; and since it was the tail end of an unusually dry season I imagined there would be few mosquitoes about. My fears were laughed at by my informant. Admittedly, there were a few mosquitoes, but they were a harmless variety, and he had forgotten how long it was since he had been troubled with malaria.

The talk then turned not unnaturally to elephants; for the whole foreground as we sat outside the tent was occupied by three vast backsides adorned with ridiculous little tails. One of them was a cow in season, and it seemed that the previous night a rogue elephant who haunted the vicinity had caused considerable panic by his efforts to make her closer acquaintance. Shots had been fired without effect. 'Elephants were more numerous than mosquitoes. Bhotia traders going north with caravans of grain and salt had been killed by elephants, greedy for a concentrated meal of grain seasoned with salt in place of their everyday unseasoned bark and branches. If I had any grain or salt with me it would be advisable to bury it deep or plant it high in a tree.

Otherwise if they winded it we should be raided for a certainty. If I had an elephant rifle (I had a .22) I should sleep with it by my side with both barrels loaded.'

It was getting dark, so hastily drinking as much whisky as politeness allowed, I made my excuses and hastened back to camp, uneasy in mind, ears well cocked, seeing elephants behind every tree as I went. We had, of course, a number of loads of rice and atta, also some salt, but I did not fancy starting to bury it at that time of night with the help of four ice-axes, and most of the trees were of the straight-boiled, high-branching variety. However, I thoughtfully passed the news on to the Sherpas so that I should not be the only one to spend an anxious night, and after reconnoitring a route up the only likely looking tree in the neighbourhood I turned in.

Sure enough it was a wretched night—due solely to mosquitoes. I comforted myself with the thought that as the country was not inhabited they were not likely to be infected with malaria, forgetting a standing camp which Lightfoot's porter corps had not far away, and the frequent passage of natives up and down the road. Rising early, after a night of heat and bites, I was surprised to find the Nepalese coolies had already gone leaving behind most of the loads. I was assured an elephant would come for these, and sure enough, like a rabbit out of a hat, a great mountain of wrinkled flesh presently walked into the clearing, dragging after it by its trunk a great length of chain stout enough for a ship's cable. A wizened little anatomy of a man climbed up its foreleg to make fast on its back a vast padded mat such as you see in gymnasiums, and then the loads were passed up and built into a neat pile. Wangdi and I exchanged astonished glances as the twelfth sixty-pound load went up, followed by two more men and the fifty-odd feet of mooring chain. Whereupon practically the whole of our outfit swayed off into the forest borne upon that one capable back. Here at last was the solution to all transport problems. Yaks, zos, goats, mules, ponies, donkeys, men might be all very well for picnics, but for serious business let us have elephants. It was with fresh respect for Hannibal that I followed admiringly in the wake of that ludicrous, swaying rump, stepping out at a good four miles an hour in the effort to keep pace.

Sherchokpa porters; the straw pork-pie hat has no crown

Mönba porters; three young men on right, two girls on left

Marching through forest, climbing hardly at all, we camped on a shelf above a wide stony river bed near a village of grass huts called Doimara. There was no sign of life, no pigs rooted, and no dogs barked. I thought at first that some frightful plague had wiped everyone out or that the Miji Akas had been doing business in a big way, but a Tibetan agent from the porter corps camp, who had come with us for the day, told me that Doimara was only occupied during the winter months. Everyone had retired to his mountain village before the onset of the rainy season. Achoong, the Tibetan, translated our 'purwana' (passport) into Sherchokpa for the benefit of the raja of Rupa three marches on. I bathed in a pool where I was astonished to see on the cliff four feet above the deep water a well-carved Buddha. There were fewer mosquitoes here, though we were still less than a thousand feet up, but in the daytime there was a new amusement in the form of blister flies or 'dimdams'. Every bite resulted in a blood blister with which our hands were soon covered. The coolies used some kind of oil, citronella I think, with effect.

Beyond this we climbed steadily, another day's march sufficing to put us beyond the reach of dimdams and mosquitoes. The porter corps marched well in a most military manner, signals for the regulation halts being given by whistle, a procedure which amused the Sherpas, who prefer to take their halts according to their inclination and the amenities of the place. On the fifth day we started early and began climbing in earnest. We soon left the maples, oaks and birch behind, and, nearing the top of the pass, the Bompu La (*c.* 9000 ft.), entered rhododendrons and bamboo through which ran many old elephant trails. While waiting for the porters to come up I climbed trees in the hope of seeing the snows, but there was too much haze. On the north side pines and juniper appeared almost at once, but unlike the trees of the dense rain-forest of the south were neither festooned with moss nor half-buried in undergrowth. We descended a lovely valley through blue pines and grassy glades to camp on a flat, shaded, grassy spur—an ideal camp site—half a mile from the Sherchokpa village of Rupa. The country reminded me of Garhwal, but the houses were of wood like Swiss chalets: the heavy beams supporting the roof were morticed to the uprights, the projecting piece being heavily notched. The gable end was decorated with a black and white machicolated pattern, and from it hung something very like a carved phallus with hairs tied to it.

Rupa was a poor, ugly, dirty village, and the Sherchokpa inhabitants were fully in keeping with it. Who they are it is not easy to say. They speak a language of their own, but they are very similar to the Mönba of the rest of Mönyul. Maize is the principal crop, but, as they do not irrigate, all crops seemed light. After I had waited in vain all afternoon for the so-called raja, Tsari Bhutia, to appear, Mahomet had to go to the mountain. I found him a shifty-looking fellow who claimed not to understand Wangdi when he spoke Tibetan, but he promised to have porters by the following evening to take us to Rahung, two marches away, at eight annas a day. The raja returned my visit in the evening bringing with him a chicken and six eggs, for which I gave him snuff and a tablet of quinine—the exchange rate seemed to be in our favour. Many of the natives were suffering from malaria which they presumably contract in villages like Doimara where they spend half the year.

The next day was a holiday. I was still very uneasy at having started at all, and half hoped that a runner from Lightfoot would catch us before we went on, bringing definite news of war or peace. I realised that I would be lucky to get any mail beyond this, for it would be passed from village to village. The Government porters were going back to-morrow (they were then busy devouring a goat I had bought them for 2½ rupees), so having written some letters I wandered down to the river, bathed, and watched some men fishing with long bamboo poles. They used a bait like a piece of carrot, and in place of a hook a running noose on the line just above the bait. I can commend this method to those who find fishing with a hook too easy; several big bronze-coloured fish had a go at the 'carrot' but all escaped. There was the usual cane bridge over the river with the less usual feature of a complete cane-ring support, which made the crossing much easier than did the rope bridges of Sikkim and Ladakh which have only a handrail. In the evening the raja took snuff with me again and warned us of the 'badmash' below the Himalaya, meaning presumably the Abors or possibly the abominable Snowmen.

We left on the 17th. Instead of our well-disciplined porter corps marching to the sound of the whistle, we were accompanied by eight

Houses in Rahung

Rahung; house and chorten in foreground;
Wangdi Norbu is in centre in slacks

men armed with bows and arrows, four women whose privilege it was to carry the heavier loads, and three small boys aged about eight, who nevertheless carried a full sixty pounds and smoked their bamboo pipes like the men. Passing through Rupa where Tibetan influence was evident from the number of mani walls and chortens, we followed a northern tributary of the Tenga river in whose valley Rupa lies. This lesser valley, the Dikong Ko, leads up to the Bomdi La (9000 ft.) which we had to cross. After two hours' march the pines gave place to rain-forest, trees coated with moss, and everywhere ferns and flowering shrubs.

At our first halt before entering the rain-forest there were some cattle, and one strange-looking beast, marked black and white, like a Frisian, with a fine head. They called it 'guru' and I took it to be a domesticated wild ox allied to the gaur of India. We sat here for an hour while our troop of tatterdemalions drank beer which they make on the spot by pouring water into a bamboo jar of fermenting maize. They seemed to have little provision for the road but this handy article and a few maize cobs or puffed maize. Their clothes were no richer than their fare—a scant piece of cotton cloth was all they wore, except for one gentleman who sported a bit of what looked like a bear skin. Watching these scarecrows sucking away at their bamboo pot put me in mind of that sixteenth-century toper's lament, 'I cannot eat but little meat, My belly is not good', with its haunting refrain

> Back and side go bare, go bare;
> Both foot and hand go cold
> But, belly, God send thee good ale enough,
> Whether it be new or old.

One of the women, 'a fair hot wench in flame-coloured taffeta', whose hair hung down to conceal a very attractive face, asked Wangdi in her uncouth tongue for a cigarette. Wangdi gave her one and in reply went through the motions of sleeping with her in eloquent sign language, which so shocked her that I fully expected Wangdi would receive a clout on the ear. These people pierce the lobes of their ears and then distend them with wooden rings like the Wa Lumbwa who used to work for me in Kenya. The songs they sang while marching, too, were in a rhythm reminiscent of Africa.

Suspension bridge, Assam type, with circular cane supports

We camped high up, an hour below the Bomdi La. It was cold, but luckily fine; for our friends had no blankets and did not trouble to build any shelters. I was early on the pass only to be disappointed once more by a blanket of mist and smoke seen through a dense bamboo screen. Unlike the Bompu La both sides seemed wet; it was not until we were down to about 5000 ft. that we came again upon grass and pines. We descended to the valley of the Digien river which, like the Tenga, runs from west to east to join the Bhareli. It is very steep-sided, more like a Sikkim valley; on some of the ridges were pine, on others deciduous trees, and forest fires were burning on all sides.

After we had paid off our mixed Rupa troop along came the raja of Rahung, a comic-looking youth who talked animatedly in a Hindustani that only Wangdi could understand. We at once started bargaining for porters for the short march to Tembang, which was the last village, or rather town, at which we could hire porters for the long stretch to our proposed base in the Gorjo Chu. Wangdi's opening gambit was to tell him that I was the Political Officer's younger brother—an inexactitude weighty enough to help us to come to terms at nine annas; the raja insisting, meanwhile, that any attempt to bilk them would be reported at once to the aforesaid brother.

We left early with a rather larger proportion of children to carry the loads. A halt was called for food in Rahung, a village remarkable only for pigs, dirt, and goitres. It is smaller than Rupa, with the usual dilapidated chortens and mani walls. There is a direct route to Tembang not shown on the ¼ in. O.S. map, which crosses the Digien by a cane bridge 500 ft. below the village. This, like the Rupa bridge, was built on the same three-strand principle as suspension bridges elsewhere in the Himalaya but with the local modification of a stout bamboo hoop every three of four feet completely containing the three main cables. The women of the party had their loads carried across by the men—a courtesy which was not done for chivalrous motives, but because it is taboo for women to carry loads across bridges.

A steep climb of 2000 ft. brought us by midday to Tembang where we camped by a spring under some trees just beyond the town.

CHAPTER III

OUR TROUBLES BEGIN

TEMBANG IS A BIGGISH Mönba village built on a commanding spur with steep sides. Round it there is a wall approached by two flights of stone steps. In spite of its apparently strong position it is liable to be raided by the Miji Aka, its nearest neighbours to the east, to whom the people of Tembang pay tribute. From here two routes lead to Tibet. The most frequented goes via Dirang Dzong, the Se La, and Tawang. This last place is a very important monastery on the direct road to Tibet and, in particular, to Lhasa. Theoretically Tawang is in Assam, but it is controlled from Tsona Dzong in southern Tibet. In turn it controls Dirang Dzong and the whole of Mönyul. Mr Kingdon Ward, who has travelled extensively in Mönyul, in a paper read to the Royal Geographical Society described the position thus: 'The political status of Dirang Dzong is ambiguous. The surrounding country is ruled by two Tibetan dzongpens appointed from Tawang. They collect the taxes, listen to complaints, and maintain law and order without the help of a single soldier or policeman. The Mönbas, who seem never to have struck a blow for themselves, are almost servile. They have definitely thrown in their lot with Tibet, and where Tibet cannot help them—as for instance against the Akas to the east—they buy immunity. The Bhutanese ignore them; the Tibetans rule them; the Akas fleece them; and the British have, or had up to quite recently, forgotten them.'

The other route north, which is more to the east and skirts the country of the Abors, goes by the Poshing La, the Tse La, and the district called Mago. This was the route I wished to follow since it led direct to the Gorjo Chu, where we proposed making our base. I was told the Dzongpen of Dirang Dzong was in the village, so after disposing of a present of 'chang' (local beer brewed usually from barley but in this case from maize), which looked and tasted like sour pea soup, I went down to meet him. Dressed in the usual dirty maroon-coloured Tibetan 'chupa', embroidered felt boots, and cheap Homburg hat,

Tembang Monastery surrounded by poles for prayer flags

from below which bespectacled eyes stared impassively, he looked like bureaucracy personified. Obstruction oozed from him. It was obviously no use telling him I was the Political Officer's brother or even the Emperor of China's son. However, over a flagon of arak we got down to business. A number of the village elders were present including the headman, or 'gambo'.

We exchanged snuff and arak amicably enough for several hours, but whenever the conversation was steered back to porters a deadlock was reached. They all insisted that it was far too early for the Poshing La, which was never open until June and which would be deep in snow. The dzongpen, who would not have to exert himself at all in the matter, kept harping on the other route via Dirang Dzong, which he hoped, I suppose, I should eventually have to follow, sprinkling a few rupees on the way. In fact, there was no sense in his suggestions, because if the Poshing La were closed so would be the passes on the western route. The upshot was that I persuaded the 'gambo' to give me a guide to the Poshing La next day to see if it were open or not. It was a two-day march there, but I hoped we might get there and back in three.

Next morning, the 30th, Nukku and I packed for three days and went up to the village where Wangdi had preceded us to find a victim for the sacrifice. Overnight the 'gambo' had repented and washed his hands of the whole affair—an inapt metaphor, for this was quite the filthiest village I had ever seen. While the discussion was proceeding in the narrow midden of a street, I looked up and saw far off, floating on a white bed of cloud, a still whiter snow peak. The natives called it Sherkhang Karbo; by its bearing I thought it might be Kangdu (23,260 ft.), east of Gori Chen. This encouraging glimpse of the snows was the first vouchsafed me.

After two hours' vehement eloquence from Wangdi, a man called Dorje consented to risk his life with us for a consideration. We got away by ten o'clock, and after five hours of up and down work reached Lagam (9000 ft.), where we camped. Here there were a small wooden monastery, a yak or two, and some hens. The solitary lama who looked after the Gompa brought us wood and lugubriously volunteered some information about the Poshing La. From the map, which at this point becomes sketchy, it looked about ten miles with a rise of 4000 ft.

We hoped to make the double journey in one day. My diary calls this an exhausting and exasperating day. It might have gone much further than that without misrepresentation, and perhaps still kept within what Swinburne considered 'language of the strictest reserve' when he called Emerson a 'hoary-headed and toothless baboon'. We were off by half-past five carrying only lunch, a sweater, and a rope. A rope, if you please! which goes to show how successfully the Tembang men had wrought upon our imagination with their account of the Poshing La in April. In forty minutes we had gained the ridge 2000 ft. above us, and then for seven and a half hours we followed an uneven, seesaw crest through silver fir, rhododendron, and thick writhing mist which allowed us tantalising glimpses of the valleys on either side. After two hours, going flat out, when we must have been well over 10,000 ft., we dumped the rope which was obviously going to be unnecessary: it seemed impossible there could be any snow pass within several days' march. Two hours later, still going fast, I asked Dorje how far it was to the pass and was told it was now just about as far as yesterday's march. I thought he was being purposely discouraging.

Having lost some height we again began to climb steadily. Our hopes rose with the ground, and presently we came upon a 'chorten' and some prayer flags, the usual signs of a pass. I asked Dorje confidently if we had arrived; he replied that we were nearly half-way. The track then descended to a pond in a grass glade, and a hut, beyond which we saw in the mist a grassy shoulder crowned by what looked like a cairn. This must be it, I thought—this wretched man Dorje does not want us to get to the pass. Dumping the rucksack containing our food, Nukku and I started for it with a rush, but Dorje, who then came up, advised us to moderate our ecstasies, for the pass was still as far distant as the spot at which we had dumped the rope. After that we toiled on sullenly. I was rapidly acquiring a headache due to the height and the exertions of our unrelenting progress. It was now midday; halts and inquiries became more frequent—sure signs of distress; moreover, if we were to get back to Lagam before dark it was time to think of turning. At length we came upon the first snow in the form of deep drifts, whereupon Dorje eagerly assured us that if there was snow here it must be lying feet deep on the pass. He said the fact was inescapable; everyone knew that snow here indicated much more snow there. I felt

Track through forest along ridge leading to Poshing La

sure he quoted to himself some hoary rhyming couplet to this effect: 'If at this point snow you find, Put the Poshing La out of mind.' This riled me, because if we failed to set foot on the pass itself Dorje would infallibly paint a gloomy picture on our return to Tembang and our exertions would have been all in vain. I determined to get there if it took all day. If need be we would sleep at the pond which seemed to be the only water on the ridge. Dorje himself had a headache by now—a piece of intelligence which I found not displeasing, reflecting that we had not come so far and so fast altogether in vain. Nukku seemed as fresh as ever.

At long last we came to a really steep rocky rise up which we scrambled, hardly daring to hope this was the pass. There was no doubt about it this time. You could feel the unmistakable free air of a pass beginning to stir. At half-past one we stood on the Poshing La (*c.* 13,000 ft.), and even Dorje had to admit that there was no snow worth talking about. Having come to a clear understanding with him on that all-important point, Nukku casually remarked that we would now return to Lagam. 'Sez you', said I, but this choice piece of sarcasm fell upon deaf ears, for the Sherpas have not had our advantages of a good modern education. A cold, clammy mist enveloped us, and there was nothing to keep us, so down we went back to the pond for food and rest. At three o'clock we set off for Lagam. As is often the way on a descent there was a great deal of climbing: at least it seemed so to me, for the gentlest rise reduced my pace to a feeble crawl, and very soon I felt sick and 'sold out', as the New Zealander likes to express it. Darkness overtook us as we began the 2000 ft. drop to Lagam. We had taken only six hours coming home, thirteen and a half for the double journey.

By half-past ten next morning we were back to Tembang, and that afternoon, which was fine and hot, we reopened negotiations for porters with the headman. He began by politely hinting that the Tibetan translation of our Government permit, which invoked the help of all whom it might concern in the matter of food and transport, was not the same as the original copy with its official stamp. However, after 'great argument about it and about', Wangdi brought things to a satisfactory conclusion, the bargain being for twenty-two men to carry our things and their food to Mago in five days for four rupees each. At

Tembang porters (Mönba); young lama in centre

Tembang porter taking snuff

this point I retired to my sleeping bag feeling very queer. As we had been sitting in the hot sun drinking the arak which inevitably accompanies these dickerings, I blamed this indiscretion for my sickness. Nukku had gone to lie down as soon as we got in, but I thought that was only due to fatigue. This was the 22nd, ten days after our camp at Tiger Flat, just about the last day that we might expect malaria to develop.

We had arranged to start on the 24th, but this was now impossible. On the 25th I was better but weak, but both Nukku and Thundu were suffering from unmistakable malaria. I had feared this from the first. I doled out quinine, of which we still had a fair supply, but the Sherpas put more faith in a great jorum of 'chang' which they had sent them daily. The headman now seemed anxious to be rid of us. He talked of his having to go to Dirang Dzong and pressed me to name a day for our start. This was not possible, for Nukku was worse and I was no better. However, on the 28th, after a night of sweating, I felt well for the first time for a week, and as Nukku, too, was on the mend, I ordered the porters for the 30th. Thundu even in full health was not exactly a ball of fire; now he did nothing whatever and I thanked God for Wangdi, who did all the camp work as well as fighting our wordy battles with the headman.

On the last day of April we pushed the two cripples off early, carrying nothing but their own kit, which I had already gone through like a destroying angel purging away the dross. I also jettisoned some of my own, in my zeal overlooking the fact that amongst the jetsam was our bottle of quinine with still some thirty tablets. Then Wangdi and I sat expectantly amongst the loads for an hour and a half, by which time the 'gambo' arrived with a few men and the tidings that no more were to be had. I had expected something like that would happen and I blamed myself for not having asked for twice as many men as we really wanted. Putting a smiling face on it we accompanied the headman through the noisome streets of the village, feeling about as charitably inclined as an old-time Liverpool crimp with a commission to complete the crew of a notoriously ill-found ship. It would have been unwise to have offered more pay, and difficult for us, who had not been there, to paint in glowing colours the delights of the Gorjo Chu to men who had.

At half-past ten we were obliged to start with sixteen greatly overloaded men instead of the twenty-two we needed. They were carrying sixty pounds of our stuff and twenty-five to thirty pounds of food for themselves. Luckily it was only eight miles to Lagam. For my part when on trek I am not averse to starting slowly and easing up as I go on, and we surely did that on this occasion. The short climb of 2000 ft. up to Lagam monastery took us three hours, the last man getting in at half-past seven.

This was the last inhabited place on our route until we reached our destination. We had been told we might possibly get an extra porter or so here, but there was still only the old Lama, who was polite but quite firm in his refusal to join us. To pass the time while Wangdi was talking to him I made an inventory of the interior of the Gompa. This is what I then wrote: 'A carved and painted beam divides the altar from the rest. In the left-hand corner housed in a crudely carved wooden box is a prayer wheel 4 ft. diameter, turned by hand. A bell rings at each revolution. The altar consists of two stone ledges running right across. On the lower, eighteen brass bowls of water, two trumpets, and an earthenware Tibetan teapot. On the extreme right an empty Castrol tin, a beer tin (Barclays), a varnish tin, and four beer bottles (empty). On the upper shelf eighteen more brass bowls, several brass vases, a china bowl, a brass Tibetan teapot, and in the centre a white cloth-covered box carrying three small brass Buddhas and a brass stupa. In the carved and painted wall behind the altar are niches holding painted clay images. Tucked away out of sight behind the prayer wheel a big wooden Buddha. In front a piece of black stone (meteorite?), weight about 20 lb., shaped like a blunted rhino horn stood on end. On a wooden bench to the right a "dorje" or "thunderbolt", a bell, prayer book, cymbals, two trumpets, and a large flat drum like a tambourine supported by a cord to the ceiling like a punch-bag. Both side walls frescoed but spoilt by age. Hung on a line in front of altar are coloured paper, coarsely woven ceremonial scarves, and several mealie cobs.'

Although we were to camp short of the Poshing La I rather feared the next day's march—a short march which you know is more tiresome than a long one you don't know. The porters had gone all right yesterday but would they go to-day? We were so near Tembang that

Tembang porter on track to Poshing La

desertion would be simple. All such fears proved groundless. The men were cheerful, marched well if slowly, and, apart from showing some inclination to halt for the night at the first 'chorten', made no bones about reaching the pond and hut, short of the pass, in ten and a half hours. Moreover, the sun shone. Strolling along the ridge through the vivid scarlet, cream, and orange rhododendrons we enjoyed some pleasing glimpses of the not very distant hill clearings made by the Miji Akas, and through the trees to our left, ridge after ridge of blue hills stretching to the distant Bhutan frontier.

That night just after turning in there was a very violent storm of thunder, wind and rain, in which Wangdi heroically went out to secure the ground sheet over our heads. This seemed to be the signal for a break in the weather, which steadily deteriorated as we approached the mountains.

Starting before seven next morning, in the hope of getting a view from the pass, I reached the summit in two hours, but was easily beaten by the mist. The descent on the north side was easy, the men were going well, and at midday we all halted for a meal of maize 'satu', which is roasted flour and can be made from barley, wheat or maize; in Tibet barley is the most generally used, as it is the only cereal which will ripen at such heights. Here it was generally maize.

At this halt Wangdi succumbed to a sudden attack of fever. He then seemed to recover and rushed on ahead by himself to the bottom of the hill where presently I found him lying. Fortunately, the camping place of Samjung was only half a mile away, so I relieved him of his load and we went on together, arriving just in time to avoid the evening storm. With Wangdi out, Thundu doing nothing, and Nukku little more, the outlook was bleak.

The camp at Samjung was by a pleasant stream, the Sangti Chu, which comes down from the Tse La. This was the 15,500 ft. pass between us and the Gorjo Chu which we had to cross next day. Samjung is just under 13,000 ft.; it was appreciably colder than the Poshing La camp: no rhododendrons were in flower and there were no Alpines to be seen.

The night was wet, and in the morning (3 May) we were shocked to find there had been a heavy fall of snow. It could not have come at a more inconvenient time, but for me the shock was mitigated by finding

Crossing the Tse La (15,550 ft.)

Base Camp at shepherds' hut in Gorjo Chu (*circa* 14,000 ft.), Lap

that Wangdi had recovered overnight. Fortunate it was for us during the evil days ahead that Wangdi's malaria was of a different type to ours. Almost every other day about noon, as regularly as a clock, he would come to me, shivering violently, to tell me, apologetically, that he was going to bed, and an hour or two later he would be up and about apparently none the worse. I am not expert in these matters, but I believe his was a benign tertiary form while ours was malignant.

His recovery was happily timed, for that morning all his forceful personality was needed to persuade the Mönba men to move. They were as reluctant to start as we were to wait, but in the end Wangdi prevailed. We still had with us our friend Dorje, of Poshing La fame, with his valuable but sometimes irritating habit of looking facts in the face, but we could have dispensed with him that morning because, besides telling us precisely how far it was to the pass, he went beyond his office to prophesy, Cassandra-like, more snow. How I hated the man—as the great Lord Halifax remarked, 'Nothing hath an uglier look than reason when it is not of our side.'

The Mönba men had Tibetan felt boots but no snow glasses, so that, within reason, snow would be more tolerable than bright sun. In the end we had both; for during the long seven-hour trudge to the pass the sun shone dazzlingly, and on top we encountered a mild blizzard. The forest ceases south of the Sangti Chu, and we followed the hidden track through stunted birch and juniper, which, at a touch, discharged on our heads the contents of their snow-laden branches. Soon we were clear of this, marching on a bare, gently sloping field of snow whose skyline ridge was always just in front of us, ever receding as we advanced.

Seven hours of dogged plodding brought us to the top at three o'clock. With hardly a pause, for it was now snowing hard, we pushed on down easy slopes into the wide, bare valley of the Gorjo Chu. The stream, which was small, was crossed by a plank, and in half an hour we reached the sheep fold called Lap (*c.* 14,500 ft.) consisting of some stone huts, one of which had a weathertight roof. It had been a trying march for all. The Mönbas had the loads, and we our fevers; Thundu lagged far behind, Nukku seemed listless, and my stomach celebrated our arrival by again 'selling out'. By the evening all but four of the Mönbas were suffering from snow-blindness which I treated with a

Gori Chen from the south side of Gorjo Chu

mixture of castor oil and cocaine. It was not as efficacious as I had hoped, but next morning although most of them were semi-blind, the pain had been reduced to more bearable limits.

I now had to decide what to do. Lap was at the very useful height of 14,500 ft.; there was shelter here; the Gorjo Chu valley led north-east in the direction of Gori Chen. These facts seemed to mark it out for our base. From it we could push a dump of food to the head of the valley from where we should be in a position to explore the Gori Chen group, and then having learnt more about the lie of the land we could carry out journeys to the higher mountains to the north-east. All this, of course, depended on how soon, if at all, we could get rid of our fever. Thundu was certainly getting worse, Nukku seemed fit but lethargic, Wangdi was all right except for his occasional midday bout, while I myself fondly imagined I had already recovered. We had no drugs for treatment, but as there was no chance of reinfection, I hoped the fever would run its course and finish. Meantime I paid off the Mönbas, who announced their intention of going on next day to the twin villages of Nyuri and Dyuri known collectively as Mago. The Tembang people seemed to have close connections with Mago, which lies on the road to Tibet. I decided that it might be useful to make contact with our nearest neighbours and to go along with them, taking Wangdi but leaving the others to recuperate.

CHAPTER IV

BASE CAMP AND FEVER

S NOW WAS FALLING WHEN WE LEFT at 8 a.m. on 4 May. A little had fallen the day before in the Gorjo Chu and that did not look as if it would lie long, but now all was white and I was sorry for the snow-blind Mönba men, some of whom had to be led by the hand on this march. The track followed the north side of the river until, after about four hours, it plunged steeply into thick forest and began climbing to the Chera La. It was snowing heavily when we crossed the pass at one o'clock. We dropped steeply, first through rhododendron and then into magnificent pine forest to the gorge of the Dungma Chu. We crossed this by a bridge and at three o'clock reached Dyuri, a little 'drokpa', or herd village, consisting of about nine wooden huts in a sea of mud. On the other bank of the Dungma Chu is another small village, Nyuri; these two together are usually known as Mago. The Dungma Chu is joined here by the Goshu Chu which comes down from the Tulung La (the main pass into Tibet), and about a mile below the combined streams enter a deep granite gorge which is impassable. There is no cultivation and the people live on the produce of their yaks and sheep eked out by a little 'satu' which they import in exchange for butter and wool. They wear skins and garments of rough wool and hair—hairiness in fact was their chief characteristic; the men were hairy in themselves, and they wore hairy caps with little tails hanging down all round.

We put up in a room festooned with pieces of drying yak meat. Bits of yak hung everywhere, we ate yak butter, drank yak milk, slept on yak skins, and were duly rewarded with a bountiful crop of yak fleas. The herdman, a veritable Esau, visited us. He promised us forty pounds of satu and the help of two men to move our stuff from Lap farther up the Gorjo Chu. He confessed complete ignorance of the valley above Lap. Devoting the next day to seeing the local sights, we walked up the Goshu Chu to a bridge where there was a water prayer wheel, a mill, and some hot springs, with pleasantly warm but rather slimy water. We returned through Nyuri to our Chamber of Horrors, which on closer inspection proved to be worse than I had thought—fleas visibly hopped about, fat white maggots crawled out of the floor, and a deaf mute mowed and gibbered at us from the corner.

When we came to pay for our board and the forty pounds of satu some confusion arose over annas and tankas. The latter is a Tibetan coin whose value was finally assessed by some hairy professor of economics at two annas. Having thus settled our obligations we set off, recrossing the Chera La. Much snow had fallen, was falling, and continued to fall all day. It was a bad march. Wangdi went well but blew like a grampus the whole way; I could not make out whether he was ill or not. I finally decided that he had Cheynes Stokes breathing while on the march—a diagnosis which did nothing to help my problem. Tea in a hut revived us to some extent and we went on to Lap without stopping. There was less snow up here at 14,500 ft. than there was down at Mago, but apart from this our homecoming was cheerless enough. Thundu seemed worse and was in bed, Nukku was ill but moving about; the one groaning and spitting, the other groaning and vomiting. What was to be done? It is easy to be wise now. Obviously what I should have done was to have taken advantage of the presence of the Tembang men at Mago and go down, although it meant giving up all our plans. On the other hand, if we hung on there was a good chance of the fever abating, and if the worst came to the worst we could probably get help from Mago. Hitherto my experience of malaria in Kenya and elsewhere had led me to believe that people seldom died of it, but I had yet to learn of the deadly 'terai' malaria of Assam.

On the 7th I went for a solitary walk up the Gorjo Chu to see what sort of a place we had come to. The weather was behaving abominably; after an hour or two of early morning sunshine the usual snow drizzle set in and continued all day. Two miles above Lap an old moraine spanned the valley except where the river came through. A mile and a half above this the valley bent sharply towards the north, and at the corner was an excellent camp site—a grassy 'maidan', big boulders for shelter, and juniper wood and yak dung for fuel. Round the corner the valley divided, and dimly through the drizzle I could see that the eastern arm held a snow-covered glacier. Coming back along the hillside I saw two herds of 'bharal' and blew some feathers out of a snow pigeon at a range of ten yards.

The following day, the 8th, we started work. Wangdi and the two men who had come over from Mago carried some loads to the proposed Corner Camp site which I had already visited, while I sweated up a hill north of our camp with the plane table to get a 'fix'. A thousand feet higher there was a cairn, evidently built by local shepherds, at which I set up shop and took sights to Gori Chen and two unidentified snow peaks. These were too close together to give good results, and I realised I should have to move to the east to bring myself broadside on to the main range. At half-past eight it was still clear. I pushed on quickly up the ridge hoping to get another 'fix'; but at nine o'clock the wisps of floating vapour coalesced with extraordinary rapidity and in a few minutes everything was hidden.

Though the mountaineer, and much more the surveyor, may revile mist and cloud, how greatly mountains gain by their effects! How their mystery and magnetism is enhanced! In mist the lowest and homeliest hill becomes a scene of adventure. Hillocks appear unexpectedly in the guise of high peaks, and nearby boulders become grim towers looming distantly through cloud. The clouds that are the almost inseparable companions of mountains lend even the best known the mysterious power of attraction of the unknown. Even when we are aware of what lies beyond the veil, the lifting of it never fails to thrill, like the raising of the curtain on the first act of a play which we have longed to see. How much greater then is the thrill when the veil of mist conceals the unknown, the unseen.

Think for a moment of Stanley in the Congo, who for weeks gazed longingly at the solid bank of cloud enveloping the Mountains of the Moon (for he must have suspected what lay behind) until one day: 'I saw a peculiar-shaped cloud of a most beautiful silver colour which assumed the proportions and appearance of a great mountain covered with snow... I became for the first time conscious that what I gazed upon was not the image or semblance of a vast mountain, but the solid substance of a real one, its summit covered with snow'; or of Lord Dufferin beating up for Jan Mayen island in thick weather, and seeing suddenly, in a rift in the driving scud, between the masts of the ship, the

Looking up the Gorjo Chu towards 'Corner' Camp at the bend

lofty summit of Beerenberg, appearing almost to overhang; or of an experience of our own on those same Mountains of the Moon, when we sat on what we hoped was the summit of Margherita in a sea of fog, which boiled up from some seemingly inexhaustible source, waiting patiently for a glimpse of the neighbouring peak of Alexandra in order to verify our position; and of innumerable dramatic revelations in the Himalaya all producing, according to our hopes, pleasure, dismay, astonishment, fright, but always exhilaration.

The tantalising visions of Gori Chen, the glacier, the more distant peaks, had filled me with impatience and made me fret at the physical weakness which prevented our coming to grips with the problems they would present. Our next day's work was a repetition of the first except that we started earlier and that Nukku turned out to carry the gear for me. This was the first work he had done and was a hopeful sign, but Thundu was the same, moaning, groaning, and eating nothing. We got to 16,000 ft., took some sights on the same peaks, and were then driven down by the mist at half-past nine. I went to bed feeling very cheap, leaving Wangdi and the Mago men to carry more loads to Corner Camp.

I meant to lie at earth next day, but it was such a wonderfully fine morning that I went to a point across the river to do another 'fix'. This was a liberty which the malaria parasites in my blood seemed to resent, and for the next seven days, when fever and headache allowed, I had leisure to reflect on the absence of our quinine and the fearful virulence of the Assam breed of malaria. It is of no interest to read of the symptoms and sufferings of others, so I pass over a grim week and come to the day when the fever departed and I was able to get up, make bread, potter about the camp, and take stock of our position. The two Mago men had gone back, having finished the job of making a food dump at Corner Camp. A herd of yaks had come up and were now grazing in the Gorjo Chu, from which all snow had now gone. Thundu seemed better, but much thinner, while Nukku's condition was puzzling. He would not go to bed, but just sat about not interested in anything, complaining only of pains in the shoulders. Wangdi was as brisk as ever though still on occasions having his midday bout of fever. He was by now getting annoyed with the helplessness of the other two, railing at them frequently, especially at the poor unfortunate Thundu for making such appalling noises and even for allowing his long hair to hang over his face.

Lying alone in my tent racked with fever I had not unnaturally thought of giving up the struggle and of sending to Mago for help, but now that I was up I thought differently—'... when the devil was well, devil a monk was he'. It was too early in the game to throw in our hands. If the fever had finally left me, as seemed possible, so it would the others. We had done nothing, and much remained to be done. So I speciously reasoned, or shut my eyes to facts, according to the point of view.

On 18 May, Wangdi and I walked up the dry nallah which entered the main valley from the north. About three miles up it came to an end under what I called the Black Cliffs, which we were not strong enough to climb. As we crossed a low col into the next nallah to the east, the mist came down and we returned to camp without having seen anything. During lunch I was amused to observe Wangdi's method of treating his ration of half a mug of pea soup. He took six large chillies, a dozen cloves of garlic, an ounce of salt, and ground them together on a stone to form a paste. This was scraped off into not more than a quarter cupful of water. Half the soup was added and then, with an occasional shake of the head and a blink of the eyes, the only indications that he was taking a powerful blister and not bread and milk, this fragrant mess was quickly dealt with. The Sherpas like their sauce piquant.

With steam rising gently from him as a result of this volcanic meal, Wangdi and I discussed plans. Nukku said he was fit enough to carry, so we decided that two of us should go to Corner Camp to explore the head of the Gorjo Chu, leaving Nukku and Thundu to follow in three days' time provided they felt strong enough. Accordingly, the next day, we moved up. We took all morning to get there and I began to realise just how weak we were. Nukku came in an hour behind and my load of thirty-five pounds felt like eighty pounds. There were a lot of yaks about, but seemingly no one in charge of them. We rigged up a tarpaulin in the lee of a boulder for a kitchen, collected yak dung and juniper, and produced a prodigious amount of smoke but little heat. The usual drizzle fell all afternoon.

We made a courageously early start next morning for a station on the south side of the river. I say courageous because a really thick mist

Gori Chen from above Lap

hid everything, and we had no good grounds for thinking it would lift. Presently it began to snow. We plodded on to the top of the ridge out of mere cussedness, sat there for some time, and then returned to camp. This fall of snow continued all the next day, but it was so light, and the weather so warm, that it had no effect at all on the appearance of the Gorjo Chu valley, which presented the same bare, brown, rather desolate appearance. Presumably the weather we were experiencing was the effect of the monsoon which, here, at the extremity of its long range, was weak and ineffective.

On the third day the dawn was murky, but the snow had stopped. We went up to the same place and managed to do a rapid 'fix' before the mist overtook us. From all these various stations Gori Chen and several 19,000 and 20,000 ft. peaks were visible; of Kangdu and its satellites to the east there was no sign. We had a fleeting glimpse of the head of the Gorjo Chu, which apparently ended in a snow ridge well to the south of Gori Chen. From this ridge we might be able to look down into the basin at the foot of the mountain, but whether I would be strong enough to get there was becoming doubtful. On the following day, one of our few fine days, I was not well enough to move, but on the day after that, after a poor night, we made a bid for it.

Had the gods been looking down that morning upon good men struggling with adversity they would have been moved either to pity or to laughter. Wangdi was going all right, but I found I was quite unable to get past a boulder (and there were a great many boulders) without sitting on it. Whatever the criteria employed to judge my rate of progression—snails, tortoises, slow-moving glaciers, or the mills of God—it was obvious I was below standard. After an hour of it, finding my pulse rate was over a hundred, we returned to camp and I to bed.

As it was only eight o'clock I sent Wangdi down to Lap, for it was five days since we had left and nothing had been heard of Nukku or Thundu. In the early afternoon he returned in the rain with bad news. Thundu was no better and Nukku, who had helped to carry our loads up, was in a very queer state. According to Wangdi he had failed to recognise him. This was decisive. I had an acute fit of ague when Wangdi returned and was shivering too hard to talk properly, but as soon as this had subsided I gave orders to Wangdi to go down again to arrange for three yaks to come up next day to take our gear from Corner Camp to Lap, and to make inquiries for a yak or yaks to take Nukku and Thundu down. He had reported that there were now two yak-herds living at Lap.

I had been living on hopes and false expectations too long and now had to acknowledge defeat. Whether we should escape even some of the consequences remained to be seen.

CHAPTER V

RETREAT

WANGDI RETURNED EARLY next morning alone except for three yaks which he had managed to collect. It was ten o'clock before we started, because owing to the yak's dislike of being handled by Europeans he had to do the loading single-handed. This discriminating beast is handsome, and I can think of no animal which serves its fortunate owner so well in return for so little. Milk and butter, hair from which clothing, rope, or even boots, can be made, and transport, are some of the by-products of this admirable ox, all at a negligible charge for maintenance. From the point of view of economy of upkeep the camel and reindeer vie with the yak. The last seems to exist on grass-flavoured gravel, the other two on thorns and moss respectively; but if one considers both his noble mien and the wide range of real necessities he provides, the supremacy of the yak is undeniable.

I crawled down to Lap in the wake of the yaks. Inside the stone hut Thundu lay in his sleeping bag from which he had apparently not stirred for some days. Wangdi at once removed him bodily to a nearby hut. Nukku lay fully dressed on the floor with his boots in the ashes of an extinct fire. He was unconscious and breathing stertorously. Thundu said he had been like that for the last twenty-four hours. We called in the two yak-herds, an old man and a lad, but for no consideration on earth could we induce the old man to let us have two yaks for the sick men: his reasons were vague but his intentions clear-cut. He went on to tell us that there were neither men nor ponies at Mago. For the time being we seemed to have reached a deadlock. In the afternoon we tackled him again and told him he must send the lad to-morrow to Mago to return with six men, and poles for rigging up litters. To clinch the thing we sent the .22 rifle as a gift for the headman. If this stratagem worked, as we hoped it would, we might expect help in two days' time; if it failed then the outlook was black indeed. I had no great hopes of saving Nukku, Thundu was too weak to stand, and in a few days I should be the same.

Next day the invaluable Wangdi went to Corner Camp to bring down some more food for the expected porters. He returned in the afternoon to find me in the throes of another fit of ague and Nukku dead. This news, though expected, was a shock; the burning question now was whether we should get Thundu down safely.

In the morning, 27 May, we buried Nukku among some large boulders where we built a cairn of stones. The old man was away with his yaks, and since I was so weak we had a struggle to carry him to the place we had chosen. In 1936 on Nanda Devi we had lost a Sherpa who had died at the base camp of some disease, the seeds of which he had had on him before we started and against which we were powerless. As he had never left the base I did not see him, but here the circumstances were different. Nukku had been our intimate companion for nearly two months. Moreover, I knew him well from 1937, when he had shared our life and done our work for several months. Now the responsibility for his death lay heavy upon me.

Malaria is depressing at the best of times, but my dejection that evening was extreme until, very late, the boy returned from Mago with word that some men would come next day. This was one of my bad days when a fresh symptom made its appearance—a feeling of imminent suffocation lasting for an hour or more. My relief when six men and four zos arrived in the evening was great. I had hardly dared to expect so prompt a response, and I felt that the rifle had at last justified its presence. The headman seemed pleased beyond words, and next morning, lying in my sleeping bag at the door of the tent, with shaking hands and throbbing eyes, I had to fire a demonstration shot.

Instead of making a stretcher for Thundu the six men decided to carry him single-handed by turn. They rigged up an Everest carrying frame with a sort of stirrup for his feet, on which he sat, facing forward, with his arms round his bearer's neck. In this way they carried him for long stretches at a time with seemingly little effort. Admittedly he was by now a mere skeleton of a man, but even so it was no mean feat, for he cannot have weighed less than ninety or a hundred pounds. As I could now only walk downhill, the headman mounted me on a zo which he led himself. The zo, which is a cross between a cow and a yak, is a milder animal in its behaviour towards Europeans. We had a very convincing demonstration of this on the second day's march when the headman tried to mount me on a yellow yak.

The snow on the Tse La had disappeared. The carriers made light of their human load, the zos stepped out, and the only halts we called were for the sake of Thundu, who was so weak that the mere effort of sitting on the carrying frame became exhausting. From the top of the pass I looked back at the stone huts of Lap, now deserted; at the place where we had buried Nukku; at the green grass and black boulders of Corner Camp. Cloud covered the snow ridge which we had failed to reach, and beyond, the dim, ghostly outline of Gori Chen showed through the drifting mists. The summit alone shone clearly, but between us there passed no nod of recognition or farewell. The bond between men and mountain who have met and measured themselves together had not been tied. We had neither trod its glaciers, nor slept on its slopes; its ridges, faces, gullies, meant nothing to us for we had never grappled. After six weeks of futile endeavour Gori Chen remained a mere peak of the Assam Himalaya, a name on the map. I turned and went down the other side.

From Samjung we crossed the Poshing La and once more camped at the hut by the pond. Everything was the same, the mist on top and the thunderstorm which struck us in the evening. Thundu seemed to be standing his journey well, and my cold fits were now merely part of the day's routine. We reached Lagam on the last day of May, our loads and sleeping bags soaked by a heavy storm, and men and animals badly bitten by leeches—another 'trifling sum of misery now added to the foot of our account'. The lush grass surrounding the monastery was so infested with these pests that the animals had to be kept away from it. We gave them a load of maize as compensation. Our old friend the Lama had now an assistant, a sort of female acolyte, who came in the evening to attend to the lamps and to empty the thirty-six little brass bowls of water into two bamboo jars. While this was going on my food was brought to me where I lay in the corner, but before I could begin to eat the woman had begun to pray and I felt constrained to lie still, ignoring the savoury smell of lentil soup and pemmican, until she had done.

The headman of Mago now left us suddenly without a word, taking with him a man and one of the zos. It was of no consequence, however, for our loads were lighter now, and the priestess stepped manfully into the breach. Tembang seemed to be empty—like London in August, no one of consequence was in Town. We camped behind the 'gompa' and immediately sent for the kit we had left behind. It was brought to us intact. Thundu and I took four tablets each from the forgotten bottle of quinine which had the immediate effect of nipping in the bud my attack of shivers. We paid off the Mago men and their zos, and in their place hired eight porters as no animal transport was available. It was, however, only a short march to Rahung, most of it downhill.

The Digien river was now in flood, flowing full and brown, and we clung thankfully to the cane hoops of the bridge as it swayed above the swirling water. The talkative little headman made us welcome, brought firewood with his own hands, and promised ten porters and a pony for the morrow. I had all the loads ready by 6 a.m. as I hoped to cross the Bomdi La, but it was not to be. The promises made in the evening, prompted by hospitality and arak, were forgotten in the cold light of morning. Eventually the party of six men, three girls, and a pony, straggled off three hours behind schedule. We made heavy weather of it with Thundu, but the track was devilish and consistently steep. I was impatient to get on, and, riding uphill on a pony, more or less at ease, I was tempted to underrate the exertions of those on foot. I always think it must have been either uncommon hardihood, or a sublime sense of their own importance and disregard for anyone else, which allowed the old traders and travellers in tropical Africa to do their 'marching' in litters borne by four or more sweating negroes—possibly many of them had the excuse that they were suffering from malaria.

There was never a chance of our getting over the pass. There was no Wangdi to encourage and browbeat with his raucous gibes and threats. That admirable man, who had the makings of a dissipated but dynamic drill sergeant, had fallen out with another of his two-hour fever bouts. The Sherpas can grow little or no face hair, but had Wangdi been able to sport long waxed moustachios he would have closely resembled a sergeant-major I had—a man in whose presence the Battery Commander (myself) became uneasy, subalterns frankly nervous, and other ranks slightly unhinged.

We reached Rupa on 4 June. There was a big 'tamasha' in progress and the headman was ill with fever. We learnt that the road leading over the Bompu La through Doimara over which we had originally travelled was now flooded and consequently we should have to use a roundabout road to the east touching the Miji Aka country. A deputy headman, remarkable for his gross, copper-coloured face, engaged to find porters and two ponies to take us to the first 'tame' Miji Aka village of Jamiri two marches away. With this business, as I hoped, satisfactorily settled we were invited to cast care aside and join the revels. It would be an exaggeration to say that everybody except ourselves was drunk, but the crowd was in that uncritical frame of mind customary in the early stages of drunkenness, and therefore very easily amused. The entertainment provided, if it could be called entertainment, made this outlook quite essential for enjoyment. The highlight was a dancing yak act performed by two men; the one in front carrying a yak's head was connected by a pole draped with cloth to his partner, to whom was attached a yak's tail. In the ring with them, as a sort of sparring partner or clown, was a man wearing a grotesque Tibetan mask. It was his part to do a few steps of Tibetan-style dancing—arms outstretched, slow turn on one foot, hop, and turn again—a manœuvre designed to bring him very frequently into collision with that ignoble caricature of a yak which would then proceed to kick him violently. The patience of actors and audience seemed inexhaustible, ours was insufficiently elastic.

Next morning when we greeted the 'Copper Portent' with whom we had arranged the details of our departure he seemed quite taken aback, as though his suspicions of the presence of strangers in Rupa were suddenly confirmed. Wangdi and I immediately sat down on the steps of his house, like a couple of bailiff's men, until we saw him saddle one pony, order another, and tell off six reluctant porters. We then went back to camp, packed up, and got under way. Thundu was now riding a pony, not because he was any stronger but because of the difficulty of finding sufficient relays of men to carry him. Keeping to the north bank we followed the Tenga river which flowed down an open arid valley of pines and oaks, apparently uninhabited. Our destination was Dahung, where the 'Copper Portent' had assured us we should find good stabling for man and beast, and possibly eggs and maize beer. At about four o'clock our porters, who were showing signs of having had enough, indicated that we had arrived. True there were trees and water, the main ingredients of a camp, but nothing else, and I realised that 'Dahung' was just a joke bought by the unsuspecting stranger. Any place at which the porters chose to stop was apparently 'Dahung', just as wherever the Macgregor sat was the head of the table.

I was not particularly happy about this forced deviation from our old route. I knew very little about the Miji Aka and nothing at all to their advantage, neither did I know how much significance to attach to the prefix 'tame' when applied to those whom we hoped to see on the morrow. I was not anticipating losing my head, for if the Mönba men could trust them so could we, but I feared they might not be quite so ready as the Mönba to provide porters, and now that we were once more in malarial country any delay was dangerous for us.

Next day, 6 June, brought us, particularly myself, many ups and downs. As we left the river to climb up to Jamiri my pony, who had just crossed a side stream, jibbed at a steep bit and stepped over the 'khud'. I rolled off quickly but one foot caught in the stirrup, and the frightened beast, recovering its footing, darted off at speed down the trail we had just climbed dragging me with it. This is a situation in which, so far as I know, there is nothing the 'dragee' can do until someone or something stops the animal. From a dragging parachute one can release oneself by a smart blow on the harness fastening, and the normal stirrup leather detaches itself from the saddle automatically; but native stirrup leathers are not so obliging, although, of course, most of them can be relied upon to break. This one did not. As we sped down the track towards the stream I realised that I should certainly get a ducking and possibly a cracked skull. By now one of the men was pursuing the pony with wild cries down the track with the sole effect of making it go faster. We took the water with a rush, missed all the worst boulders, and breasted (man and beast) the opposite bank. Luckily this was extremely steep, the pony faltered, and the Mönba caught it. Even before I was released I had determined on walking to Jamiri no matter how weak I might be, so I was unlucky to find when I stood up that the only injury sustained was a bruised thigh.

We came to the Aka village of Jamiri at three o'clock after a long uphill slog. There was no very striking difference between these 'tame' Akas and the men I had with me except their very independent attitude.

The performing 'yak' at the Rupa 'tamasha'

They appeared to live in communal huts of which there were three, each 150-200 ft. long, rectangular, with a grass roof. The men carried a sword like a Burmese dah, and bows and arrows. The last are said to be bated with aconite. In the first years of the British occupation of Assam these Akas were very troublesome, and in 1883 they broke out again. A small expedition under a General Sale Hill was successful in quieting them; since then there has been no serious trouble. According to the Assam Census Report they are divided into two clans bearing the very suggestive names of Hazari-Khoas or 'eaters of a thousand hearths', and the Kapah-chors or 'thieves that lurk in the cotton fields'.

Our reception was of the coolest. 'There was no camp site near the village, and we had better go back to the main river from which we had just come, where we should find water and wood. There was none for us here. Moreover, they had no porters or ponies to hire out even if the road to Charduar was passable, which it was not. And, finally, it was no use my flourishing the Government "purwana", which asked all whom it might concern to help us with food and transport, because this particular village did not recognise any Government.' The headman who delivered this declaration of independence was a prim, severe little man in a smart Tibetan coatee of yellow silk. Of course, taken as a whole, our party was not calculated to impress. The Mönbas could be written off as potential slaves. Thundu looked like a wasted effigy of Death on the Pale Horse, Wangdi a disreputable Nepali (which in fact he was), and myself one of the poorer 'poor whites'. But when our gorgeous friend tried to put us in our proper place he over-reached himself in asserting in such a very offhand way that he had no truck with any Government. As we found later, he was lying about his status because he was one of the 'tame' Aka chiefs who received a small subsidy from Government. He visited Charduar shortly afterwards, and having the bad luck to find me still there, received a severe 'rocket' from the Political Officer for his ill manners.

To camp on the site indicated for us, some three miles from the village, was obviously equivalent to putting ourselves in Coventry, so we camped as close to the village as due regard for our health allowed in order to give our nuisance value full play. When we had thus settled in on his doorstep, so to speak, the headman came off his high horse and sent word that we should write in English what we wanted and he would have it sent to Sadeyo, a rajah of a neighbouring village. In the evening this prim little man paid us a swift visit in person to tell us that six porters would be here next day and that he himself might supply the other six at the rate of six rupees to Charduar, cash strictly in advance.

Jamiri was most unsavoury, flies abounding. Our policy of letting our nuisance value have full play acted also in reverse like Lend-Lease. By midday the prim rajah and I were paying each other social calls, and having exchanged presents—eggs, a chicken, and a load of wood on his part, and some sugar and a Balaclava helmet on mine—we began pouring libations. Although he had thus mellowed towards us the rajah was careful to point out, as he refilled my bamboo mug, that this condescension was only due to a personal regard for me and the weak condition of our party, and that Sadeyo rajah, who was a creature of the Government and heavily subsidised for it, was the man to whom I should have gone for help in the first place. At this moment a small, stout, but majestic figure appeared in the doorway. What with the dim light of the hut and the maize beer I was not seeing too well and at first thought it to be a reincarnation of Napoleon dressed as a Ghurka officer, but it proved to be Sadeyo himself fully accoutred with hat, revolver, belt, shorts, boots, and puttees. He was voluble but efficient, having brought the porters along with him; and, having cadged a water-bottle which he had seen in my camp, he departed as suddenly as he had come, wisely declining to join in a party which obviously had had a long start. From this I managed to extricate myself before nightfall, taking with me as a parting gift a bushel or so of bamboo shoots.

For one reason or another that was a bad night. Outside the tent there seemed to be more midges in the air than oxygen, and shutting the tent merely meant including the midges and excluding the air; from the men's hut came the most maddening, prolonged singing, which at times reached such a pitch of frenzy that I almost thought the prim little man was inciting his warriors to assert their independence by massacring us on the spot. Malaria and maize beer have a lowering effect on one's morale.

However, dawn came at last, as dawns do, and we got under way by seven o'clock with ten porters, men and girls, six of whom had to carry Thundu. Between Jamiri and the Bhareli river there was a 6000 ft. pass to cross, and having climbed over that we camped by a side stream short of the Bhareli. The going was bad—a succession of steep, thickly forested valleys. Lush, damp, sunless jungle, with its smell of decaying vegetation, depresses me. A botanist or naturalist might find such a march enthralling, but, for one who is neither, it is just a matter of one damned thing after another—stinging nettles, thorns, beans which produce a painful rash, tree ticks which bite venomously, and worst of all leeches. The foliage overhanging the paths, and the paths themselves, are the springboards from which they leap on to the passing traveller; and seeing them weave their lithe bodies hungrily in mid-air as they scent their prey (if scent is the means by which they work) arouses in me almost as much horror as does a snake—possibly more, because a snake can at least be struck down with a stick or kicked.

The next day's march brought us to the junction of the Bhareli and Sessa rivers, the latter being crossed by a bamboo bridge. Ever since leaving Jamiri there had been much talk of an unfordable, unbridged river, and on the third march we met six rivers in succession. Every time we approached one of these I expected to be held up, but one by one, by bridge or ford, the difficulty was surmounted until I began to think the local men were mistaken. However, as we approached the seventh there was a decidedly menacing murmur of fast-moving water. There was no sign of a bridge, and the experts pronounced it unfordable. I made one or two tentative attempts which soon satisfied me that for once the experts were right. We moved upstream a few hundred yards to where just round the first bend two single strands of cane, one directly above the other about three feet apart, spanned the river. Three of the men forthwith crossed at the double like so many monkeys, hardly troubling to use their hands. It looked so easy that I thought I would try, but there was so much play in the ropes, which were too close together for my comfort, and so much nervous strain, that I barely got over.

It was obviously impossible to take loads across, particularly loads like Thundu, whom it would have been a pity to have lost after having carried him so far. I wondered how the Akas manage, but they proved fully equal to the occasion. Quickly selecting a tree near the bank, they skilfully felled it, so that it spanned the water. It was rather too high on one side, so they fixed stakes on each end of the tree and ran a handrail of cane across. In a short time the whole party was over. An hour later the last river was behind us, and we camped that night in some grass bandas on a flat above the Bhareli—a favoured picnic place called Balipung, only twenty miles from Charduar.

Capt. Lightfoot had heard of our coming and met us half-way with a car. This was not the least of his kindnesses. Thundu was packed off to hospital where he was found to be suffering from kala-azar, or black fever, as well as malaria, from both of which he made a good recovery. Wangdi and I were taken to the Political Officer's bungalow where we received every kindness and were soon restored to normal by good food and quinine.

So ended my 1939 journeying, and a more unqualified failure has seldom been recorded. Sometimes we climb the wrong mountain, cross the wrong pass, or find ourselves in the wrong valley, but that can be laughed off provided we get somewhere or do something. Here we got nowhere except to a starting point and achieved nothing but a sense of endurance.

It will be seen that the Assam Himalaya are not easy to reach, but neither were Christian's Delectable Mountains, nor is any place that is worth reaching. By this I mean country which is more or less unknown, sparsely or not at all inhabited, inhospitable, difficult to move in, and, of course, mountainous. I admit there are many parts of the Himalaya which do not fulfil all these exacting conditions, but there the magnificence of the mountains covers any deficiencies and still leaves a credit balance.

The malaria difficulty could, I think, be overcome if strict precautions were taken for the first week's marching—that is, everyone under a net before sundown, long trousers instead of shorts, and mepacrine. It would be at least as difficult to supervise Sherpas as British soldiers to ensure that these precautions were carried out, but if they were, parties would be able to reach the mountains unhampered by sickness. Porters will always be difficult to obtain owing to the few villages and the small number of inhabitants. Small parties will therefore be, more than ever, essential. In this group of the Himalaya there are nearly twenty peaks over 20,000 ft., none of which has been looked at closely, much less climbed, and only four of which bear names. To those who understand, this will perhaps be some measure of our disappointment and of our eagerness to try again.

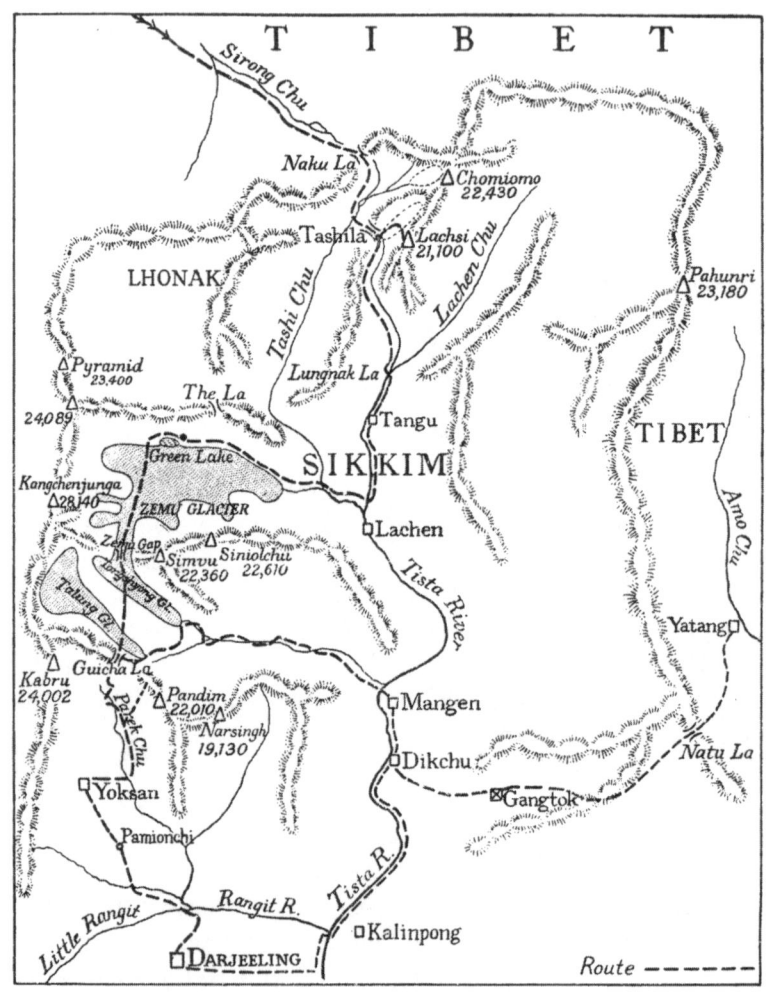

Map 2: Sketch map of Sikkim to illustrate Zemu Gap and Lachsi journeys (not to scale)

CHAPTER VI

THE ZEMU GAP—FAILURE

If, slightly to amend a remark of Chateaubriand, the mistakes of our nearest and dearest are not altogether displeasing to us, then, *a fortiori*, the mistakes of those we do not know must be highly gratifying. Nothing can be more bitter than the controversies of divines and explorers, and the rivalries of mountaineers. Of the quarrels of divines I shall say nothing—there are so many—but I recall the bitterness evoked by the explorers Speke, Burton, and Grant, over the Nile sources; by Peary and Cook over the North Pole; and by Whymper and the Italians on the Matterhorn. In the writings of these men, particularly in the Journals devoted to their exploits, there is often found a regrettable harshness as they refute or demolish the theories or claims of their rivals. In the following chapter there is no theology, the exploration and mountaineering are pitched in a minor key, but the illustration will serve to explain, if not excuse, an occasional gibe at the mistakes of others.

The small native State of Sikkim in north-east India, bounded on the west by Nepal and on the north and east by Tibet, has been open to explorers and mountaineers for nearly a hundred years. Sir Joseph Hooker, the great botanist-explorer, was at work there in the years 1848–9. Many have followed him, and after the 1914–18 war hardly a year passed without several small parties and possibly one large expedition either attempting some of the few unclimbed peaks or traversing its passes and glaciers. In spite of this activity there were still a few minor inaccuracies on the map of Sikkim, particularly with regard to the less frequented glaciers. It is probable that these have now been corrected, for in 1938 and 1939 the Survey of India was engaged on a new map of Sikkim. This chapter tells how one or two of these inaccuracies were detected.

The mountainous part of Sikkim, that is, the regions of snow and ice, is confined to the eastern and northern borders and the north-west

69

Mani wall and chorten, Sikkim;
mani walls must be passed on the left

corner. The giant Kangchenjunga (28,146 ft.) on the Nepal border, with its twelve-mile-long Zemu glacier, is the main attraction. A complete map of the Zemu glacier had been made by a German party in 1931, but there remained one pass, supposed to have been crossed but once, whose south side was little known. This was the Zemu Gap (19,276 ft.), a deep notch on the ridge between Simvu (22,360 ft.) and the most eastern satellite peak (25,526 ft.) of Kangchenjunga.

The two great advantages of climbing in Sikkim are the accessibility of the mountains and the ready supply of Sherpa porters in Darjeeling. If those in the first flight are engaged, as they usually are, then there are others who are glad enough to earn a few rupees in a less degrading way than by pulling the rickshaws of people too idle to walk. The gambling and drinking habits of the Sherpas provide an ever-present stimulus to work. This may offend the moralist but it helps anyone in search of porters. It is therefore easy to make a short impromptu trip. So in April 1936, having some unexpected time on my hands and wishing to try out some porters for the Nanda Devi expedition, I thought I would cross the Zemu Gap. According to an article in an old number of the *Geographical Journal* which I found by chance in that hospitable place, The Planters' Club, there seemed little to prevent it.

In May 1926 the author of this article had crossed the Guicha La, gone down the Talung and up the Tongshyong glaciers, and had then crossed the Gap to the Zemu glacier and back again—the latter part before breakfast. The main difficulties were encountered on the two glaciers which, owing to stone and ice bombardments, resembled a road near the front line on one of the more unquiet days on the Western Front. Only two other parties had interested themselves in the Zemu Gap. One in 1920 had visited the Talung glacier but had decided against going on by reason of the unpleasantness already referred to; the other in 1925 with Mr N. A. Tombazi, who claimed to have ascended to the Zemu Gap from the south. He had not crossed it.

A photograph taken from the Guicha La suggested that the ridge separating the two dangerous glaciers could be crossed in a direct line between the Guicha La and the Zemu Gap. If this were so there would be no necessity to remain for long under the barrage of stones and ice which apparently played constantly on any party foolish enough to traverse these glaciers. There seemed to be no insuperable difficulties in crossing the Gap itself, so I was tempted to give orders for my mail to be forwarded to Lachen, the village by which I expected to return after a triumphant crossing of the pass. Fortunately, being naturally pessimistic, I gave no such hostage to fortune.

The party, consisting of four Sherpas, two ponies, and myself, left Darjeeling on 1 May bound for a place called Chakung. This plan necessitated a double march, as we wished to avoid sleeping in the hot, malarial valley between. One of the Sherpas, Pasang Kikuli, deserves special mention on account of his magnificent record. Born in 1911 in Sola Khombu in north-west Nepal, the home of most Sherpas, he carried on the three Kangchenjunga expeditions of 1929, 1930 and 1931. In 1933 he reached Camp V on Mount Everest, and was one of the survivors of the terrible Camp 8 on Nanga Parbat in 1934. He stayed with his sahib, Uli Wieland, until the latter's death at Camp 7, and then, with three other Sherpas, eventually got down badly frost-bitten. In 1936 he was with us on Nanda Devi, where snow-blindness prevented his going high, and he was the only porter to accompany Houston and myself on the crossing of 'Longstaff's Col' on the way back. In 1938 he accompanied Houston and the Americans on the highly successful reconnaissance of K2. A year later, on the same mountain, he and two other Sherpas perished in a gallant attempt to bring down an American, Dudley Wolfe, marooned at 24,700 ft. He was a great-hearted mountaineer if ever there was one.

From Chakung the ponies returned, leaving us and a local man to shoulder the loads for the next thirteen-mile stage. Travelling on the beaten track in Sikkim is delightful. The sight of heavily forested valleys contrasting with the green and brown patches of cultivated fields, the well-spaced stages, the comfortable rest-houses, make a pleasing introduction to the sterner work ahead. Most important of all is the fresh food such as hens, milk, butter and eggs which can often be obtained. I like eggs, and on this hilly thirteen-mile stage had acquired a dozen which I intended eating as soon as we camped. Like Jane Austen's Mr Woodhouse I am of the opinion that 'an egg boiled very soft is not unwholesome', but on this occasion Pasang blotted his copy-book by hard-boiling the lot.

From the Pemayangtse bungalow, reached by doing five miles down and then five miles up, Yoksam, the last village on our route on

Sikkimese—a lama on the right

The ex-Lama from Yoksam monastery

the other side of the Rangit valley, seemed to be within shouting distance, but such is the valley-seamed nature of the country that it takes two days' marching to reach it. The last stage to Yoksam is a short one, so short that we arrived at eleven o'clock in the morning. I had hoped to camp beyond it, for camping for the day at that hour of the morning seems to me to be almost as abandoned as to go to bed in the afternoon, but the Sherpas would not suffer themselves to be torn so rudely and so unnecessarily from their last hold on civilisation and the good things which it meant. At Yoksam the former Lama of the now defunct monastery proved to be one of the most obliging men we had met with in Sikkim. He produced an overpowering brew of 'chang' and a chair, and undertook to find a couple of men to help us with our loads as far as the Parek Chu, the valley below the Guicha La. It can be taken, I think, as a general rule that the nearer they live to mountains the better the men; which may be one of the reasons why in so many mythologies mountains are the home of the gods.

Rising at five next morning I was staggered to find our two local recruits, provided by the ex-Lama, waiting to start. This keenness was no flash in the pan. They proved to be an admirable couple, indifferent to rain and not averse to snow. It rained all day, but low down the Parek Chu we found a 'lean-to' built against an overhanging rock. We were soon drying ourselves in the comfort of a fire. Having had previous experience of Sikkim weather I had brought with me an umbrella from the Darjeeling bazaar. I found it extremely useful, as it kept both rucksack and shoulders dry. Under its shelter and clad only in shirt, shorts, socks, and gym shoes, I found that rain, provided it was not cold, became a matter of indifference to me. I found too, odd though it may seem, that bare legs and shoes are no bad anti-leech measure. The leeches attach themselves, of course, but they are easily removed long before they have time to settle down to serious drinking. On the other hand, if boots and putties are worn they are not discovered until the end of the day by which time the blood has almost to be wrung from one's socks.

Next day we reached the grazing alp of Dzongri (13,000 ft.) on a plateau above the Parek Chu valley out of which we had been forced to climb. Scorning the warmth and shelter of the yak-herd's hut, and in spite of a cheerfully persistent drizzle, I obstinately put our camp a quarter-mile beyond it in order to get a view of Pandim (22,010 ft.), a peak just south of the Guicha La which had an added interest in that as yet no one had attempted to climb it. My obstinacy was rewarded when, towards sunset, the mountain drew back its cloud curtain, and revealed first the south ridge with its forbidding defences, then the summit, and finally a section of the long north ridge under which we should have to pass next day. The light was poor, but it was good enough to show why Pandim's summit had enjoyed such a long period of seclusion.

Some four inches of snow fell during the night, but the two local men turned up barefoot but smiling for their last march. We dropped down again through rhododendron forest, now a blaze of colour, to the Parek Chu and followed its left bank. Through the lowering clouds bits of the north ridge of Pandim furtively disclosed themselves, as if aware of our intentions. We camped under a rock below the ascent to the Guicha La, within reach of the last of the juniper bushes.

In the evening we had a clear view of the north ridge of Pandim. The lower end, near the Guicha La, was decorated with formidable gendarmes, but I observed that these could be outflanked by means of a snow gully, which led to a deep cleft in the ridge above them. This was undeniably long, and even if it were reached at this point I was by no means certain that the remaining two-thirds of the ridge could be climbed. However, the invitation of this conveniently placed gully, just above our camp, though it might be declined could not be ignored. I wrestled with temptation for most of the night and finally gave in. The Zemu Gap could wait for a day. Even if we got no farther, it would be good to get on to the ridge and see what the difficulties were.

I felt as if I were Jorrocks stealing out for a surreptitious by-day in Pinch-me-near Forest. Nevertheless, we took most of our loads. It would be foolish to reach the ridge, find the going good, and then be unable to camp there in readiness for exploiting success the following day. Kikuli and I could sleep there and the other two could go down. We got off early, I still clutching the umbrella with one hand and an ice-axe with the other. There was a long grind up scree to about 16,500 ft., where the gully narrowed and snow appeared. By keeping well to the side we were able to avoid the snow for another 500 ft., until at length the snow impinged against the steep rock wall and we were

A Lepcha from Sikkim

driven on to it. The notch must have been still about 500 ft. above us, but through the mist we could make out to the right of it a high gendarme, and to the left a crazy-looking pinnacle which seemed as unstable as a house of cards or a 'serac' on a hot day. The snow in the middle of the gully appeared likely to provide better going, but between us and it was a water-worn runnel of ice, three or four feet wide, across which I had to cut steps. The time had come to discard the umbrella, which I forthwith stuck in the snow by the runnel to fall to work cutting steps. Three of the Sherpas were still below, well into the side of the gully, when Pasang and I stepped across the runnel. There was no warning sound, but some instinct made me look up, and there, coming straight for us out of the mist, were half a dozen large boulders. They hit the snow above with a thud and then took the line of the runnel in a series of menacing bounds, some in the runnel itself, some outside. There was nothing to be done, and in a flash the crisis was over. The umbrella disintegrated as a rock hit it, and Kikuli and I remained staring stupidly at one another, rather white about the gills. There was no need for debate; the decision was immediate, silent, unanimous. We recrossed the runnel, cast a thoughtful glance at the place where the umbrella had stood, and went down the gully.

That afternoon I climbed to the Guicha La, whence I saw the Zemu Gap and the intermediate snow saddle between the Talung and Tongshyong glaciers. Even at that distance the steep ice-fall leading up to the Gap and a rock wall crowning it roused misgivings.

Once more we found that time spent in reconnoitring is seldom wasted. When we crossed the Guicha La next morning snow was falling so thickly that we had to steer by a compass bearing I had had the sense to take. There was a fairly steep snow slope down the north side where three of the Sherpas showed themselves to be novices by a good deal of unsteadiness, one of them even parting company with his load. By the time we had reached a grassy shelf a few hundred feet above the Talung glacier the snow had stopped. We spent an hour in crossing to the moraine on the other side, where we found more grass, a little juniper, a herd of bharal, and, most fortunate of all, a pool of water.

The daily fall of snow was becoming a nuisance. Snow fell continuously that night, but the morning broke fine and clear. Weather in the Himalaya that spring was worse than usual. The Mount Everest party led by Mr Hugh Ruttledge had found the upper rocks white with snow on 30 April, and, although the arrival of the monsoon in southern India was not officially reported until 19 May, the weather throughout the month was mild with occasional heavy falls of snow. It was very similar in fact to what we were experiencing, except that in Sikkim snow fell nearly every day.

A weary trudge through deep powder snow brought us to the saddle on the ridge whence a gently sloping field of névé led down to the Tongshyong glacier which we quickly crossed. It is here about half a mile wide. As we steered for the foot of the ice-fall of the small tributary glacier which descends from the Zemu Gap, snow began falling heavily again. The map showed the Zemu Gap as lying at the head of the Tongshyong, but it is in fact half a mile short of the head and has a small glacier of its own at right angles to the main one. There were two ice-falls on this subsidiary glacier. The first was so steep and intricate that we were forced to traverse off to the left and take to the rocks. We camped at about 18,000 ft., nearly level with the top of the ice-fall, taking a lot of time and trouble to find accommodation on a little patch of rock still clear of snow—trouble that was largely wasted because snow fell throughout the night. The Sherpas are masters of the art of digging out or building up rock platforms for tent sites. They turn themselves into human bulldozers, lying down with their backs against a rock for purchase and their feet firmly wedged against the half-ton rock they mean to shift. A series of back-cracking heaves then does the trick.

We could now take stock of our position. The two stone-throwing glacier-valleys had been crossed without trouble—not so much as a pebble had fallen. Indeed, they were wide and open enough for us to avoid anything but an avalanche on the Kangchenjunga scale. Actually there were no slopes to give birth to such except at the head of the Talung. A thousand feet above us was the Gap, guarded first by the even steeper and more intricate ice-fall, and finally by 100 ft. of ice-wall.

The snow froze on the tents in the night, so next morning, since packing these would be troublesome, I left the men to follow later and pushed on alone to reconnoitre. The snow terrace between the lower and upper ice-falls was so badly crevassed that I was forced to

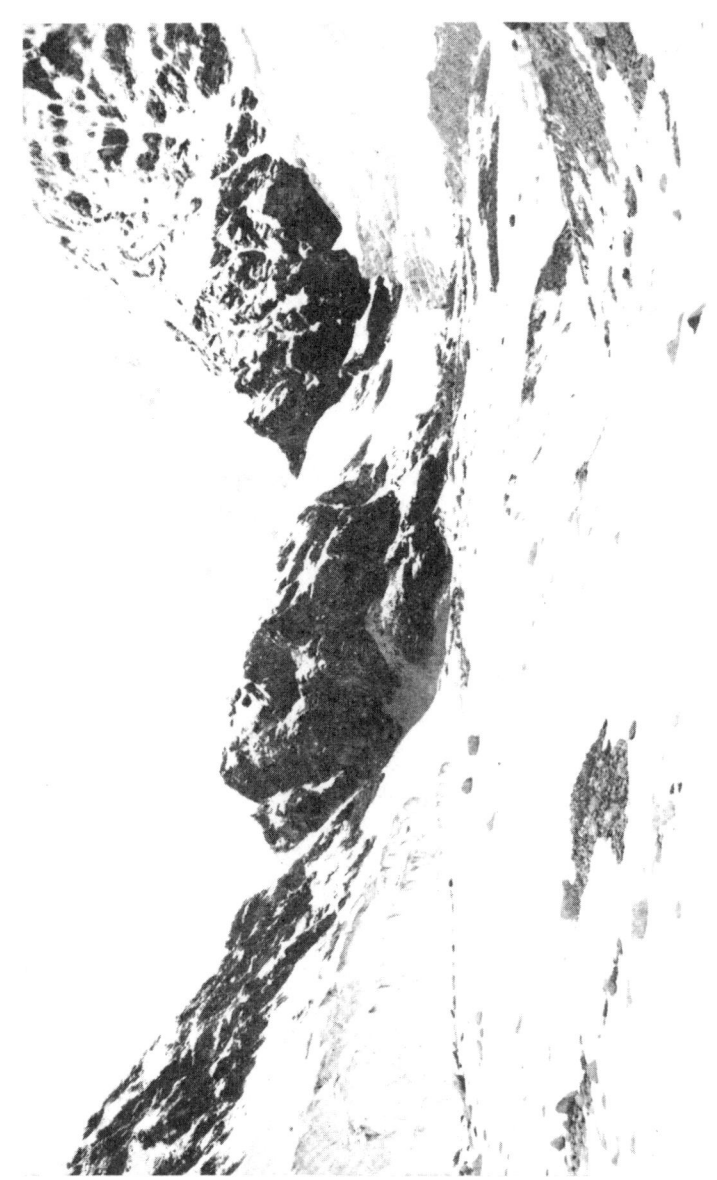

Head of Tongshyong Glacier—Query Boustead's 'Zemu Gap'?

wait on the lip of the first big one until the porters arrived. We roped up and crossed, camping a little higher right at the foot of the upper ice-fall. Shut in as we were between two high rock walls we found the heat and glare so overpowering that it was essential for us to get some food and drink before having a look at this formidable affair. Owing to the nature of the ground and the crevasses there was hardly room even for our two small tents, and we were too nearly under the Simvu slope for comfort. Small trickles of snow, incipient avalanches, kept hissing down, but all came to a respectful halt about ten yards from the tents. At an occasional louder roar the Sherpas would rush panic-stricken from their tent, so frightening me that I did the same. The Sherpas bore me no ill-will for the Pandim gully incident, but this was trying them too highly. It was obviously no place for a prolonged sojourn.

These alarms ceased about three o'clock, when, feeling stronger, I kicked and cut steps up the ice-fall for about 100 ft. Here a doubtfully flimsy bridge over a large crevasse led to a steep wall of ice which would certainly take a long time to climb, so after casting about vainly for an alternative, I left it for the next day. Although we were loath to give in, defeat seemed imminent, for beyond these obstacles lay the final ice-wall which from below appeared impregnable.

Pasang Kikuli joined in the assault next morning, and together we hacked a big staircase up the thirty feet of steep ice, a job which took two hours. Above that we were able to kick steps, but there were only a few inches of snow overlying the ice, and we realised that when the sun had done its work the snow covering would not hold. A little higher we came to a horribly frail bridge over a deep crevasse. Moving gently with the utmost circumspection we crossed in safety by crawling. Whether or no this bridge would hold the weight of a man with a load was a nice point which I had already half decided ought not to be settled by experiment. A short snow slope led to yet another bridged crevasse from where we had a good view of the final wall two or three hundred yards away up a gentle snow rise. It was fully as high as we had feared, all iced, and appeared to overhang in places. An icy gully on the Simvu side might have been forced from a camp on the plateau, but it was beyond the strength of our weak party even had we come safely over the two dangerous crevasses.

THE ZEMU GAP—FAILURE 81

If the Sherpas had any regrets at leaving the Zemu Gap uncrossed they managed to conceal them. Not a moment was lost in packing up and standing away from the threatening slope of Simvu. We took to the rocks on the north side of the ice-fall. We had funked this route on the way up—justifiably, too, as it happened, because in order to get from the rocks to the glacier we had to 'rope down'; that is, to suspend the doubled rope over a convenient rock and slide down it, hoping that the rope will *not* slip off, and then hoping nearly as much that when everyone is down, the rope *will* slip off and *not* jam.

The weather thickened as we camped early in the middle of the glacier, for I wanted to examine the head of the Tongshyong. The Zemu Gap of our experience differed so widely from the one about which I had read that I was inclined to believe that a mistake had been made and that the genuine Gap lay concealed behind some corner near the head of the glacier. But, as I found that evening, there was no other break in the mighty east-southeast ridge of Kangchenjunga, and the easy, low col at the head of the Tongshyong obviously led into the wide bay at the head of the Talung. It occurred to me that in the thick weather which prevailed when the first alleged crossing had been made, this, and not the Zemu Gap, was the place which had been crossed.

There is something eminently satisfactory about a circular tour. It rounds off the journey and is as satisfying in its way as the complete traverse of a mountain. We therefore decided to go back down the Talung Chu, a river valley which joins the main Tista valley route at Mangen. The only Europeans who had followed it down were Messrs Raeburn and Tobin in 1920. From the map it seemed about three days' journey—it had taken them eight, but of that I was not aware or I might have forgone the satisfaction of a circular tour.

It was a glorious morning on the 14th when we walked down the Tongshyong. The rough surface of the glacier was now covered by a smooth carpet of frozen snow along which we strolled, enjoying the easiest glacier walk I have ever had. The Tongshyong was narrower than the Talung and perhaps stones did fall from its steep containing walls (though we neither saw nor heard any), but a party that steered a reasonably central course could not possibly be hit. We had some bother getting down the steep, high, terminal moraine to the river. I

Sherpas moving down Tongshyong

Looking down the Tongshyong Glacier

slid—intentionally I think—and the porters roped down. Having with some trouble crossed to the right bank of the swiftly flowing Talung Chu we plunged at once into a tangle of dense rhododendron, where we had a gruelling time. There was no vestige of path but there were signs that native hunters, probably Lepchas, came here occasionally; we found a dead buck in a recently set snare and a single log bridge spanning the river.

A fine night, which we spent round a gigantic fire, was followed by another glorious morning. By midday, after three hours of heavy going, we were driven down to the river, which was crossed by a snow bridge. Shortly after we had to go back, this time by a natural rock bridge. This place was a most astonishing cleft, barely three feet wide, with the river boiling through the gorge 100 ft. below. A difference of ten feet between the take-off and landing sides made it a fearsome jump.

The third day gave us a ten-hour bush-crawl along the right bank, with midges, tree ticks, and leeches doing their best to enliven the proceedings. The tree ticks were in the minority but by far the most troublesome. They were strategists. When they dropped on one, instead of attaching themselves at once to the first handy bit of skin, they invariably sought out the soft underbelly before burying their heads deep in the flesh.

On the 17th, although we had found a track of sorts, we had another bad day. An hour was spent in roping the loads over a rickety three-span bridge, then the track petered out and the going became atrocious, until at last we spotted another bridge. We crossed this and camped. We had only covered a mile in nine hours.

Next morning we found that by crossing this bridge we had made a false move. The track disappeared and no progress was possible, so we crossed back and picked up a good path which at long length brought us to a new field of maize surrounded by dense forest. There was no one there, but a mile or so farther on we came to a small village where there were a few women. We got nothing out of them, not even curiosity, which was surprising, not to say disappointing; for I had begun to feel that this Talung Chu journey of ours was fast becoming epic. It is mortifying to appear, apparently from nowhere, feeling that you have done something remarkable, to find that the first person you meet, and that a woman, ignores you completely.

The path we now followed had evidently been constructed empirically. It went up and down with the most damnable reiteration and frequently scaled steep rock 'pitches' which were cunningly roped and laddered like a popular Dolomite climb. One particularly fierce place was a bamboo suspension bridge over a 100 ft. drop—'for those free from dizziness only', as Baedeker puts it. Presently we met a man, but he, like the women, was dumb and spake not. It would have been interesting to know more precisely where we were, for our dead reckoning must have been wide of the mark. After twisting about high above the valley in a hesitating manner the track suddenly made up its mind and without more ado dived straight down to the river, 2000 ft. below. Somewhat dazed, we camped there in a field of cardamoms. We were now down to about 4000 ft., but here there seemed to be fewer pests than in the forest higher up.

If we were anywhere near where we thought, we might expect to emerge at the end of the Talung Chu on the 19th. The track maintained its vagaries and even introduced us to a new method of surmounting steep rock 'pitches' by a single slippery bamboo on a slanting traverse. At the next houses we reached, the only woman in residence ran away but a man stood his ground and even told us where we were. The rest was plain sailing, except for a memorable thousand-foot slog up to Mangen, a small town on the Tista valley route.

On the way back to Darjeeling we called at the Residency, Gangtok. Dressed as I was in torn shirt and shorts, with bare legs and a beard not yet strong enough to conceal the dirt beneath—in short, travel-stained—I was rather surprised that I got past the servants at the door, resplendent in their scarlet and gold livery. And it was unfortunate that there should be a dinner party that night, where, with the Resident's spare trousers hitched up to my armpits (he was a very big man) and his coat sleeves turned up several times, it was difficult to feel really at ease. Contrast, no doubt, is the relish of life. Comfort is only valued after hardship, luxury after squalor, riches after poverty. If experienced in the reverse order the appreciation is, perhaps, less keen; and, I reflected that evening, the transition should not be too violent.

CHAPTER VII

THE ZEMU GAP—SUCCESS

THE EARLIER INTEREST IN THE ZEMU GAP was provoked by the thought that it might provide a more direct route to Kangchenjunga than did the Tista valley-Zemu glacier route, but, once the south side of the Gap had been seen, this possibility could be ruled out. Any further interest that I took in it was therefore academic, the unprofitable solution of a problem in mountain travel and a desire to tidy up the map. I now doubted very much whether the Gap had ever been crossed and it was therefore more necessary for me to try. From what I had seen, the crossing from the south was not to be undertaken singlehanded, but from the north side it might be easier. It might be possible to rope down the ice-wall or one of the flanking rock walls, and there would be no need to run the risk of avalanches by camping on that narrow overhung glacier below the menacing slopes of Simvu.

Accordingly, on the way back from Mount Everest in the summer of 1938, I resolved to devote a fortnight or so to a journey in Sikkim, including if possible a return home by the Zemu Gap and the Guicha La. The monsoon would be in full blast, but in Sikkim there appears to be no pre-eminently 'best' season for mountaineering. Climbs have been undertaken before, during and after the monsoon, even as late as November, and the weather has been uniformly poor.

As is usual with a party returning from Mount Everest, we soon began to break up, like rats leaving the sinking ship. We had seen quite enough of each other for a time, and delays in getting transport were trying the patience of all. The crowning blow fell at Tingkye Dzong, where a box belonging to the eminent mountaineer and geologist, N. E. Odell, was stolen. The box contained valuable geological specimens, and the surprise and chagrin of the thief must have almost equalled the fury of Odell. It was a serious matter from every point of view. The results of several months' work had gone, and, if the thief talked, the Tibetans would learn that we had been collecting stones against their express wishes. They quite rightly object to people going about knocking their rocks to pieces with a small hammer, thus releasing any spirits which may happen to be in them. Of course, the thief would probably be feeling too much of a fool to advertise the fact that he had risked his life, or at any rate the skin on his back, for a box full of stones.

Shipton had already left to do some survey work in the Nyonno Ri, happily brandishing a theodolite instead of an ice-axe; Smythe, sniffing the fleshpots from afar, disappeared over the plain, leaving behind a cloud of dust and small stones; Odell and Lloyd intended returning by a pass called the Choten Nyima La: I was bound for another, the Naku La. Dr Warren alone stuck to the ship, having to look after a porter who had been struck with paralysis while on the mountain.

My relief will therefore be understood when, on the last day of June, leaving Karma Paul, the Tibetan interpreter, to wrestle with transport problems, I escaped with two Sherpas, rejoicing in the knowledge that our progress would depend on our own exertions and not on the whim of a Tibetan official.

In Tibet one marches at will over a seemingly endless expanse of bare, brown, gently undulating plain, steering as often as not by some distant landmark, under a pale blue lucent sky, perhaps lightly flecked with cloud. These conditions contrast strongly with those in Sikkim. There, under a leaden canopy of heavily charged rain clouds, men and beasts follow a roughly paved mule track winding through deep-cut valleys whose high, steep, densely forested sides shut out all but the highest peaks.

The two Sherpas I took with me were Renzing, wild and unruly, but a first-class man and an Everest 'Tiger'; and Lhakpa Tenzing, quieter and with less fire in his belly, but also a 'Tiger'. We succeeded in hiring a pony to carry our extra food, and set out for the Naku La, an 18,000 ft. pass on the main Himalayan range between Tibet and Sikkim. The pass is used by Tibetans who graze their sheep in the Chaka Chu valley on the Sikkim side. The map of the Tibet-Sikkim Himalaya is pleasingly sketchy hereabouts, and it was impossible to identify the group of villages at which we halted for the first night. We were told that from here the pass could be crossed by a long day's march, so we started early, travelling over gravel and sparse grass up

Camp by the boulder in the Parek Chu

the flat Sirong Chu valley. There is a beautiful lake half a mile long and a quarter wide on the Tibetan side, and a smaller one on the Sikkim side. Before one reaches the lake a curious thing is seen. Spanning the valley floor from hill-side to hill-side, a distance of about three-quarters of a mile, is a roughly built, dry stone wall about four foot high and 6 foot thick at the base. Doubtless it is of Tibetan construction, but when and why it was built I have no notion.

The rise to the pass is so gradual that it is almost imperceptible. A fierce wind blew, and when we reached the grass-covered summit we ran immediately into rain, mist and cloud, which were to be our constant companions throughout the trip. I particularly wanted a view from the top because I had designs on Lachsi, a 21,100 ft. peak lying west of Chomiomo (22,430 ft.). We were completely ignorant of the mountain and its approaches, and I did not know until later that an ascent had been attempted in 1936. According to the map, the valley into which we were looking was bounded by Lachsi on the east, but although the clouds were thick, I could see enough to convince me that no high mountain bounded the valley on that side, but only a low rock ridge.

The descent was as gradual as the climb. After passing a glacier flowing down on our left from Chomiomo we camped with some Tibetan shepherds at a place called Naku, about four miles from the top of the pass. To the north-east a depression on the ridge bounding the valley invited me to cross into the next nallah, which, I argued, must lie immediately below Lachsi. We crossed this the next day. A Tibetan volunteered to help us with our loads, which were still very heavy, since we were carrying a fortnight's food. Going up to the col we found cairns and learnt that it was known as the Tashi La and was used by the Sikkimese with their yaks. It leads into the Tashi Chu nallah by a descent which is exceedingly steep, even for yaks.

Here we had one great stroke of luck. It was the usual cloudy, drizzling day, but, just as I reached the col, a rift in the clouds disclosed for a bare minute, immediately opposite across the valley, a peak which I took to be Lachsi. It appeared very similar to the mountain which we had noticed some months before on the way into Tibet—a long snow ridge, almost a plateau, crowned by an unmistakable snow pimple. This momentary glimpse had also revealed a possible route up; but the Sherpas who reached the col a few minutes later saw nothing of this, so that next day, when we climbed it, were quite bewildered. We descended, camped in the moraine trough below the col, and sent our Tibetan friend home to his sheep.

Starting at 5 a.m. and moving north, we skirted the ice-fall at the head of the small Tashi Chu glacier and then turned round a half-circle until we were heading almost south. This intricate manœuvre was designed to land us on the main ridge, but, when hitherto unseen peaks began to loom up through the mist on our left, I began to wonder whether we were really on Lachsi. The snow was very soft until at a height of about 20,000 ft. signs of an irresolute attempt at freezing appeared. We progressed slowly and the 'pimple' obstinately refused to show itself. At the same time the so-called plateau became less like a plateau than ever. It narrowed to a knife-edge, which on the right fell away in a steep and broken ice-fall, and on the left in a rock precipice. At last we came to a notch which yesterday I had welcomed as a landmark. Now a closer view showed that it needed consideration. Lhakpa, not liking the look of things, decided to stay where he was, but Renzing and I descended by a steep and tortuous way into the notch and, what was infinitely more important, succeeded in climbing out the other side. The snow was good. The pimple, which now appeared, was about 100 ft. high, and with care we managed to reach the summit by a ridge of very unstable rock covered with snow. There was just room to stand on top. During the ascent, which had taken six hours, the increasing warmth of the day had reduced the snow everywhere to a uniform softness compelling us to take almost as long over the descent. It was so warm that we even had rain at 20,000 ft.

The first part of our programme thus completed we headed for Tangu on the main route from Sikkim to Tibet, reaching it on 4 July. A traveller's first feeling on seeing that the Rest House where he proposes to stop is already occupied is one of disgust, his second one of curiosity about those whom he will shortly meet. Mules and other signs of activity near the Tangu Rest House had warned me that this had happened, but I was not prepared to see the Nazi flag flying and the members of a large German scientific party led by a Dr Ernst Schaefer. He was a tough-looking, interesting man who had travelled much in western China and Tibet, and had written two books about it. The party was

Pandim from the north-east (22,010 ft.)

spending several months in Sikkim collecting birds, insects and plants, and doing other scientific work; later, as already related, they 'infiltrated' into Tibet. The party included every breed of scientist known to man: ornithologist, zoologist, entomologist, anthropologist, and many other 'ologists' of whom I had never heard. There was also a photographer whose special subject was Alpine flowers. I think they were genuine enough. They were not a party of those German 'technicians' of whom we were to see and hear so much a year or so later.

Next day we took the Lachen road and then turned up the Zemu glen, camping with some cowherds near Yaktang. Their rough wooden shanty rose like an island out of a sea of mud and was amazingly squalid inside, but we passed a pleasant night with the cowherd, his wife, and some female relations. There were seven of us and a hen in a hut ten feet by ten feet. Our next camp was in a cave about a mile below the glacier snout, which like most caves could be summed up as 'draughts and drips'. Still, we were much better off than outside in the rain.

In the morning, through mist and rain, we could see the snout of the glacier only about 500 yards above. There was some very rough going in the trough for about a mile, until the river which we had been following, the Zemu Chu, disappeared under the ice. I was glad to see the last of it; for two days it had been a close and terrifying companion. After crossing another stream, which at that early hour was not very formidable, we reached the old German Base Camp in three hours. Here there was a collection of tins and rubbish which would bear comparison with the collections to be found on any of the more popular beauty spots of England, but here it had the shock of unexpectedness. We should be thankful that Tibetans are such thorough scavengers. Anyone walking up the East Rongbuk glacier past Camps I, II and III, on the way to Mount Everest, would not realise that here there had probably been more tins opened in the last twenty years than anywhere in India. On the Rongbuk there is not a trace of a tin to be seen. The grimness of life at Camp III would be greatly increased if the accumulated debris of seven expeditions was still to be seen.

We pushed on to the Green Lake the same day. In good weather this must be a glorious walk among grass and flowers, with the glittering precipices of Kangchenjunga and the great peaks of the Nepal border in full view. Unfortunately we could see less than a mile ahead.

There was a little furze growing here, which the Sherpas used to get a fire going in the lee of a boulder. Lhakpa nursed it as if it were a sick child, not caring how wet he became. From here a cairned track led to the foot of the Northeast Spur, the route by which the Germans made their attempts on Kangchenjunga. Before reaching this we took to the glacier again and crossed to the arm which descends from the Zemu Gap. Again we were in luck. This was the only day on which the clouds conceded a view for any length of time. Never at any time did they rise above the 19,000 ft. level, but that was just enough to resolve any doubts we had about our being on the right track. Two glacier arms on our right, one of which I at first thought might be ours, obviously ended under the cliffs of Kangchenjunga, but of this mountain, or of Simvu, or of Siniolchu, or of any other landmark, we saw nothing.

We had started at five o'clock with the intention of tackling the Gap that day, but we did not reach the foot of the approach glacier until eleven. The col, barely discernible under the cloud canopy, looked near enough, but taking into account the time and the weather I decided to wait until the next day. I had, for once, decided wisely. Unfortunately our Primus stove, like the Dutchman's anchor, had been left behind, not for the sake of lightening our loads but for the more usual reason of forgetfulness. However, Renzing went back to the foot of the North-east Spur and presently returned with some sort of fuel, so that our camp on the ice was not so cheerless as my carelessness deserved. It is surprising how far up the eastern slopes of Kangchenjunga fuel can be found.

I roused the men at 3.30 next morning and we started making tea in the open in a drizzle of rain. Two hours later this became worse, driving down the glacier from the Gap. Within a quarter of an hour of leaving, on reaching the névé, our expectations were realised—the snow was rotten. At this season, below 20,000 ft., the sun's effect upon snow conditions needs little consideration, for whether you start at midnight or midday the snow will still be soft. It took us four hours to reach the Gap (19,200 ft.) although I suppose we had not more than 2000 ft. to climb. There were no great difficulties, but the approach was narrow and subject to avalanches from both sides—the remains of two very big ones were seen. As the day drew on the drizzle changed to snow, and a fierce wind from the pass driving this in our faces so obscured our vision that I had to remove my snow-glasses to find a way through the crevasses.

We noticed one thing which I hesitate to mention for fear of reopening old controversies. A single track of footsteps, which in view of the weather conditions could not have been more than two or three days old, led up the glacier as far as the crest of the Zemu Gap and then disappeared on the rocks of the Simvu side. On returning to Darjeeling I made inquiries, but so far as was known no party had been out anywhere near Kangchenjunga. The last known visit to the south side of the Gap was made by John Hunt on 18 November the previous year. Moreover, lunatics are scarce, and who would go 'swanning' about alone on the Zemu glacier?

The last time I had reported having come across strange tracks in the snow (in the upper basin of the Biafo glacier, Sir Martin Conway's Snow Lake) on my return from the Karakoram in 1937, considerable comment had appeared in the correspondence columns of *The Times* from both learned scientists and experienced mountaineers. This correspondence, illuminating but inconclusive, should be read by students. G. K. Chesterton has remarked on the loving care and patience bestowed by the professors on their building up of *Pithecanthropus*—a bit of skull here, a few teeth there, and a thigh-bone from somewhere else—until at last they produced a detailed drawing, carefully shaded to show that the very hairs of his head were all numbered. How amused he would have been to see the ferocity with which the professors fell upon *Homo Nivis Odiosus* and tore him (and those who believed in him) limb from limb.

In the present instance there were no tracks like 'soup plates' which, according to fancy, could be conveniently attributed to bears, snow leopards, otters, leaping hares, or gigantic one-legged birds, but plain tracks of large boots. Of course, for this there is only the word of one man, albeit an unexaggerative man of scrupulous veracity. Given the existence of an Abominable Snowman, there is no reason why he should not have picked up a discarded pair of climbing boots at the German Base Camp and put them to their obvious use. We are not to suppose that a Snowman, or an animal if you like, has not wit enough to keep its feet dry if they happen to be the shape that go into boots. These tracks were in fact so real that the Sherpas and I discussed the possibility of one of Schaefer's party having preceded us and crossed the Gap; but whoever or whatever it was had certainly not descended from the crest. I was pleased to recall the friendly hint I had given to the anthropologist of Schaefer's party—an earnest, inquiring man—over a few glasses of Kummel, encouraging him to spare no pains in solving the problem of *Homo Nivis Odiosus*, and begging him not to be put off by the zoologist, who would infallibly tell him that any tracks he found were not those of our abominable friend, not even of a Snark or a Boojum, but only those of a bear.

To return to the crest of the Zemu Gap where we were now standing, craning our necks to see if those mysterious tracks went down the other side, and if so, which way they went. The weather was too bad and I was too anxious about our descent to start looking for the pair of crampons which Tombazi (see chap. vi) had reported having left on the rocks on the north side when he ascended to the Gap from the Tongshyong glacier in 1925. Instead we addressed ourselves at once to the problem of getting down.

From our visit in 1936 I knew of the steep ice-wall on the south side, and had taken the precaution of bringing 240 ft. of Alpine line. Even so on first looking over the top I got a shock. There was a wall, over 200 ft. of it, and overhanging sufficiently to prevent one from seeing where one would land. We could not use the rope down this. However, search revealed a very steep and narrow gully descending from the junction of the crest of the pass and the precipitous shoulder of Simvu. Between two runnels of ice was a thin ribbon of snow. It was loose and wet, but with careful handling ('footing' would be better) steps could be made in it. I will not guess at the angle for fear of being called a liar, but it seemed to me that a man with a long nose, standing upright, could have wiped it on the snow. I went down a rope's length and hacked out a platform in the ice for Lhakpa, who followed me. It was so misty below that I was not at all sure whether we could reach the plateau short of the wall on which Pasang and I had gained a footing in 1936. There was a bergschrund at the foot of the wall, but another rope's length sufficed to see me over this.

Having climbed back to the platform where Lhakpa was, I got Renzing, who was still on top, to begin lowering the loads down the ice runnel to our level so that we could drag them on our platform by

Zemu Gap from across Tongshyong Glacier—showing lower and upper ice-fall and final ice wall

making a long arm with our ice-axe. Lhakpa was then sent down over the bergschrund, Renzing joined me on the platform, and the load lowering began again. To save time I sent my own load, which was lighter than the others, down the runnel under its own steam. Leaping the 'schrund' it disappeared across the snow into the mist at the rate of knots. I thought I had seen the last of it, and the probable loss of sleeping bag, mat, spare clothes, tobacco, camera, and ten pounds of sugar, was offset to some extent by the certainty of having no load to carry. The remaining loads were lowered.

Crossing the little snow plateau we found my load, which had stopped just short of the next obstacle. This was the upper ice-fall which had given us trouble in 1936; since then it had altered out of all recognition. A great chasm more than 100 ft. wide and 100 ft. deep had opened up across the glacier. We found a place where an 'abseil' of fifty feet would have done the trick, but the edge overhung slightly and at the bottom of the chasm was a crevasse into which there was an even chance of landing. A situation in which one found oneself dangling at the end of a fifty-foot rope over a crevasse instead of over firm ground was full of possibilities, but as we had a second rope with us I think that even that situation would not have been irretrievable. But in such places, employing rope tactics, one of the difficulties is to make the man above understand what is wanted. In the gully we had just descended my shouted instructions to Renzing were lost in the wind.

This overhang was of no use to us so, moving over to the right, I reconnoitred another route. It started in an unorthodox manner with a 15 ft. jump, and it was therefore essential to know whether the rest of the route would 'go' before committing the whole party; we had in fact already burnt our boats, or at any rate set them alight, by our descent of the gully, for to climb that with loads on would have been a hazardous performance. The lower part proved possible. The Sherpas jumped, and down we went. The last 30 ft. to the floor of the chasm was a steep, icy funnel which terminated very close to another crevasse. I well remember the plaintive cry of the first man, Lhakpa: 'Do you want to kill me?' on being told to trust to the rope. One load on being shot down did finish in the crevasse, but it stopped on a ledge from which we fished it up. Having lowered the Sherpas down I cut steps for half the distance and then, being in a hurry, slid the rest. Having climbed out the other side I was half afraid there were other surprises in store for us, for the mist hid everything; but as we went down the ground became easier, and presently we reached the spot below the ice-fall where we had camped in 1936. It was now hidden by the debris of a colossal avalanche. It can be assumed that most big avalanches take place after the first heavy monsoon snowfall when the temperature is rising rapidly; but avalanches are very much an Act of God, and behave, in spite of our knowledge, in an incalculable way. Especially is this so in the Himalaya, where they also assume an unimaginable size and travel unbelievable distances. The only safe rule is to take every precaution, trust nothing, and expect one day to be caught out.

We reached the Tongshyong glacier at 3 p.m., having taken five and a half hours to come down from the top, and nine and a half from our camp on the other side. The crossing of the Gap in the reverse direction with heavy loads would be extremely difficult, although conditions undoubtedly vary considerably from year to year. Even so the alleged crossing in 1927, on which I have already commented, must have been a remarkable feat. The party left their camp on the Tongshyong at 3 a.m., crossed the Gap, descended to the Zemu glacier, and returned to camp in time for breakfast at 9 a.m.!

We were getting tired, our loads and we ourselves were wet through, and the thought of finding abundant fuel at the snout of the glacier led us there rather than cross at once to the Talung glacier by the snow-saddle route we had used in 1936. We had had enough snow wallowing for one day; we were in that frame of mind which recoils shudderingly from the mere thought of going uphill again, and we had not yet made up our minds to abandon the original plan of returning by the Talung Chu route. In 1936 that journey had not been easy and now the weather was much worse, but it was the most direct route to Gangtok which I had to visit before going on to Darjeeling. We found some fuel late that evening, but it was the wrong kind of shrub, and nothing would make it burn. In monsoon conditions in Sikkim only wood like juniper or 'chir', full of resin, would have consented to light. We dined austerely on cold water, sugar and satu. The whole, mixed and squashed together in a cake, is palatable. I had just written up my diary, commenting on the really remarkable fact that, although I had gone practically the whole day without snow-glasses, my eyes

Lower ice fall and Zemu Gap beyond
—snow slope on right is descending from Simvu

seemed to have taken no harm, when they began to smart; presently I was in all the agony of snow-blindness. There was little sleep that night either for me or for Lhakpa, whose eyes were also affected. Next morning the pain was less, but I could only bear to look at the ground at my feet. Under the circumstances this was not a great handicap, for only someone blessed with infra-red eyes could have pierced the prevailing mist.

We started off, stumbling in the wake of Renzing, intending to cross the foot of the dividing ridge in order to get on to the Talung glacier. Once there we would make for the Guicha La, for, what with our blindness and the weather, the Talung Chu route was unthinkable. The very few who know that trackless vale of tears will agree that this decision was wise, but it soon became evident that in trying to reach the Talung by the route we had chosen we were extremely foolish. We kept too low, as tired men will, and soon we were fighting a losing battle with rhododendron and other close-growing abominations. After a six-hour struggle, in which we gained about a mile, we found ourselves above the snout of the Talung. As we were unable to get down to it at this point on account of the very high, steep moraine banks which are a feature of the country near the Talung-Tongshyong junction, we had to continue bush-crawling to the right and soon found ourselves spread-eagled on a rocky cliff. By this time we were getting desperate, so using a rhododendron root as a dubious anchor, we lowered the loads and roped down after them. Tired, wet, and cross, we trudged over the glacier to the moraine on the other side and followed it up until five o'clock when we camped. There was plenty of scrub about but none that would burn, and we dined as frugally as before. However, the pain had gone from our eyes, and in spite of having wet sleeping-bags we slept well—he who sleeps, dines.

The mist was as thick as ever next morning when after more satu, sugar and water, we set out to look for the Guicha La. We had been there before, but I feared there would be much 'trial and error' work before we hit it off in the mist. But our luck still held. We had not been going an hour before I spotted a wisp of mist with a decidedly bluish tinge. I dared not suggest that it was smoke for fear of rousing false hopes, but presently the Sherpas, who had probably noticed it long before, announced that it was smoke. In a few minutes we were drinking sheep's milk, and warming ourselves in a matting shelter with some very astonished shepherds camped at the foot of the Guicha La. They had come over the previous day.

Our misadventures were not over yet. We toiled up grass slopes for an unconscionable time until we all agreed we should have reached the pass. Casting about, we hit on a path and eventually reached the pass—but not the one we were aiming for, which must have been nearly a mile to our right. This one was the higher Guicha La at the foot of Pandim. We dropped down to the Parek Chu, seeing the sun for the first time in many days. We draped our sleeping-bags outside our loads to dry, and set off at speed down the valley, bent on reaching Dzongri before nightfall.

The glacier stream, swollen by melting snow and rain, looked formidable so, certain that Dzongri was on its other side and uncertain whether the bridge lower down still existed, we decided to cross while the going was good. On the far side we picked up a half-hearted track down which we proceeded gaily enough in spite of the heavy rain which had begun again. The track became more and more tenuous until finally, in the heart of a thicket, it petered out. Having noticed some sheep and a shepherd's hut on the other bank about a mile back, we decided to return and ask about the bridge, though we feared that by now there would be too much water to recross in safety. Retracing our steps until we were opposite the hut, we plunged into what had become an angry river; we could get no wetter and death by drowning seemed preferable to another night in the open. The hut appeared to be empty except for a heap of blankets, but in response to our shouts the pile of blankets stirred and a boy came to the surface. He was a lad of prompt decision and had evidently at once made up his mind that we were not desirable guests. In reply to our question he answered unhesitatingly that Dzongri was a bare two miles away. We sped away in the rain, hardly stopping to thank him for his glad tidings. A long two miles brought us no farther than the bridge, and for another three we climbed steadily for what I thought must be 10,000 ft. but which was probably only 2000.

I was well ahead of the Sherpas when, just about dusk, I took up quarters in a muddy, leaking, derelict yak-stable, which seemed to be the only shelter in Dzongri. By hacking bits off the less wet parts of the underside of the roof I managed to get a fire going just as the others arrived. They seemed surprised and a bit disappointed at our poor quarters and meagre fire. The pan was put on for tea, Lhakpa went off to look for juniper, but was back in a minute to tell us that just round the corner was a billet with a roaring fire. We moved over and spent a luxurious evening in the company of a young yak-herd and half a dozen still younger yaks. In three days more we reached the Tista valley again at a point eighteen miles from our destination, Gangtok. The Sherpas were now lagging. Leaving word for them to make their way to Darjeeling, I procured a car the same afternoon and reached Gangtok.

We had climbed a mountain and crossed a pass; been wet, cold, hungry, frightened, and withal happy. Why this should be so I cannot explain, and if the reader is as much at a loss and has caught nothing of the intensity of pleasure we felt, then the writer must be at fault. One more Himalayan season was over. It was time to begin thinking of the next. 'Strenuousness is the immortal path, sloth is the way of death.'

PART TWO

Wartime

CHAPTER VIII

THREE CLIMBS IN WARTIME

◆

Irak

In wartime there are few opportunities for mountaineering. Normally an army avoids mountains as far as possible, and even in a war embracing the whole world it is remarkable how little fighting has taken place amongst them; by which I do not mean just mountainous terrain, where there has been fighting to spare, but mountains of interest to the climber. The Himalaya, in any case, would be given a wide berth by even the most enterprising army; the Caucasus were never really reached; Switzerland has been out of bounds on the last two occasions; while in Norway the campaign was over before the mountaineer, who felt that here at last was his opportunity, had had time to send off his first appeal: 'Sir, I have the honour to forward this my application for transfer, etc., etc.' to whomsoever might be interested or influential.

This business of trying to adapt a war to one's own ends can be overdone. At least such was my own experience in the first two or three years of this war. It is better to lie passive, neither helping nor hindering the current, but drifting with the stream of events as directed, or so one likes to think, by Higher Authority. You may well find yourself in a backwater or spinning round and round in a whirlpool, but if you stick in an oar in an attempt to stem the stream or to explore some interesting looking creek, anything may happen. After returning from Dunkirk I moved heaven and earth to get myself sent to East Africa, a country about which I knew a good deal. The result was that I found myself in a regiment earmarked for Singapore, of which I knew nothing. I had the very greatest difficulty in extricating myself from this ill-starred unit only twenty-four hours before it embarked. I lay quiet for a long time after that until I was tempted to make some passes at a job in a mountain battery, whereupon I received orders to report forthwith as an instructor at a school of mountain warfare. I escaped being left high and dry on that barren reef by submerging quickly again in the sea of regimental soldiering.

Irak is not a country which I would recommend to mountaineers; indeed I should hesitate to advise anyone to go there unless, as the Shipping Agents say, 'sufficient inducement offers'. No special inducement was offered to us (a Field Regiment R.A.) to go there in May 1941 except that all expenses were paid. After a diverting voyage up the Persian Gulf in a thirty-five-year-old 'City' boat, which was too slow to keep up with the convoy even though we lent a hand with the stoking, we were cast ashore at Basra, driven twenty miles into the desert, and invited to make ourselves at home. Apart from its heat, the desert outside Basra has some unusual climatic features. The most noteworthy is the violent gale which begins before 8 a.m. and continues with unrelenting fury until late afternoon. It is, of course, accompanied by a great storm of sand, so that it is impossible to do anything between those hours except cower inside a tent until it collapses, and then to continue cowering under the flapping folds until the wind abates.

After a week of this we dug out the half-buried trucks and marched in three stages up the Tigris valley to Mosul to take an inglorious part in the tail end of the Syrian campaign. The march was notable for the mortality rate of the tractors due to overheating by day, and for the number of Arab rifle thieves in the night. Many stories are told of the uncanny skill of Pathan rifle thieves on the North-west Frontier, but I believe that the Arabs of Irak have little to learn about this difficult and hazardous art. On this march two men with a Bren gun buried it and slept on it, and next morning were facing a charge of 'losing by neglect' one Bren gun. Rifles were taken from men who slept with them stowed in a specially constructed pocket inside the blanket, with the sling wrapped round their wrists. In consequence of this the leaguer* after dark was like No-man's Land. Verey lights soared into the sky and bullets zipped across the ground fired both by our own sentries and by the sentries of neighbouring units. It was safer to sleep below ground-level.

Having crossed the Syrian border west of Mosul on the Aleppo desert-track, we speedily reduced two small towns which were still

---

*   Camp, *cf.* laager—Ed

hostile. The guns were laid on the white, red-roofed house of the French Commandant, who was given until eleven o'clock to march out with the garrison. At five minutes to the hour nothing stirred but the Tricolour, still fluttering from the roof. On a little hillock close to the battery, the Commander of the Brigade Group, our Regimental Commander, and 'back-room boys' like myself, waited expectantly; those who had them nonchalantly brandished brightly coloured horse-hair fly whisks. The layer sat at his gun, squinted again through the sights at the distant house, and put his hand on the firing lever. For it was one of those rare and pleasing occasions when in the absence of anything bigger than a machine gun on the other side, one can come into action in the open in full view of the target to work one's wicked will without fear of retaliation—just as at a practice shoot, in fact, without umpires or safety officers, and instead of dummies in the danger zone with real people and real houses. It was a pity that on this occasion they happened to be French.

At one minute to eleven a cloud of dust appeared in the gateway of the fort, and a small car bearing a white flag shot out of the town and came tearing towards us. It was fortunate, I reflected, that during the pourparlers the synchronisation of watches had not been forgotten. The other town, El Haseke, some miles south, was even more of a disappointment for our fire-eaters. Our fast-moving light column, rumbling across the grassy plain in tactical formation, breathing only fire and slaughter, had barely covered ten miles before word came back that El Haseke had surrendered.

We showed the flag to the Sheiks of the Shammar tribe of Bedouins, ate vast trays of mutton and rice with them and drank little cups of cardamom-flavoured coffee; calmed some frightened Armenian villagers who every moment expected to have their throats cut by the Shammar; soothed the excited Syrians and saw that some sort of civil government was functioning; and then retired to Mosul to dig ourselves in against the arrival of the Germans. The contingency might be remote, but it served as an excuse for the digging which kept us occupied for the rest of our stay in Irak. The men, unversed in higher strategy, did not appreciate it. We had spent the winter of 1939 digging gunpits on the Belgian frontier and now we were to do the same on the borders of Irak. I can only remember one occasion when a previously prepared position was occupied, and then we had our guns pointing in the opposite direction to that for which the pits were built—a trifling but irritating circumstance.

Reconnoitring the defences on the border west of Mosul was more amusing than digging them. The architect, the Colonel of a battalion of the Frontier Force Rifles, employed me as his artillery adviser. We made our H.Q. in the buildings of a railway station near Eski Mosul. From this comfortable billet we made extensive surveys of the proposed defences in the Colonel's station wagon, accompanied by a bearer with tiffin basket, an orderly with sun-umbrella, the Colonel's shotgun, and his dog. If a bustard or a pack of sandgrouse was seen, the siting of company localities, battery positions, anti-tank guns, and machine guns had to wait. After lunch we would forgather on some convenient 'tell', or burial mound, and survey the scene of our labours through closing eyes. To call this part of the world the Syrian desert is a misnomer. At that time of year, early summer, it was like the Sussex Downs; great sweeps of gently rolling country were covered with flowers, iris, anemones, and periwinkles. The climate conformed to the country, for the nights were cool and the days sparkling.

It was an unwelcome change to leave these pleasant uplands for our camp at Mosul between the river and the railway. It is true that there was the Tigris with its attendant strip of green cultivation; but beyond that narrow strip the desert was true desert, arid and stony; the hills were distant, and the heat was severe. Sickness made its appearance. Sandfly fever was the chief complaint from which, I think, the whole regiment suffered at one time or another with the exception of an officer who drank a bottle of whisky a day, and myself, who drank none. The Trade and the Temperance Societies may make what they can of it. There was a little malaria, and jaundice was a prevalent complaint which preferred to attack officers rather than men.

I attributed this invidious distinction to our over-eating and under-working. We certainly lived very well. A Syrian contractor, efficient but of imperfect morals, looked after the mess and the men's canteen. Every Sunday he put on a chicken curry for which guests used to come in from far and wide. It was best eaten with a towel or sweat cloth round the neck. Turkeys were even more plentiful than chickens, for this part of Irak seems to be the home *par excellence* of the turkey. The

Syrian wished me to go into partnership with him after the war in the turkey export business, but whether this was a tribute to my honesty or my gullibility I never decided. Peaches, apricots, and grapes were cheap and plentiful, as was the local wine, which was thick, sweet, and very strong. For special occasions we imported a superb walnut brandy from a monastery in the hills.

The river was a great boon because, apart from football, excursions to Nineveh or Erbil, or getting drunk in Mosul, there was nothing for the troops to do but watch the Taurus Express go by every other day. Kind-hearted passengers used to fling newspapers on the embankment just above our camp. The Taurus Express, linking two such fabulous cities as Baghdad and Istanbul, seemed to me in wartime the quintessence of romance. I liked to think that most of the passengers were German spies, 'technicians', British secret agents; that every woman was some wicked but glamorous 'Lucy Felucci', and that every man, equally wicked but less glamorous, was known only by a cipher number in the most obscure room of the Foreign Office or the Wilhelmstrasse.

The river was dangerous for poor swimmers, like any other river, and acquired an undeserved reputation. I used to make the whole battery trot down to it for an early morning bathe; some disliked the trot down, more disliked the bathe. The great event was a swimming gala which, appropriately enough, included a race for home-made boats. A boat made from the petrol tank of a Messerschmidt, insubordinately called 'Tilly's Filly', won easily.

For those who preferred to think of the remote past rather than the uncertain and probably distasteful future, there were excursions to the nearby Nineveh or the more distant Erbil. The great earth mounds of Nineveh are just across the river from Mosul, but for the inexpert there is not much to see. Of more interest is the shrine and mosque of Nebi Yunus close by, where there is the spurious tomb of the prophet Jonah. Some pieces of bone, apparently from the sword of a sword-fish, are exhibited as part of the backbone of the famous whale. Archaeologists, it is said, roll their eyes at the mention of Nebi Yunus. It is believed to be built on the site of the palace of Sennacherib but, because of the fanaticism of the Moslems of Nebi Yunus, no excavation can be done. Erbil, the ancient Arbela, is on the Kirkuk road forty miles east of Mosul. Here the last Darius buried his treasure before the battle in which he and his empire were overthrown by Alexander. The present town is on a great mound which presumably consists of the remains of successive Arbelas from the first foundation thousands of years ago. It is the oldest inhabited city extant.

The winter in northern Irak is severe. By mid-November the hills to the north and across the river to the east, six to seven thousand feet high, were coated with snow. Around Mosul itself winter brought cold, wind, prolonged rain, and flooded camps. This year just after Christmas there was really bitter weather, when a foot of snow fell and lay for a week. At night it froze hard and the crackling of snow on my tent roof reminded me of better times. The only form of heating we could find for the tents was charcoal braziers. All the cooking in Mosul is done on charcoal, so that when we came into the market the price rocketed from five shillings a sack to a pound. The supply came from the forested hills near the Turkish border north of Mosul, to which my thoughts, stimulated by the snow, now began to turn. An official inquiry into the charcoal business at the source was as good an excuse as any for a week in the mountains.

In Mosul I had met a climbing friend from India who had thoughtfully come to war with his ice-axe, and I was able to borrow that essential implement. Tents were no difficulty, for every man had his bivouac tent, and the Mosul bazaar supplied thirty foot of clothes-line for a climbing rope. The lack of suitable boots was more serious, but 'with bread and iron one may get to China'.

In the summer, about seventy miles north of Mosul, there had been a convalescent camp. From the accounts and photographs of those who had been there, I felt sure that in winter something in the nature of real mountaineering could be done there, and that Amadia would be the best centre. With that object in view three of us left Mosul in a fifteen cwt. truck in the first week in February. No precise information about the state of the road was available, but we started under the impression that we would be able to reach our destination by truck. Much depended on our doing so, for we had only a week's leave. I had with me my own driver-batman and a bombardier from the 'Q' stores.

Thirty miles from Mosul the plains gave way to the foothills of the tangled ranges of Kurdistan, the home of Kurds, Assyrians, and

Armenians; the Kurds are Sunni Moslems, the Assyrians Christians. Amadia was once the headquarters of the Turkish administration and is entirely Moslem, but in the same valley there are many Christian villages. The Christians of these parts have suffered for their beliefs as few others have. They are always subject to oppression, and up to as recently as 1923 were liable to be massacred. In that year several hundred Assyrians of Dohuk and Simmel were murdered by the Iraki army and the local Kurds.,

After leaving the small trading centre of Dohuk the road climbs the Charkevi Dagh range, the last barrier before the Khabur valley in which Amadia lies. For the most part the hills were studded with stunted oaks, but occasionally my eyes were gladdened by clumps of juniper forest, as refreshing as the sighting of land after a long voyage. As we neared the top of the Charkevi, drifts of snow appeared on the road. One by one these were rushed until at last the inevitable happened and we found ourselves stuck up to the axles in snow. A road gang helped us to dig ourselves out and told us that half a mile on the road was blocked. Beyond this, for the remaining fifteen miles to Amadia, there was three foot of snow. These men, lithe keen-faced Assyrians, looked as though they should have been carrying rifles rather than long-handled shovels. They were dressed in baggy trousers of coarse grey wool with a thin green or purple stripe. Round the waist they wore the voluminous cotton cummerbund, said to contain seven yards of cloth, and on their heads untidy grey turbans. One or two had sheepskin jackets, others army greatcoats, which from their appearance must have been relics of the 1914–1918 war.

We selected a camp site by the road and turned the truck round with difficulty. Leaving the men to dig a site for the tents, I went off to a village above the road of which we had caught a glimpse. This proved to be a Christian village with a tiny stone church and half a dozen flat-roofed houses. I asked the black-bearded priest for two mules to carry our stuff to Amadia. He promised his assistance and begged us to sleep in the village.

Next morning, instead of following the road which winds round the southern slopes of the wide Khabur valley, we struck down into the valley with our mules and across to the northern side. After a tiring march we camped about four miles short of Amadia in a spot which had few attractions other than its proximity to the shapely snow and rock peak on which I had had my eyes all day. Snow lay everywhere, and one place was as good as another. Camping in snow, and using snow for cooking, was a new pastime to my two gunners, who were not at all enthusiastic until we made friends with some nearby Assyrians, who brought us loads of wood and promised chickens and eggs.

In the morning, leaving the men to recover from the long march, to which they were unused, I climbed the peak. It was about 6500 ft. high and of almost Alpine standard. When later on I took the men up they were extremely steady and did very well until the spectacular summit ridge was reached, which they promptly decided would be, in the language of Baedeker, 'fatiguing and not repaying'. Our two remaining days were devoted to a long snow walk towards the Turkish border and to visiting Amadia. I have never seen a town so situated. It is built upon the summit of a great knoll whose limestone sides are so smoothly precipitous that they appear to have been quarried. A long winding staircase, cut in the living rock, leads up through an arched guard-house to the town, which is further defended by a wall built upon the edge of the cliff. Within the walls, the mean, narrow streets and squalid houses form a town altogether unworthy of the strange and imposing pedestal on which it has been built.

After our return to Mosul the regiment moved from the river to Qaiyara where there are a number of oil wells. The crude oil, which we were allowed to draw freely in buckets, was used both for fuel for cooking and for surfacing the roads in the camp. Digging was given up for the time being. Instead we carried out exercises in the desert to the west which, at this time of year, early spring, was as pleasant a place to drive about in as one could wish. A smooth surface of young green grass ran for mile after mile, broken only by small and infrequent wadis, a rare burial mound, or the tents and herds of some wandering bedouin.

Fifty miles out in the desert, untenanted except for the goats of the bedouin, were the ruins of the Parthian city of Hatra—Al Hadhr as the Arabs call it. Here, to my mind, is something far more astonishing than the earth mounds of Nineveh. An immensely thick wall encloses an area of perhaps half a square mile within which are ruined houses and streets, and in the centre a massive stone building of two stories known

Ruins of Hatra

Hatra: Entrance to Temple of the Sun

as the Palace of the Sun. A dark barrel-vault connects two great halls, on the wall of which are sculptured heads, partly defaced by stones from the slings of Arab urchins. On the perfectly cut ashlar can be seen the private marks of the masons. To see the remains of this once powerful fortress rising so incongruously from the surrounding wilderness lends forcible emphasis to the contrast between the Irak of the past and that of the present. To support the numerous inhabitants of such a fortress, the desert in the vicinity must then have been in a high state of cultivation. It was an important place in the second century A.D., an outpost of the Parthian Empire. Two Roman Emperors, Trajan in A.D. 116 and Severus in A.D. 178, besieged the city, but failed to take it. It was eventually sacked, and afterwards abandoned, by the Sassanian king Sapor seventy years later.

Still moving southwards the regiment was next halted at El Fata where the oil pipe-line from Kirkuk crosses the Tigris on its way to the Palestine coast. This must be one of the hottest places of a hot country. At this point the Tigris breaks through the Jebel Hamrin range, and the barren rock ridges on both sides of the river radiate heat like a hot-plate. Sandy, stony desert hugs the river. Here the desert has come into its own, and though the river flows broad, strong and deep, it is powerless to nourish on its sterile banks the hardiest of trees or even one vestige of greenery.

Sandstorms occurred daily and no vehicle could move without creating a local sandstorm of its own. Here, every day, we dug fiercely against time, constructing an all-round defensive position on each bank; for, by now, Higher Authority had announced a date by which all these positions were to be ready. We were not the first who had dug and suffered at El Fata. The place was honeycombed with trenches dug by the Turks when they took up a defensive position here towards the close of the 1914–1918 war. These old trenches were the home of innumerable scorpions, small snakes, giant centipedes, and giant spiders, all of which seemed to transfer themselves immediately to the holes we had dug for our tents. We had learnt by experience that the plan of digging down four or five feet before erecting tents not only gave more headroom but made for warmth in winter and coolness in summer.

The only relaxation we had from digging was a forty-eight-hour exercise in the desert to accustom us to move in desert formation and

Inside Temple of the Sun

Inside Temple of the Sun

live on a pint of water a day. A month later we were doing this in the Western Desert in earnest, where the heat was admittedly of no consequence, but where there was no time limit to the exercise. On this occasion we struck an uncommonly bad spell with the wind blowing in the same direction as that in which we were moving, with results similar to those of a following wind in the Red Sea. Before the exercise was well started the water ration had to be doubled, and later, as more heat casualties occurred, all restrictions on drinking had to be removed. Finally the whole Brigade had to halt, facing into the wind, to wait for evening, as few of the engines could run for any length of time without boiling.

Persia

On the eve of our departure from El Fata a stroke of luck came my way when the Brigadier took me with him on a tour of the Persian defences. There, too, some unfortunates of what was then called the 9th Army had been busy throughout the winter altering the Persian landscape. Their lot, however, had fallen to them in a more pleasant place for both climate and scenery than had ours. A hasty glance at our proposed route on the map showed me that near one of our stages, Kermanshah, there was a 10,000 ft. peak called Bisitun, so I determined, if it was possible, to tarry there awhile. The Brigadier, who knew on which leg I halted, was quite agreeable. He, and another major who was coming, were keen fishermen, and they had heard of a river near Kermanshah which, whatever might be its merits as a defensive line, was excellent for trout.

There is no bridge across the Tigris between Baghdad and Mosul. At El Fata it is crossed by a light transporter bridge, built by the oil companies, which takes single trucks, but our Sappers supplemented this by a cable ferry like the 'bacs' of the Congo basin. In such ferries a pontoon, attached to a pulley running along the cable, is driven across by the action of the current. Having crossed the river, we drove for two hours over the desert to Kirkuk, the centre of the oil industry and itself a large producing centre. A few miles from Kirkuk, in a small hollow in the desert, is the reputed site of the 'burning, fiery furnace' which was heated seven times for the benefit of Shadrach, Meshach and Abednego; here the gas, which escapes from the oil below, burns with a perpetual, bluish, lambent flame.

We spent the night in a dry river bed south of Kirkuk, and next morning drove happily along the wrong road for some seventy miles. When such mistakes occur the responsibility lies with the senior officer but the blame automatically falls on the junior, whether he happens to be driving, reading the map, or merely sleeping in the back. It was not until we reached the Persian frontier beyond Kanaqin, where the only formality was the signing of a book, that the constraint occasioned by this untoward happening began to wear off. After staying so long in Irak we were not disposed to be hypercritical, but nevertheless our first impressions of Iran were far from favourable. The custom-house was a terrible rococo affair, but the greatest eyesore were the men, who were one and all dressed in shoddy European suits and cloth caps. I believe the late Shah was responsible for this dismal uniformity, who not only decreed that European clothes should be worn, but himself, through his agents, sold them to his unlucky subjects. Thus attired, the people looked so incongruous that, for me, even the nobility of the Persian background was qualified—the wide flat valleys, filled with fruit trees and fields of corn; and the great, sweeping, sparsely wooded hills, transmuted by a soft, clear atmosphere reminiscent of Kashmir.

From the frontier the road climbs steadily to the foot of the Paitak Pass (5300 ft.), the gateway through the Zagros mountains to the Iranian plateau beyond. The road up to the pass is steep, loose, and has many hairpin bends. We camped that night near the top and reached Kermanshah next day. As we approached the town from the south we looked straight at the lofty, serrated ridge of Bisitun, the black rock face slashed with the white of snow gullies, the whole rugged mass rising abruptly from the green plain beyond Kermanshah. The town itself, which is modern, commercial, and tinny, holds nothing of historic interest, but a few miles out where the main road meets the mountain barrier and turns east, are the grottoes and rock carvings of Tak i Bostan. The place was a pleasure retreat of the Sassanian kings. The grottoes and carvings are cut on the face of a limestone cliff from whose foot a mighty jet of water gushes into an artificial rock basin

Rock carvings in the grotto, Tak i Bostan

Rock carvings in the grotto, Tak i Bostan

fringed with trees. One noble old 'chenar' tree looks as though it must be almost contemporary with the carvings. Of these there are several, the principal being a colossal figure of Chosroes (A.D. 400) in armour mounted on a horse. Twelve miles along the road to the east, on the rocks of Bisitun itself, are other carvings commemorating the life of Darius.

We sampled some cheese and wine in a fly-blown hotel whose name, the Bristol, had aroused false hopes, and then drove out to the local military H.Q. which was sited not far from the deep, azure pool of Tak i Bostan. As if that in itself was not enough, their tents were pitched right under a magnificent face of rock, while up a narrow side valley we caught a fascinating glimpse of peak after peak receding into the wild highlands of Kurdistan. They had been several months in that delightful spot, surrounded by some of the noblest works of God and man, and seemed surprised when we failed to express sympathy with their hard lot. The Brigadier left next day to examine the defences of his trout stream, leaving me, with an officer from the H.Q., to examine the defences of Bisitun.

The mountain consists of a hogs-back rock ridge, broken by a number of towers, and running for several miles in an east-to-west line. A deep notch high up on the Tak i Bostan end of the ridge seemed the obvious jumping-off place for a complete traverse of the mountain, which was the ambitious project I had in mind. It would involve sleeping on top, finishing the traverse on the second day, and 'jumping a lorry' on the main road at the eastern end to get back to Kermanshah in time.

By means of a narrow gorge between the west end of the mountain and the cliffs above Tak i Bostan we penetrated to the back, or north side of Bisitun, where grass and shrub covered the steep slopes stretching up to a scree gully below the notch. A convenient sheep track led us to some sheep folds high up on these slopes before leaving us to find our own way to the scree. Although we were carrying only light loads, food for the night and a blanket, my companion soon began to show signs of distress. Before the scree was reached he decided to turn back. About midday I reached the notch where serious climbing began. The rock was sound and I had taken the precaution of bringing rubber shoes. The towers presented the main interest on a seemingly endless ridge; many of these would not yield to a frontal attack and had to be turned from the south, as the north side is precipitous. It was four o'clock by the time I reached the foot of what I hoped was the final peak. After several unsuccessful attempts to climb it direct I had to go down 500 ft. to find an easier way. As I stood on its summit it seemed to me that another tower half a mile away challenged our superiority, but I had had enough for one day, and so descending a few hundred feet I bivouacked by a patch of snow, lit a fire from a few scarce twigs, and dined off water, chapatties, cheese and chocolate.

There is no more satisfying ending to a climb than to spend the night on the mountain, preferably on the top. The bond between man and mountain, forged in a day-long struggle, never seems so strong as when at its close you seek the meagre shelter of some rocky overhang near the summit with which you have been striving all day to get on terms. But usually this happy consummation is not possible—the weather, the site, the ability to carry even the most modest necessities, conspire to prevent it. But if it be possible, and we spurn the delights of tea, beer, baths, and a warm bed, in favour of cold stones and hard fare, we may remind ourselves, as we lie shivering, that 'abstinence from low pleasures is the only means of meriting or obtaining the higher'. To protest, as we often do, that our pleasures are derived simply from being on the mountain and not from reaching the top, and then, having inadvertently, as it were, arrived on the summit, to hasten down after the briefest of halts, is surely to give ourselves the lie.

Such may have been my reflections as I lay alone on Bisitun watching the shadows creep down the slopes and then stretch across the valley to mingle with the golden haze still lingering on the distant hills. With a companion it would have been perfect. Society has not yet condemned the man who sleeps out alone, but it regards the activities of the solitary climber and the solitary drinker with distaste. The one is unsafe, the other unsocial, and both are likely to lead those who indulge in them into difficulties. A man who habitually climbs alone for preference is liable to be misunderstood. The state of mind of men like Maurice Wilson who died when attempting to climb Mount Everest alone, and the young American, E. F. Farmer, who lost his life similarly on Kangchenjunga, must be regarded with suspicion, and as a confirmation of a part at least of Dr Johnson's dictum, that

The pool and spring, Tak i Bostan

Rock carvings: Chosroes in armour mounted

the solitary mortal is certainly luxurious, probably superstitious, and possibly mad.

In such cases, the disaster, if there is one, involves only the responsible person, unless it happens that a search party has to go out to find the remains; while the rash but orthodox climber involves others besides himself if he comes to grief. The practice of climbing alone teaches self-reliance and caution, though the critic may cavil at the paradox of learning caution while performing an admittedly incautious act. But, from my own experience, it is true that one is far more cautious when alone, even too cautious. No normal person would, I think, climb alone from choice; it is usually the absence of a suitable companion which drives one to solitary climbing and afterwards to its justification: and in wartime the opportune occasion was more frequent than the man. Inaction in the face of fleeting opportunity is a crime, whereas climbing alone rather than not at all is but a venial impropriety.

I was up at five next morning and by seven had reached what I thought was the higher peak. Now, of course, it looked the lower. Without instruments it is often impossible to say which of two points on a ridge is the higher. You can go backwards and forwards from one to the other and still be in doubt. I did not propose doing this. I did not, in fact, propose continuing the traverse. From the point I had now reached its completion might take almost another day. I had no food left and not a great deal of energy so, with an uneasy feeling of having left undone something which I ought to have done, I turned to go. I took a direct line to the road down the south face, which was a mistake. I had forgotten, or I had never noticed, that for a thousand feet above the road there was a long rampart of steep cliffs. Taking the first gully which offered, I was soon brought to a stand by impossible water-worn slabs. I tried the next three or four successive gullies to the west but met with no more success, and it was two o'clock before I got off the mountain and on to the road. The lorry drivers must have been taking their siesta. I trudged the whole length in the hot afternoon sun, buoyed up by the thought of the cold, blue pool of Tak i Bostan.

Here one more was added to my already long but exclusive list of memorable bathes. To qualify, the first essential is for the bather to be really hot and tired. Then, if not sea-water, the water must be clear, deep, and cool (or otherwise have some unusual compensating feature), so that as it closes over one's head the whole body seems to absorb its clean, refreshing goodness. To make this clear, a bathe in the Dead Sea, for example, would not be refreshing but might qualify as unusual. Lastly, and this is important, one must be stark naked, with no clinging costume to impair the unity of body and water.

These exacting conditions were fulfilled on several occasions: in the Atlantic off Kribi on the West Coast after a cycle journey in the Congo; a deep pool in the Indus during a hot march; under the spray of a 100 ft. waterfall in Kashmir where Shipton and I danced wantonly for a full quarter hour; the first dip in the Mediterranean after a month's marching and fighting in the desert; in a glacier pool amongst young icebergs (very memorable but short-lived) during a hot climb in the Dauphiné; and in the lake at Habbaniya where at all times one might enjoy the 'cool silver shock of the plunge in a pool's living water'.

When we returned to Irak at the end of May the regiment had moved to Habbaniya, the R.A.F. station west of Baghdad. The battle in the Libyan desert was approaching its disastrous climax of 8 June, when we lost two or three hundred tanks, and soon afterwards Tobruk. Losses in 25-pr.* batteries, either overrun or cut off in 'boxes' (the origin of the 'hedgehogs' of the Russian front) were so serious that almost every day field regiments were leaving the 9th Army for the desert. Seven days after quitting Habbaniya we joined an Indian Infantry Brigade near Mersa Matruh over 1000 miles away. In two days we had crossed the Syrian desert, the Jordan, and Palestine. After a much-needed halt of one day on the coast for rest and maintenance, we carried on southwards through the Sinai desert to the Canal, jammed in a stream of reinforcements moving down from Syria. We moved on to Cairo and thence westwards along the coast road, all the way jostling against a double-banked stream of traffic escaping from the advancing Germans—administrative units, R.A.F. ground staffs, mobile cinemas, and all the 'cankers of a calm world and a long peace' in the back areas.

There are no mountains in the Western Desert. There is scarcely a hill until the Green Belt west of Derna is reached, unless one counts Himeimat, a curious excrescence on the edge of the Qattara

---

*   25-pounder—Ed

On the summit ridge, Bisitun

Bisitun summit ridge

Depression where we had an observation post in the early days of July before the Germans took it. In the desert the eyes of the mountaineer acquire a troubled look, searching for something that is not there. Stale, flat and unprofitable indeed seems a world which is smooth, wrinkleless, and uninteresting as a death-mask, spacious as the sea but as empty, where no distant line of hills speaks of some yet more distant soaring range, 'a grayer portion of the infinite sky itself... permanent above the world'.

In the desert the first six months of 1942 were the heyday of 'Jock' columns, small columns formed as a rule of a battery of 25-pr. guns for hitting power and a troop of 2-pr. anti-tank guns and a battalion or company of infantry to protect them. They were named after their inventor the late Brig. 'Jock' Campbell, a Gunner V.C. In the confusion of the retreat to El Alamein after the fall of Tobruk, such *ad hoc* formations were used extensively with doubtful wisdom or effect to delay the enemy until the El Alamein line was prepared.

Two days after we joined the Infantry Brigade my battery was detached to form such a column, and found itself 'swanning' about in the desert west of the undefended minefield which ran from Mersa Matruh to Siwa Oasis. We had with us a platoon of Punjabi infantry, a troop of 2-pr. guns, and orders to stop 'at all costs' an approaching enemy tank column. As hitherto we had only done this sort of thing against imaginary tanks we moved around in some trepidation, scanning every moving vehicle or cloud of dust with nervous expectancy. The first shots fired came as something of an anti-climax. Although there was a thin screen of armoured cars a few miles to the west between us and the enemy, whenever we halted we invariably brought the guns into action ready to fire. During one of these halts, a vehicle, apparently a British 2-pr. *portée* (a gun carried on a three-ton lorry), was seen approaching. An officer drove out to exchange news and promptly had his truck (an armoured O.P.[*]) holed by the 2-pr. The whole battery of eight guns incontinently opened up, but the stranger escaped untouched. Our difficulty was that the Germans had captured so many of our vehicles that we could never quite believe what we saw.

---

[*]   Observation Patrol—Ed

Greatly to our relief we got permission by wireless to retire behind the minefield for the night, but we were given to understand that from that position there must be no retreat. The minefield was undefended except for odd columns like our own, each fighting its own battle in complete ignorance of what was happening on its flanks. Next afternoon our observation patrol was driven in and we were attacked by artillery and some thirty tanks, which stood off and shot at us from 'hull down' positions. After three hours' fighting we suffered forty casualties. All our guns were still firing, but so were the enemy's, and it was impossible to see whether we had inflicted any damage or not. It seemed probable that we were on the way to joining the many other batteries which had been overrun or otherwise extinguished. However, at the last minute, as the sun went down and the tanks might be expected to begin to close in, reprieve came in the form of permission to withdraw. We did this successfully under cover of our own smoke screen. We had saved all the guns and it was, therefore, all the more galling to lose one of them during the subsequent night march when it parted company with its trailer. The surprise and chagrin of the sergeant of the gun when, at the first halt, he discovered there was nothing behind his tractor, would in other circumstances have been funny. The other battery of the regiment, some miles north of us, was overrun by German infantry in British lorries and lost four guns.

The next serious engagement took place two days later on 28 June at Fuka after the fall of Mersa Matruh; but this time the whole of our Brigade Group was involved in an effort to stop the advance. The Germans, following their usual practice of attacking towards dusk with the sun behind them, speedily overran the position. Luckily for us the value and scarcity of 25-pr. guns had by now been fully realised by whoever was directing the storm in that corner of the battlefield. The guns were to be saved, and when the enemy tanks were about 500 yards away we received orders to pull out. The whole of the Infantry Brigade and our own Regimental H.Q. were put 'in the bag'.

We went into the 'box' position of Abu Duweis in the extreme south, and marched out again next day when it was discovered that the water supply could easily be cut. From 1 July, for the next fortnight, the battery was again the nucleus of a 'Jock' column supported by a company of the West Yorks. Alarms and excursions at all hours of the day and night, retreats and advances, shelling and being shelled, with on the whole never a dull moment, was the order of our existence. One can laugh now, but at the time the laughter was a bit hollow. I remember driving up to within two hundred yards of a tank, in response to a beckoning figure on the turret, before spotting its black cross; and at another time approaching on foot a ridge which we had intended using as an observation post and hearing an enemy vehicle coming up the other side, obviously with the same intention; and I recall how we lay in close leaguer on a dark night watching an enemy column pass a few hundred yards away.

There is no doubt that if a good word can be said for any form of warfare then the war in the Desert, as in the days of small columns, had much to recommend it. There were no long periods of boredom and waiting and no long periods of being harassed in static positions. Provided one had a little experience, a lot of luck, and kept wide-awake, then it was possible to have plenty of shooting without being shot at too much in return. Moreover, in those days the 8th Army was small, most of its units were known to one another, and all felt like members of a family; so that when we were having a bad time, or in retreat, there was, as there always should be with good troops, a more comradely helpful spirit abroad than the 'devil take the hindmost' air of a successful advance.

At no time, to descend to a more material plane, did the battery ever live so well as during the days on column. There was no interfering H.Q. to blunt the edge of initiative, to ask silly questions, and to demand irritating, tell-tale returns. Wandering about as we did in a more or less trackless waste, here one minute and gone the next, it may seem odd that we fed so well, or that we were able to draw adequate supplies of petrol, water and ammunition; but so it was, and the Supply services of the Indian Division with whom we served were always able to meet our requirements once we had established contact. We were blessed in having a battery captain without a conscience, a man of small body but Falstaffian mind, who scoured the desert for supply points and overdrew freely from each. It was very easy, because no one really knew where or what units were operating. We no longer wondered whether we had enough milk or sugar for tea with each meal. The amount we drank was limited solely by the amount of water available, and every halt which seemed likely to last longer than twenty minutes was the signal to 'brew up'. The spare vehicles which we had somehow acquired in the course of the retreat were used for fetching water, and the only time we went short was when one of these mistook west for east and was picked up by the enemy.

All good things come to an end. By mid-July the El Alamein line was becoming firmly established, and the days of small mobile columns were over for good. We realised that our free-booting life had ended when we dug ourselves in on Ruweisat Ridge and connected ourselves by telephone to various inquisitive and interfering headquarters from division downwards. Once more life became real and earnest. Rations were counted, ammunition was counted, and when we were not harassing or being harassed by the enemy we were pulled out to train for the mobile warfare we had so recently and reluctantly concluded. Only once, immediately after the break-through in early November, did we come near to recapturing that 'first fine careless rapture'. But our share in the pursuit was shortlived, and we spent a bleak, cheerless winter at El Adem, near Tobruk, clearing the old battlefield of Knightsbridge. In the course of this at least sixty or seventy of our 25-pr. captured that summer were salvaged and made serviceable.

In February we made another long forced march to take part in the battles of Mareth, the Gabes Gap, and the Wadi Akarit, until at length we were detached to support the 19th French Corps in the final stages of the North African campaign.

Tunis and Zaghouan

We took over positions from a unit of our 1st Army. It was pleasing to be treated with the deference they thought due to men of the 8th Army but, since solid pudding is better than empty praise, it was even more gratifying to be given the run of their canteen—to buy real matches that lighted instead of Monkey or Crocodile brands whose heads flew off before they were struck; to smoke English cigarettes instead of the notorious 'V's; and to eat English chocolate instead of the mottled desiccated substitute from Palestine. We really felt we had at last shaken ourselves clear of the East—both Middle and Near.

The French Corps had little mechanical transport. Their artillery was horse-drawn and their infantry relied on mules, but in the heavily wooded hills of the Djebel Mansour, where they were now fighting, animals were of more use than motors. The infantry of the division on our front consisted of battalions of the Foreign Legion, of Tirailleurs Marocains and Algériennes, and of Goums. In the division on our left there were also Senegalese. The Foreign Legion came up to my expectations; they looked tough, lived simply, and observed remarkable discipline. I visited a battalion in the line and was surprised to find that, whenever possible, men sprang up and saluted; a great number of them seemed to be Spaniards. For lunch the officers had coarse bread, dates, and wine—a simple satisfying diet which was, in my opinion, preferable to the white bread, tinned stews, jam and margarine of our army, besides being healthier, cheaper, and no trouble to prepare.

The Goums were irregular Arab troops, mostly recruited from a tribe called the Shaamba, who are hereditary enemies of the Touaregs. They draw pay, but find their own food and clothing—a system which possibly accounts for their informal appearance and their predatory habits. 'Find' is the right word. Their officers and N.C.O.'s, whose job must be no sinecure, were French. These troops were not often employed in set battle pieces, but were held in leash and turned loose in the event of a break-through—'Cry havoc and let slip the Goums' was possibly the Corps Commander's order when he thought the situation ripe for exploitation. Whether it was true or not I cannot say, but it was common talk that for a prisoner they received a hundred francs and for an ear twenty-five francs. An ear is an ear, whether German, Italian, or British, and twenty-five francs is twenty-five francs, so one had to exercise more than ordinary care when operating with Goums.

The attack on the Djebel Mansour went according to plan and resulted in an advance by the whole Corps to a line south of Pont du Fahs, where we occupied as usual the flat plain and the Germans the high ridge. It was difficult enough to find gun positions which were not in view from this ridge, but behind it towered the rugged limestone massif of Zaghouan, nearly 4000 ft. high, which dominated the country far and wide. The French put in another very gallant but ineffective attack against the ridge and the foothills of Zaghouan, but it was not until the Germans withdrew, as a result of pressure by the 1st Army on the left, that we advanced beyond Pont du Fahs to come into action in what was to be our last position in the African campaign.

As we moved along the straight road which led through Depienne to Tunis, the wide, flat, cultivated plain on either hand seemed uncommonly devoid of cover. At last we spotted a winding shallow wadi, deep enough to conceal the guns, if not to hide their flash. We dived into it like rabbits into a burrow, dispersed the vehicles, and returned to the road to await the coming of the guns. Their arrival was the signal for considerable shell-fire, probably directed from O.P.'s on the lower slopes of Zaghouan, which now frowned at us on our right flank. So long as we remained here in action any movement of vehicles in or out of the wadi was discouraged by both sides. The wadi soon became uncomfortably crowded, for we were not the only ones to covet the shelter of this natural trench, so that when a shell did fall fairly inside someone usually got hit. Meantime the French on our right were trying to force their way along the foot of the mountain to the small town of Zaghouan, but for the last two days the position of the shell-bursts of the 75 mm.'s on the slopes had given no indication of any progress.

However, in conjunction with the general allied assault, another attack was put in beyond Depienne, and as early as 10 o'clock on the morning of 12 May, it was clear that the enemy was going back. Thin columns of smoke from burning vehicles and mushroom-shaped clouds from exploding ammunition dumps could be seen behind his lines. At dawn the regiment had fired a barrage in support of a battalion of the Foreign Legion, but now the battle had rolled on and, as yet, no orders had come for us to advance.

At last, towards midday, came the welcome signal 'Prepare to advance'. Skirting Depienne, as the road was mined, we soon crossed the Zaghouan-Tunis road and ascended the two hills that the French had taken earlier in the day. A couple of long Russian 5 cm. anti-tank guns, some weapon pits and a machine gun or two, marked the first enemy defences. There was no one about, dead or living, but a mile or two farther on the scene was lively enough. From three Valentine tanks, part of the small tank force used by the French in their attack, smoke was ascending cheerfully, while the crews stood around discussing the phenomenon. A stream of Senegalese infantry with pack mules was moving up. Below, in a narrow valley, were three abandoned batteries, one of captured 25-pr. and two of 10.5 cm.'s The guns had been destroyed, and their vehicles were still smouldering. Strewn around was the usual litter of clothing, blankets, ammunition, rifles, food, equipment, letters and newspapers. The Senegalese loitered hopefully on passing these riches, but the French N.C.O.'s would stand no nonsense. A short burst from a Tommy gun was directed at the feet of the loiterers as a hint to keep moving. Across the valley a white flag was being waved anxiously.

Reports from our forward armoured O.P. indicated that all resistance had ceased except in Zaghouan itself. The French wanted us to push a troop forward to deal with it, but this was unnecessary as it was within range of all our sixteen guns from where we were. But as surrender was in the air it seemed a pity to fire needlessly on those pleasant white walls lying at the foot of the mountain.

We dropped our trails more or less where we stood. My choice of site for Regimental H.Q. was possibly influenced by the presence of two German field kitchens, one with its copper full of a stew ready for dishing up, the other containing a slightly overdone rice pudding. By late evening the Germans in Zaghouan had come to heel, but the French Commander mistrusted them, and insisted on our remaining at a half-hour's notice. Naturally, since coming into those parts from the 8th Army front near the coast I had had my eye on Zaghouan, the only mountain I had seen since Bisitun. Many long broken limestone ridges help to form a striking mass which, on the north and west sides, rises abruptly from the Tunis plain. It seemed to be a case of now or never; we were only three miles away; to-morrow we might be anywhere.

One of the battery commanders, who was full of enterprise though not a mountaineer, was of the same opinion. Promising to be back soon after dawn, we got the C.O.'s permission to absent ourselves for the night. A well-graded track, or even road, appeared to lead to a white building perched jauntily on the face not 1000 ft. below the main ridge. George said we would take his Jeep, and suggested starting at midnight. I said we would start at nine, one of the only two sensible decisions we made that night. The other was to take the German equivalent of a Verey light pistol. The big idea behind this was to have a Brock's benefit on the summit to celebrate the victory. Even while we discussed ways and means, coloured signal smoke was going up from all directions. This was customary in the desert after a successful action. The Germans were equipped on a lavish scale with all manner of light signals which our men delighted to fire off when they got hold of them. I was soon equipped with a captured pistol and a supply of coloured signals.

At 9 p.m. the Jeep proved to be a non-starter, and obviously the fifteen cwt. truck we had to use would only take us to the foot. To uphold my principles I pointed out that this was far more satisfactory than being driven almost to the top. George was more honest. He heartily regretted the absence of the Jeep.

I was rather worried about mines, for the French were less experienced and less particular about removing these than the sappers of the 8th Army; but we got safely to the main road and soon passed through Zaghouan behind a stream of captured lorries full of Germans. A mile beyond, following a road which appeared to lead round the mountain, we met some Goums. They had with them an enormous Boche who was not unnaturally apprehensive of the green turbans and bandit-like accoutrements of his captors. Our appeal to their French N.C.O. was immediately successful. His patrol had just crossed the mountain and he would put us on the track. A few hundred yards on we parked our truck while the N.C.O. pointed out a rough mule track leading upward into the gloom of the woods at the foot of the slope. 'You can't go wrong', or words to that effect. 'Montez toujours, toujours montez', was his parting admonition. The aptness of his words impressed me, so we decided to adopt them as our watchword for the night.

At 11 p.m. we started climbing. An hour later the moon went down, and the bridle path lost its usefulness, for it disappeared over a col. This was evidently the route by which the Goums had crossed from the south to the north side of the mountain. Another well-marked track led off to the right, but it was impossible to tell whether it trended up or down. George, whose mind seemed to run tourist-like on tracks and roads, thought it would lead us by 'une pente insensible' to the summit, and I was weak-minded enough to consent to try it. After a good fifteen minutes at a cracking pace, for we were going downhill, even George admitted that we were not abiding by our watchword. Back we went to the col, and this time struck boldly up the slope.

We soon found there was some difference in moving on a path and moving on an unknown boulder-strewn hillside in the dark. Presently the slope narrowed to a ridge whence sharp rocky teeth loomed up vaguely against the black sky. It pleased us to think we were now on the summit ridge, but from what I could remember of that, having only seen it from some distance away in daylight, I had misgivings. However, as always in such cases, when one feels the country is not all it should be, we could hope for much from time and chance. The east side of our ridge now began to fall away sheer. Keeping as far from danger as possible we groped our way along until brought up short by a chasm of unknown width and depth. The firing of a success signal was perhaps premature, nevertheless a red Verey light soared into the air disclosing, some twenty feet below us, a knife-edge ridge, the only link with the opposite side of the chasm. Such a questionable place at such an hour in the morning called for consideration and another light. Suitably enough this one was green. The revolting colour it lent to the surrounding rock and my companion's face, gazing curiously into the depths, tipped the scale in favour of retreat.

The turning of this obstacle cost us some loss of height and several more cartridges. Some of these broke into pleasing clusters of stars, but these were not of much value as pathfinders. I have since learnt all about German light signals. By a simple system you can tell by touch, in the dark, the various colours and types. A white flare has the edge of the cartridge base half milled, green is smooth, red is fully milled. The 'Sternbundel', a white rocket bursting into stars, has six studs on the top of the cartridge. The 'Fallschirm', or parachute flare (which would have been just the thing for us), has a parachute in relief on the top. There is also a 'Pfeifpatrone', or whistling flare, which has a point on the top. Unluckily we had none of these. A shriek of dismay from the light as it hovered over the chasm would have been an artistic touch.

This gap or cut-off was the first and worst of several others, but using our light pistol freely, we reached the highest point of the ridge. It was 4 a.m. now and the sky was perceptibly lighter. Across a valley we could see the outline of the summit ridge, and the two familiar rock towers at the top. We used the last of our lights finding a way down into the valley, and then we wearily climbed a steep slope to the foot of the final tower. Up this a mild scramble led to a wooden beacon marking the top. A tricolour flag was fluttering proudly in the dawn wind, and at the foot of the beacon lay an unexploded 75 mm. shell. There was no Boche O.P. on the top; most of these were on the lower ridges, but evidently some French gunner had felt it incumbent on him to drop a round on the top. As a gunner this interested me, for to land a shell on such a place is extremely difficult.

We lay on the top exhausted by the night's work. I ate some 'Knackebrot', the German ration biscuit, each packet of which carried a slip of paper eulogising the properties of the biscuit and beginning with the rhetorical question 'Kamerad, kennst du Knackebrot?' It is, in my opinion, very good, much better than our own. George was past eating, even if he had shared my passion for Knackebrot, which he did not. Away to the east some battery fired fitfully for a time and then stopped—the last shots of the African campaign. I should like to be able to add that far to the south the pine forests of the Djebel Mansour, which we and the French had cleared so gallantly a week ago, lay dark and sombre, that eastwards the sea threw back the rays of the rising sun, and that to the north the Tunisian plains stretched like a carpet of green and gold to the black olive groves and white walls of distant Carthage; but unluckily a blanket of cloud hid everything.

The rest is mere disillusionment. From below the tower fifteen minutes' walking took us to the road we had seen from below. Our fifteen cwt. truck would almost certainly have made the grade. An hour's zigzagging down another mule track brought us to the truck, which we found had been pillaged unmercifully by the Goums. The driver, not unexpectedly perhaps, had chosen to sleep during the night, and roving bands of Goums, who had already found numerous abandoned enemy vehicles, had acted on the wise and plausible assumption that ours was merely one more. One might say of the Goums, as Stonewall Jackson said of his Texans: 'The hens have to roost mighty high when the Texans are about.'

CHAPTER IX

ALBANIA

Their habits are predatory—all are armed

BYRON

It MAY BE AN ODD VIEW, but I think one drawback to the army is that promotion is almost inevitable. No one is allowed to remain where he is; once having set foot on the slippery slope of promotion he must either go up or down. That is possibly why so many good men refuse to accept a stripe, and prefer to remain in a position of important permanence at the bottom. In the Artillery the command of a battery is the best that life affords. It is a post a right-minded gunner would wish to hold for ever; once beyond that he feels that it is a case of 'farewell the tranquil mind, farewell content'. Even at the head of a battery he still has both feet on the ground, in close contact with his men and the seamy side of war; he is still on the right side of the gulf which separates those who plan from those who act, and which is crossed immediately he becomes part of a Headquarters—even the modest headquarters of a regiment. From the throne to the scaffold is a short step; short and equally decided is the transition to Second-in-Command of a regiment—the ultimate end of the senior Battery Commander. Though the appointment carries with it an extra 6d. a day, it is the equivalent of the Chiltern Hundreds so far as any active responsibility is concerned. It is a stagnant pool, from which in the fulness of time and chance he may be fished up to command a regiment himself, but the unlucky or unworthy may float there for long enough gathering seaweed and barnacles. Having drawn my 6d. a day in such an uncongenial post for several months I was prompted to answer an advertisement in General Routine Orders, which, in the Army, corresponds to the Agony Column of *The Times*. Volunteers were wanted for Special Service of a kind which involved almost complete independence. Better to reign in Hell than serve in Heaven, I thought, as I wrote out my application.

Various qualifications were essential, or at least desirable, but unlike the alluring posts offered in the advertisements of civil life, no capital was required.

So it came about that one moonlit night in August 1943, after a month's training, I found myself flying over the Mediterranean bound for Albania in company with a sapper sergeant and a corporal wireless operator. My known predilection for mountains had possibly accounted for my being sent to Albania—reputedly a mountainous country. We counted ourselves fortunate in having been dispatched so promptly, but even so we feared there would be little for us to do but dissuade the Albanians from massacring the helpless Italians, and to arrange for the transport of prisoners back to Italy. Italy was already on its knees and appeared likely to throw in the towel at any moment.

There was already one British mission in Albania. This had moved up from Greece in the previous May, and we were to be dropped to them before proceeding to our own particular area. Two other independent missions were also in our aircraft. We had an uneventful flight, but if there is any charm in flying at night, which I doubt, it is quite spoilt if you know that presently you will have literally to take a leap in the dark. However, the pilot of the Halifax found the signal fires with a precision which was admirable or disgusting according to one's feelings at the time. At the energetic prompting of an efficient dispatcher we dropped through the large hole in the floor and, shortly after, we had all landed safely but rather wide of the target. We must, I think, have been dropped at over 2000 ft. and consequently drifted too much. The usual height for dropping is from 600 to 800 ft., but in hilly country at night there is no doubt a strong tendency for the pilot, unless he is supremely confident, to maintain a liberal safety margin.

This mission to which we were dropped consisted of a major and a captain. They had been playing a lone hand in Albania for three months and were, I think, as pleased to see us as we were to arrive. We had a warm reception, and having walked from the dropping ground to their village headquarters, we sat down to fried eggs and sweet champagne at three in the morning. My principal feeling was one of intense satisfaction at having at length got back to Europe, even though it was enemy-occupied, after so long in the wilderness. I could almost have hugged the ground.

Map 3: General map of Albania

We spent a few days there organising the mule transport to take us to our respective areas, and acquiring some very necessary knowledge of the situation. If it is true that 'happy is the nation that has no history', then Albania must be one of the unhappiest. Her history is an unbroken record of invasion, oppression, and wrong by Turk, Greek, Austrian, Italian, Serbian, Bulgarian, and German. Few countries can have been so ravaged and so subjected to oppression at the hands of its stronger neighbours, and yet have retained its will for independence unbroken as did the Albanians for 500 years, from the time when Skenderbeg, their great national hero, first made head against the Turk. After the 1914–18 war, after various interested countries had been forced to relinquish their claims, Albania was declared an independent Republic. The first President was Zog, a landowner and politician, who in 1928 was proclaimed King. Mussolini had long had an eye on Albania—there are small deposits of oil and chrome ore there—and in the years before the war had by means of loans acquired a considerable hold. In Holy Week of 1939 he presented Zog with an ultimatum which, if accepted, would have made Albania an Italian colony. The ultimatum was rejected. On Good Friday the Italians invaded the country and Zog fled to England.

The country can be divided socially and physically into northern, central, and southern Albania. In the north, which is wild, mountainous, and therefore the most backward, feudalism is blended with a clan organisation, and the Roman Catholics outnumber the Moslems. Central Albania is more open and less mountainous; the great families are less powerful, and most of the land is in the hands of small farmers with a leavening of country squires. Roman Catholics are few, and there are more Moslems than Orthodox Christians. As Tirana, the capital, is in central Albania, it is here that communications are the most developed; but there are no railways* anywhere in Albania and not many motor roads. South Albania is mountainous also, but the mountains follow a simple plan. Two wide open valleys running from south-east to north-west provide an easy through route, and since the

---

*   The fact that there were no railways in Albania was not so widely known as it might have been; for Base were in the habit of sending us explosive charges designed specifically for blowing them up.

Old Turkish pack bridge, south Albania

frontier between Greece and Albania is not naturally difficult for travellers, the south is open to Greek influence; this may be one reason why the people there are the most progressive, the most educated, and the most democratic. Here also the Moslems outnumber the Christians. For Albania as a whole the proportions are 70% Moslem, 10% Roman Catholic, and 20% Orthodox (not the Greek Orthodox Church, for the Albanian Christians have their own head). But in Albania religious tolerance is the rule and nationality comes before religion. As Byron observed, 'The Greeks hardly regard them as Christians or the Turks as Moslems.' One reason for this is that, except in the central coastal plains, where there are some fanatics, the majority of Moslems belong to the Bektashi sect, or reformed Moslems, which is a philosophy rather than a religion, whose members neither observe the Moslem fasts nor abstain from strong drink. Albanian is an Indo-European language of unknown origin. The vocabulary, in which there are many Latin words, is largely borrowed. There are two different dialects, spoken by the Ghegs of the north and the Tosks of the south, the dividing line being the Skumbi river south of Tirana. As with all other languages I was dismayed by its difficulty, but more so than usual.

At the time of the Italian invasion, when King Zog fled and left the country to its fate, the Albanians, in the absence of any leader or rallying point, offered little resistance to the invader. But after the initial shock of surprise had worn off, a resistance movement began to take shape, at the instigation, as in most of the invaded countries, of a few Communists. This became known as the L.N.C. or 'LevizjaNacionalClirimtare'—National Liberation Movement—and embraced all classes, all political opinions, all religions, and a good three-quarters of the people of south Albania. It identified itself with the Allies against Fascism and Nazism, and had for its first objective the freeing of Albania from Italians and Germans, and for its second the establishing of a 'free, independent, democratic Albania'. For these aims they were prepared to sacrifice everything. Unhappily, as in other Balkan countries, one such single-minded movement was not enough. There were others who looked beyond the immediate struggle, who, it could be argued, paid more regard to the material welfare of Albania. The principal rival party to the L.N.C. was the Balli Kombetar, or National Front, which regarded the Greeks and the Yugo-Slavs as the real enemies and preferred, therefore, to husband its resources until the war was over. Under an outward show of resistance they were prepared to temporise with the Axis powers, and were not willing to incur suffering by an unnecessary display of zeal in a cause which would probably triumph without the aid of Albania. If it did not triumph so much the better for them, who would then be in a position to crush their rivals. There was a third group, of little importance in 1943 but becoming more prominent later, which comprised supporters of the absent King Zog. They too were chiefly concerned with party, and were not prepared to antagonise the Germans to please the Allies. Both these latter parties took Mr Facing-both-ways as their model. They were ready to help us if it could be done without embroiling themselves with the Germans, and they would co-operate with the Germans up to a point short of offending us. Unfortunately our official policy, the guiding principle of which was to avoid the appearance of taking sides in local politics, enabled them to do this, and both received our support without doing anything to earn it.

In August of that year there was suspicion but no open hostility between the two main groups, while Abas Kupi, who later became leader of the Zoggists, was still a member of the L.N.C. It was obvious, however, that their differences were irreconcilable and must soon become wider. Meanwhile, the British Government, anxious to remain neutral in these local squabbles and to assist anyone who professed to be willing to kill Germans or Italians, proposed having British liaison officers with all parties with the laudable intention of persuading them to sink their differences and to unite in the common cause. It was the peculiar tragedy of Albania that this well-meaning policy was persisted in after it had become clear to most observers that these differences were fundamental, and even when only one of the parties was fighting and suffering while the other two were either actively hostile or feebly neutral.

In the week I spent with the mission at Stylle, near Korca, it became evident to me that the L.N.C. alone had war aims similar to our own, and were ready to go to all lengths to attain them. Accordingly I elected to go to the Gjinokastre area which promised to become the centre of the L.N.C. movement. The small mule train necessary to carry our wireless stores and kits was provided by some nearby Vlachs.

These interesting semi-nomadic people, who are widely distributed over the Balkans, call themselves Romani and speak a language akin to Roumanian. They are muleteers by nature, horse-copers by intuition, and live the life of shepherds, travelling in the spring with vast flocks of sheep to the high uplands, where they pass the summer, and then in the autumn returning to their scattered settlements in southern Albania and the Greek Epirus. Showing no interest in politics or war, they seem to be the one unchanging, untroubled race in the Balkans which knows enough to meddle only with its own affairs and to let the great world go by.

Our cross-country journey took three days. It was pleasant to stroll along behind our sleek, active little mules through the sun-drenched countryside, stopping perhaps at a village where we were elaborately entertained, or perhaps with some Vlachs who pressed on us maize bread and bowls of 'kos', similar to the Bulgarian 'yoghourt'. In a village the entertainment always began with 'meze'—a sort of grace before meat consisting usually of soft white cheese and 'raki', which is the fiery brandy they distil from grape juice, plums, mulberries, or even figs, often flavoured with aniseed. This was followed, after a formal interval, by eggs, mutton, pastry dishes of various kinds, and concluded with thick sweet Turkish coffee. For a few leks we bought luscious purple figs and bunches of grapes, and once we were made free of a tree laden with the largest mulberries I have ever seen—from this orgy the three of us emerged stained from head to foot a rich and royal purple.

There was no sign of the war until we reached the town of Permet; but of past wars there were many, for in this troubled country there are few places free from scars. The village of Frasheri, for example, which we passed had been ravaged by the Greeks in 1914 in company with 150 other Albanian villages; and on the highest mountains one would find stone sangars and heaps of spent cartridges fired by the Greeks in their campaign against the Italians. Permet itself had suffered in that campaign, and had recently been burnt again by the Italians as a reprisal for some partisan action. It was now garrisoned by Italians who occupied newly built barracks.

The town lies in the Vjose valley on the motor-road from Jannina in Greece to Berat. In addition to this there is the road from Jannina to

Korca; another to Gjinokastre, Tepeleni, and Valona; and a coast road from Saranda to Valona. There are but two short east-west roads; one linking Tepeleni with the Permet road, and one linking Saranda with Gjinokastre. This scarcity of motor-roads made southern Albania an almost ideal country for partisan warfare. Enemy garrisons were confined to towns on the roads, while the country in between was more or less under partisan control; and the necessary strengthening of garrisons and the collecting of mule transport were ample warning signs that a drive through partisan territory was in preparation. The partisans would have been even more favoured had there been extensive forest or thick scrub, but most of the south is singularly bare of trees. There are patches of oak, pine, and beech forest between Korca and Frasheri, but eastwards the forest gradually thins out to stunted oak scrub, so that west of the Vjosa one finds a country of high bare ridges where wood of any sort is of almost famine scarcity.

In order to avoid the Permet garrison, we crossed the road and forded the river about a mile above the town. From the west bank a steep stony path zigzags up to the 6000 ft. pass over the Nemercke range into the upland valley of Zagori. Dawn overtook us still below the pass. We halted for a moment to look down upon the fertile flats on the banks of the Vjose, the blackened skeleton of Permet half-hidden among cypress trees, and the blatantly unscathed Italian barracks inside their barbed-wire perimeter.

On the pass we had to give an account of ourselves to the partisan band or 'cheta' on guard there. With one exception they seemed suspicious of our *bona fides*. The exception was a voluble little man, not unlike Charlie Chaplin, who had once owned a restaurant in Tirana, and who now attached himself to us, unbidden, in the role of chef to the mission. Though not unmindful of his own wages and trade perquisites, he filled this post very satisfactorily for three or four months. His pastry was ethereal, his soups substantial; and the mission at Shepr, where we lived, earned a well-deserved reputation for good fare. His long and successful reign came to a sudden end with the discovery in his house of various bits of parachute silk. For this he was condemned to be shot. In saving him, which I did with difficulty, I acted from purely altruistic motives, for it was unfortunately impossible to re-employ him.

The village of Shepr where we established ourselves consisted of about one hundred houses. It lay on the eastern slope of the wide and rather barren valley of Zagori, between the long, level, almost unbroken ridges of Nemercke and Lunxheries which rise to over 6000 ft. The floor of the valley is about 3000 ft. above the sea. Some fifteen miles to the south is the Greek frontier, and a few of the villages south of Shepr have a Greek population.

The Greeks are in the habit of making extravagant claims to most of southern Albania, including Gjinokastre, Korca, and Valona, but it appeared to me that a very slight adjustment of the present frontier or a small transfer of population is the most they can fairly ask.

About five miles south of Shepr the Lunxheries mountains are cut by a wild and difficult gorge, by which a paved mule track leads down to the Dhrino valley and Gjinokastre, about six hours' march away. The people of Zagori are mainly Orthodox Christians, and most villages enjoy the blessing of a venerable time-mellowed stone church of a uniform pattern, with an arched cloister on one side, and a high tower of which the upper part and belfry are built in the form of three open arches, one above the other. The houses are of stone with stone roofs and are enclosed by a high wall. Large double wooden doors under a tiled porch lead into the flagged courtyard and the stables, which usually occupy the ground floor of the house. Stone stairs lead to the living rooms above. The old alluvial fan on which Shepr stood had been built up into terraced fields where wheat and maize were grown in rotation, while in the village itself were many fruitful terraced vineyards and orchards. However dirty the narrow alleys between the high walls might be, there was no dirt inside the houses, and over the whole village lay an air of pride, modest well-being, and content.

We hired an empty house for one gold sovereign a month, and there awaited the arrival of the partisan command—the Shtab—which was then located at a village called Kuc, south of Valona, two days' march from Shepr. The whole area, from the Greek border north to Valona, and east as far as Frasheri, was called the 1 re Zone. The commander was Islam Radowicke, a middle-aged, competent, cautious soldier, liked and respected by all, but no Communist. His political commissar, for they were organised on the Russian model, was Badri Spahiu, a man younger than Islam, and a fiery patriot and Communist.

House in Shepr used as headquarters

Typical hill country, southern Albania

Both were ex-officers of the Italian-trained Albanian army. Badri's house in Gjinokastre had already been burnt and his wife and child forced to lead an unsettled precarious life between various villages. He was able and tireless, and spoke forcibly and persuasively, using a wealth of quiet gesture. Albanians, like Irishmen, seem to have a natural genius for fighting and generalship. Most of them have carried a rifle from their youth up, and until fairly recent times the national pastimes of brigandage and blood-feuds necessarily made the survivors cunning in the use of ground and cover. They served as valued mercenaries and janissaries with the Turks, from whose ranks came Skenderbeg, the Albanian Alexander, Taut Gaiola, the great Pasha of Constantinople, and Mehemet Ali of Egypt. We see them serving under the miserable Ferdinand of Naples, and against him in Sicily, where both before and after the arrival of Garibaldi and his Thousand the Albanian colony played a part fully in keeping with Byron's estimate of their race, 'faithful in peril, indefatigable in service'.

At this early stage the partisan movement was weak. Apart from the arming and equipping of the 1st Brigade by the mission then near Korca, nothing had been done. Nearly every man had a rifle, captured, stolen, or inherited, which might be of Italian, German, Greek, Russian, Austrian, or French origin; but except for a few Italian light machine-guns there were no automatic weapons. The riflemen wore broad leather belts supported by cross straps in which they could carry 150–200 rounds. Almost as serious as the lack of automatics was the shortage of boots. Normally Albanians wear very stout hand-made shoes with slightly turned-up toes which slip easily on and off, or a sandal with a rubber-tyre sole. Now there were neither the leather, the tyres, nor the cobblers to turn out footwear in the required quantities. In the 1 re Zone there were about 3000 poorly-armed men organised in five groups—Berat, Mesoplik, Kurvelesh, Malakastra, and Zagori—and in addition to the 'active' battalions, there were reserve battalions which only turned out in the event of a levy *en masse*. The 1st Brigade of Korca was the forerunner of some dozen mobile brigades which were recruited from the active battalions as arms and ammunition became available. Just before I left the country in May 1944 I attended the inauguration ceremony of the 8th Brigade, by which time the L.N.C. forces of southern Albania were believed to comprise

Partisan leaders outside H.Q., Shepr:
back right, Shefket, Cdr, 5th Brigade; next, Radowicke Cdr of 1st Zone;
next, Tahir, Cdr 3rd Brigade, with bandaged face

Two Albanian partisans; note ammunition belt and red star in caps

Hakmarrje, or Vengeance Battalion;
the Albanian National Flag carried on right is a black eagle on red ground

Albanian girl partisans

nearly 20,000 men, most of them well armed, organised as a Division under a General Staff.

Even in those early days I was impressed by the camaraderie and *esprit de corps* of the various battalions and 'chetas', the easygoing relations between men and leaders, and the severity of the discipline. For immorality, theft, looting, or even failing to put into the common pool what had been captured from the enemy, the penalty was death. On one occasion five boys of Shepr who had found and sold some drugs, which they had picked up near the dropping ground long after they had been dropped, were sentenced to be shot. Only their youth and the strenuous pleading of every family in the village saved them. And one afternoon, just before I left, three men were tried in Shepr, two for immorality and one for stealing cigarette papers from a comrade. The British officer who happened to arrive that day to relieve me had to step over the bodies lying in a lane by the church where they had been shot. He reached our house perceptibly shaken, wondering among what sort of cut-throats he had fallen. Military offences were punished by disarming and dismissal—a disgrace worse than death—and such was the exalted feeling of dedication to a noble cause that they were willing to accept or exact the stern penalties of this Draconian code.

To show their boundless admiration for the Russian army, and to distinguish them from the Balli Kombetar (or Balli as we called them), the partisans of the L.N.C. wore a red star in their caps. Otherwise they looked like any other Albanians—perhaps a trifle more travel-stained. They seldom shaved but, on the other hand, they did not grow beards. Later we were able to clothe most of them in battle-dress, but for the time being the townsmen wore something 'off the peg' and the peasants their rough natural woollen homespun, with trousers like badly cut Jodhpurs. A few had German uniforms, more had Italian, and after the Italian collapse the appearance of partisans in white naval rig with straw hats added a touch of originality to a far from uniform body. The unalterable and obligatory form of salutation was 'Death to the Fascists', to which the reply was 'Liberty to the People', or in Albanian 'Vdekje Fashizmit—Liri Popullit'. This rigid formula helped to smell out anyone of Balli tendencies, whose own particular slogan was 'Death to the Traitors', by which they meant the L.N.C.

The partisans had little to occupy them when not on patrol. They sat about endlessly but animatedly discussing the war, politics, or the next meal, smoking hand-rolled cigarettes, and singing. Their songs, which were all about partisans, were melancholy, tuneful, and pleasing. When in particularly good heart they danced. This always took the form of a ring dance in which a file of men, of any length, imitated the slow steps and actions of a leader who flourished a handkerchief and crooned an improvised topical catch which the chorus emphasised at the appropriate place. If any women joined in they formed a separate ring. I enjoyed watching the comical steps and actions of the leaders of these dances.

There were a number of young girls with the partisans, some working as clerks or interpreters, some in the ranks. The arms which they carried were symbolic, for their job in action was to tend the wounded. Those who were clerks led a busy life, for, as I discovered later with the Italian partisans, the amount of paper circulated would not have discredited a real army. A duplicating machine which I procured for them considerably augmented the ammunition supply for this war of words. Having so much time on their hands the partisans, I thought, might well have benefited the country and improved their already good relations with the villagers by helping in the fields. But they left all the ploughing and the fetching of wood and water to their wives, sisters and mothers; for, like most amateur soldiers, they considered that fighting alone was consistent with dignity. In Albanian society the women's place is fully on a level with the men's, and they earn it by doing most, if not all, of the work.

CHAPTER X

THE ITALIANS COLLAPSE, THE GERMANS ARRIVE

I FIRST SAW THE PARTISANS IN ACTION in a night attack on Libohov, a small town on the opposite side of the Dhrino valley to Gjinokastre. A garrison of fifty Italians lived there in the Citadel, and it was the home of many prominent Balli. My part in the action was to prevent the arrival of reinforcements from Gjinokastre by mining the earth road which connects Libohov with the main road, but from what I had heard of the Italians in Albania, the last thing which the garrison of Gjinokastre would be likely to do was to stir from their barracks after dark.

We found Islam Radowicke with two or three hundred partisans lying concealed on a hot afternoon in the wooded bed of the river which cuts through the gorge from Zagori to the Dhrino valley. The strictest precautions to avoid observation from the air were enforced. This was, of course, sound practice, but the Italian Air Force had done little to deserve the exaggerated respect shown to it by the partisans. One bomb had been dropped on Shepr, and the effects of it were still felt. I remember how puzzled I was on the morning of our arrival, when the only man in sight, to whom I wanted to speak, persisted in cowering flat in a maize field. The hum of an aeroplane a good ten miles off was responsible for his odd behaviour. But aeroplanes could not be entirely discounted. The mission at Stylle told us how on one occasion an Italian plane had followed one of ours over their dropping ground and off-loaded a bomb on to the signal fires, to the great surprise of all concerned. The Germans frequently used an aeroplane during their drives, and my successor at Shepr, who was living outside the village in tents, had his camp bombed. Lt.-Col. Leake, who was on a visit from our H.Q. in Italy at the time, was killed there.

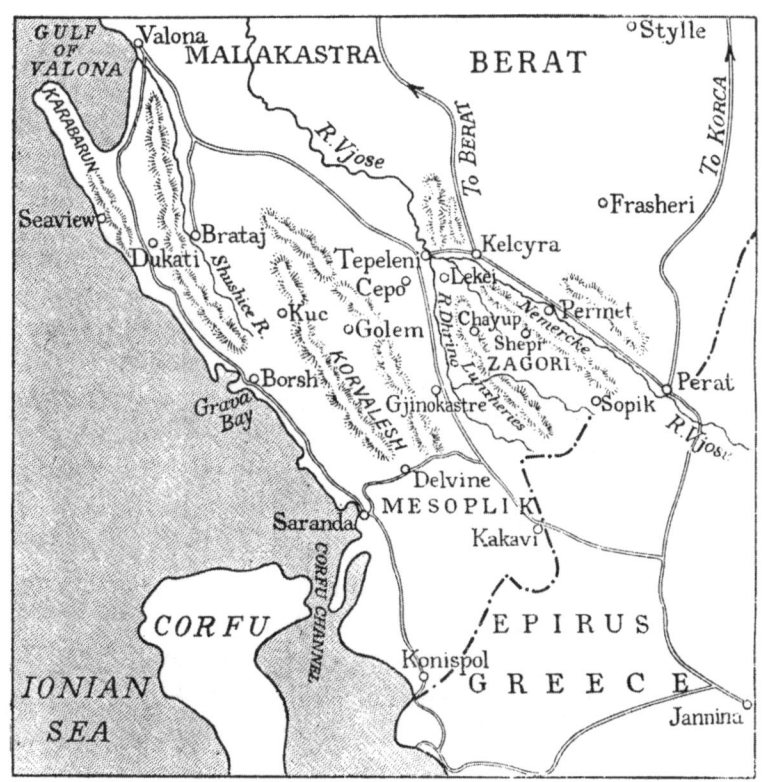

Map 4: Sketch map to illustrate south Albania

At dusk, after a meal of bread and cheese, the men filed out of the river bed for the three hours' march to Libohov. In spite of the secrecy imposed prior to this night attack, someone had warned the Italians who were waiting for us inside their fort. Their morale was known to be low, so perhaps the partisans thought that if sufficient noise was made the walls of the Citadel might oblige like those of Jericho. A hot fire was opened with all the rifles and the few machine-guns available, to which the Italians replied with machine-guns and mortars. The darkness was intense, but with so much stuff flying about some of us who were not behind stone walls were bound to be hit. Six of the partisans were killed. The bugle sounded a charge, the attackers closed in through the town towards the fortress, set alight the houses of the most-hated Balli, and withdrew in good order before dawn. It was a bold but quite futile effort.

A grim scene was enacted next morning in the little village of Labove on the way home. Under the mellow red brick walls of an old Byzantine church, one of the partisans who had died of wounds was buried. Badri delivered a funeral harangue. As he finished, a trembling wretch was led to the open grave and almost without warning shot to death by the partisans standing round. He was a spy captured in Libohov during the night.

After this abortive action Radowicke returned to Kuc and Badri to a place called Cepo, six miles down the Dhrino valley from Gjinokastre, where a subsidiary headquarters was established. On 8 September, preceded by only twenty-four hours' warning, there came the news of the Italian collapse, and orders for me to get from them all the arms I could by fair means or foul—even purchase was allowed. Having dispatched a letter to the Italian commander asking him to meet me at Cepo to discuss surrender terms, I went there post haste on foot, leaving my wireless at Shepr. In the Gjinokastre area was the Perugia Division, commanded by General Ernesto Chiminello, with a strength of 5000 men and a mule battery of eight 75 mm. mountain guns. The bulk of these were at Gjinokastre itself, but there were small garrisons at Permet, Saranda, Delvine, and Tepeleni, a strategic point commanding the gorge at the junction of the Gjinokastre-Valona road and that from Permet.

I crossed the Lunxheries range by the pass and grazing alp of Chayup, forded the Dhrino, and crossed the main road in daylight. On a concrete bridge spanning a small tributary of the Dhrino were two German trucks and three dead Germans, who had been ambushed by partisans on the previous day. Following an earth road up this tributary valley, I found Badri and 200 partisans at the monastery of Cepo, built on a commanding spur about 3000 yards from the bridge and the main road. The monastery was a rambling, ramshackle old building in a courtyard enclosed by a high stone wall. A fig tree, a fountain, and a little chapel, in which were some old uncared-for frescoes, faced the living quarters. The presiding genius was a striking figure—a tall, robust priest, clad in a black cassock and a high stiff black hat, who conversed loudly and energetically in Greek or Albanian with equal fluency. Although old, grey-bearded, and spectacled he radiated vigour and decision, and was one of the stoutest, most warm-hearted and hospitable men I have ever met. He was an impressive, imperious blending of Mr Pickwick and Friar Tuck.

The monastery staff consisted only of an old mad woman and a few decrepit men, but under one of such commanding personality it provided an overflowing abundance of the good things of life equal to anything found in wealthy well-staffed monasteries—great hunks of fresh wheat bread, bowls of white liquescent cheese, honey from the hundred hives lining the south wall, figs as big as pears, grapes, wine, raki. Fortunately the Albanians take no breakfast—they say their stomachs are too coated with chalk to function properly at that early hour—so we could face with perfect equanimity the rich oily stew served up twice a day in an enamel bowl the size of a baby's bath.

General Chiminello proved elusive. He failed to attend a meeting we arranged half-way between Gjinokastre and Cepo, having been frightened, he said, by the presence of a Balli patrol on the road. Meanwhile the leaders of the Balli Kombetar were in touch with him demanding his surrender to them in the name of the Provisional Albanian Government of Tirana. At length our patience was exhausted and on the 14th we all marched by night towards Gjinokastre. The partisans, whose numbers had swollen to 500, took up positions in a ravine about 1000 yards from the northern perimeter of the barracks, and Badri and I with a small escort climbed up to the fortified outpost ridge and passed through the wire under a white flag. From the ridge, which was strongly held, we looked down on the fine modern barracks,

Some L.N.C. leaders: on left, Shefket Pezi, Cdr of 5th Brigade, next to him Baba Faze, a Bektashi priest and partisan leader

Shefket Pezi and author in Permet

the vehicles and guns neatly parked. Our mouths watered, like Blücher's at the sight of London. The company holding the ridge were bewildered but friendly. They conducted us to the General's office, which was situated on the main road. We were afraid of the arrival at any time of Germans from Jannina or Valona, in fact some German trucks had stopped at the barracks the previous day, so the first request I made of the General was to take us somewhere where we could talk without fear of being surprised. He was a tall, thin, weak-looking man. With him were five of his colonels. They were all very smart, in shiny black riding boots and much beribboned uniforms. In a distant corner of the barracks Badri, who like many Albanians spoke Italian fluently, opened negotiations.

It had been reported that a small German force was attacking the Italian garrison at Tepeleni, so we proposed to the General three courses: to join us in attacking these Germans, to hand over everything to us as representing the Allies, or to burn everything. His counter-proposal was that he should be allowed to march his whole force to the port of Saranda where, when transport to Italy had been arranged, he would surrender all he had. He said that he had received no orders, that he was not in touch with Rome, that his men would certainly not fight the Germans, and that he would not consider handing over any weapons until he was safely at the coast. To receive the arms at Saranda did not suit us. Here at Gjinokastre, where men were available, we could quickly disperse and hide all the material, for time was the all-important factor. It was strange that the Germans had not already come. Badri assured me that the Saranda road would be blocked by partisans, and as we could stop any move in the direction of Valona, we told the General he must make up his mind by five o'clock that evening, although it was obvious to all that if he refused we could not impose our views. I threatened to have his barracks bombed, Badri swore at them in Italian, and the colonels raved about their military honour. The party broke up in a temper and we repaired to the outpost company to await the issue. They sent up lunch for us, and while we ate, Shefket, one of Badri's trusted henchmen, took on one side the company commander who had privately intimated that he was ready to 'sell the pass'. This was treachery, and I was not sure that the Italian could be trusted to carry out his part of the bargain or that we would not have to fight the rest of the garrison afterwards. Down below the Italians appeared to be packing up and at five o'clock came a terse note from the General: 'I will give up my arms to nobody.'

Feeling rather foolish, we left, and we had not got back to our lines before heavy firing broke out on the main road. For reasons that were obscure the company on the ridge opened up in our direction with all they had, while the mountain battery started plastering some empty fields across the river. The partisans held their fire and presently the Italians calmed down. Badri agreed with me that an attack on the garrison would be too expensive, but we hoped that they would move out, when we should be better able to deal with them. To hurry them up we arranged to cut off their water supply, which was piped down to the barracks from the town above, and the same night I returned hotfoot to Shepr to report progress. When I got back at dawn on the 16th I found the worst had happened. Finding the water cut off, the thirsty Italians, after burning what they could not carry, had marched in the night, and had reached Saranda unhindered. Elsewhere, after burning their equipment, the garrisons of Permet and Kelcyra had surrendered, and the partisans had taken and were holding Tepeleni.

Instead of at once following the Perugia Division to Saranda, which was a long two days' march for the partisans, Badri arranged for a somewhat premature triumphal entry of Gjinokastre. The town, the capital of the Province, had a population of over 10,000. It is a lovely old place, straggling terrace-wise over the steep slopes of three spurs or buttresses of the high barren mountains which bound the Dhrino valley on the west. Led by Badri on a white charger, recently captured from the Italians, the partisans filed slowly up the narrow cobbled streets between old-fashioned houses, stone-arched doorways, trellises of vines, minarets, and cypresses. The people were wildly excited, casting bouquets of flowers, and embracing long-lost relatives and friends in the ranks of the procession. At length we reached the massive walls of the citadel. This was built in 1808 by the notorious Ali Pasha, the cruel Lion of Jannina, and completely dominates the town. The great crowd which had gathered in the sun-baked square outside the walls of the gloomy fortress now gave themselves up to an afternoon of undiluted oratory. First the mayor, then Badri, then myself, faced the delighted crowd, and after that anyone who felt he had something in him demanding utterance. One of the L.N.C. representatives from Zagori, a spectacled student called Shemsi, embarked on a long harangue which appeared to be nothing but an all-embracing Ernulphus' curse directed against the Balli Kombetar. A Balli leader, Bahri Omari (for the rupture between the parties was not yet final), was standing next to me fanning himself with his Homburg hat, as much to cool his rising indignation as to mitigate the hot blast reflected from the blazing white square. Hemmed in as he was by partisans and L.N.C. adherents, his position was delicate, but he stood his ground stoutly enough and even attempted to raise his voice against some of the more outrageous accusations. At this point, fearing trouble, I begged Badri to silence the exuberant Shemsi. More certain help, however, was at hand. The appearance of an ancient and solitary biplane sailing sedately through the sky far to the south, dispersed the crowd in disorder and brought the celebrations to a timely, if undignified, end.

We dined and slept that night in one of Gjinokastre's oldest houses. Most of these are two- or three-storied buildings with projecting wings and a balcony between. The ground-floor windows are small and barred, those on the second floor are high and latticed. Above them the broad eaves are supported by wooden struts projecting from the wall. The stone floors and stone walls of the ground-floor rooms make them delightfully cool and dim, and the austerity of the stone is relieved by brightly painted fireplaces and by red and blue pointing between the stones of the floor. Upstairs the wooden ceilings are carved or painted in red, green, or yellow designs, and adorned with an abundance of crude stars and crescents. We dined in Albanian fashion from a common dish of 'pillau' placed in the centre.

In the morning I set off for the Greek frontier in a war-weary Italian truck with six partisans and seventy pounds of explosive. As the road from the north was barred by partisans at Tepeleni, we thought that if we could blow the bridge near Kakavi on the road to Jannina, we might delay the Germans sufficiently to save some of the booty we expected to get at Saranda. Badri and his men were already en route for the port. Between Gjinokastre and Kakavi on the Greek border the road runs through flat open country, and is more or less invulnerable to sabotage. There were three bridges spanning mere dry river beds which formed no obstacles, but a mile or so beyond the border we had been told of a more promising place where the road crossed a deep ravine. We trundled along the dusty road, half expecting to run into a German column, crossed the Greek frontier, and reached the unguarded bridge without incident. It appeared to be a recent replacement of one destroyed in the Greek-Italian campaign, and consisted of three massive concrete piers supporting a wooden roadway. The piers were 6 feet thick, but the builder had thoughtfully provided holes in them for demolition charges. With my six partisans acting as a covering party I hastily rammed thirty-five pounds of powerful explosive into each of two piers and connected the charges with a length of detonating fuse. Just as all was ready some Greeks from the nearby village appeared, took in the situation at a glance, and launched an indignant protest on behalf of the doomed bridge. It was of no particular value to them, they said, but if the Germans found the bridge blown they would certainly burn the nearest village, which happened to be theirs. I quite saw their point, but war is war. Lighting the safety fuse, I told them to run, and set them the example myself. A few minutes later there was a satisfactory roar and bits of bridge shot high into the air. When the last piece had fallen I ran back to survey the work of my 'prentice hand with the modest pride becoming to an amateur in crime. The bridge had 'had it in a big way', but the ravine was not so difficult to cross as I had hoped, and it was clear that a diversion could be quickly effected.

We returned to Gjinokastre, burning a small wooden bridge for good measure on the way. I made another forced march to Shepr to report to Base, returned almost without stopping to Gjinokastre, and from there reached Saranda by car on the 22nd. It is about forty miles away over bleak uplands.

Saranda is a small town almost opposite the northern tip of Corfu which is only about ten miles distant. This small, modern, dusty and indefensible town lay on the shore of a deep and sheltered bay. Steamers could lie out about 300 yards from a wooden jetty on which, however, there were no cranes.

Chiminello and his staff were installed in an office building on the water front. Badri had already seen them, and since neither side chose to offer recriminations for recent past events, they were on good terms with each other. Moreover, the Italians were jubilant, for 2000 had been embarked in an Italian ship the previous night. Chiminello said he was now in touch with Ambrosio, the Italian Chief of Staff at Rome, who had ordered them to retain their rifles. We agreed to this and, in return, the General agreed to defend the town if the Germans came—a promise which I felt sure would not be fulfilled by the thoroughly demoralised men waiting impatiently to be taken home. Meanwhile the handing over of vehicles and mules, of which there were 300 belonging to the mountain battery, had begun, and the partisans worked furiously to remove to Kuc and Cepo as much of the stores, arms and ammunition as they could handle.

While this went on I made a quick journey on foot to Konispol to see what was happening there. This is a small town on the Greek border twenty-five miles south of Saranda to which it is linked by a motor-road. I was pleased to note that a blown bridge had stopped all traffic, and that the unbridged, fast-flowing river looked likely to present a more formidable obstacle than our ravine at Kakavi. I was surprised to hear afterwards that the Germans had reached Saranda by that route. The few partisans at Konispol were jumpy. They explained their fears by taking me to a high hill whence we looked down upon a small jetty on the Greek side of the frontier where, through glasses, I could see a large number of naked Huns sporting in the sea. Across the narrow Corfu Channel columns of smoke were rising from a town which the Germans had been intermittently bombing during the day.

On our return we forsook the road for a footpath which, winding through low hilly malarious country, past dirty, fever-stricken villages, eventually brought us out near the mouth of the narrow Vutrinto channel which links the long lagoon of that name with the sea. Hard by were the ruins of Buthrotum, a very ancient Greek settlement, and before the war a centre of archaeological research. It was dark when we pushed through the last reeds bordering the channel. We hailed the ferryman, who at length grudgingly consented to take us across to his hut, where we dined off fat juicy mullet while a boat was being prepared to take us up the lagoon. All night we pulled quietly over the black glassy water under silent wooded hills, until with the dawn wind puckering the calm surface, now growing pallid before the oncoming day, we landed at a little jetty at the northern end.

A German reconnaissance plane making a dawn patrol passed overhead, and when we topped the rocky neck of land separating us from Saranda bay, I was amazed to see a steamer lying peacefully at anchor a few hundred yards from the town. I went straight to the General's office and heard his tale of woe. Only a few more men had got away, and the ship lying there, a rusty Italian tramp of about 3000 tons, had fouled her cable and was unable to move. The crew had deserted her, wisely, I thought, in view of that German 'recce' plane. As we talked inside the room, idly regarding through the open doors of the balcony the lifeless ship, we were startled by the familiar sounds of a diving plane, and the whistle of falling bombs. The ship disappeared in a cloud of smoke and spray, and when this had subsided I saw that I was alone and that the ship was undamaged. I went to the house where we were stopping, which was not quite so close to the harbour, but found it empty. Saranda was deserted. At intervals throughout the day six Stukas returned five times to the attack, dived low, released their bombs, and flew off for more. From this target practice the ship sustained one hit which set her on fire and she eventually sank at five in the evening. It was a pity, I thought, that so few partisans had stayed to watch such a pitiful performance.

I never saw General Chiminello or his officers again. When the bombing started, all the Italians, realising that Saranda's brief day as a port of embarkation was over, fled north to Porto Palermo. I heard later, and believe it to be true, that the Germans found them there and shot the General and 150 of his officers. The remnants of the Perugia Division I was to see once more living on berries in the woods near Kuc. Leaving the partisans to deal as they could with the enormous booty they now had, I walked once more to Shepr and back again to Gjinokastre on 29 September. There seemed to be an air of gloomy expectation over the town which I was at a loss to understand. The Germans had been so long in coming that I thought they must have decided to abandon Albania; but this morning it was rumoured that Konispol and Saranda were occupied and that a large column was even then on its way from Jannina to Gjinokastre. At eleven o'clock I left for Cepo and at midday the head of the column arrived.

At Cepo there was more definite news, most of it bad. The Germans had entered Saranda two days after I had left, where they had found large quantities of stores, mainly grain and petrol, which the partisans had not had time to remove. From there they had advanced up the coast road, and were now attacking the H.Q. and depot at Kuc in the Shushice valley south of Valona where Radowicke was stationed. Coming up the road to the monastery I had seen, at the foot of the spur, a big dump of grain, rice, forty-gallon petrol drums, some trucks, and two 40 mm. antitank guns. It was probable, however, that the Germans were unaware of the importance Cepo had thus acquired. The Tepeleni position astride the main road a few miles north of Cepo was strongly held. It was Badri's intention to fight the Germans there and to 'lie doggo' at Cepo, but as a precautionary measure some 200 partisans were occupying a long horseshoe-shaped position on the low hills commanding the approach to the monastery.

Having been told that a bridge in the gorge south of Tepeleni had been prepared for blowing, Badri and I went down by car to see it. It was a concrete arched bridge which carried the road over a small nallah with steep cliffs on one side and the Dhrino on the other. These cliffs, at the foot of which the road is cut, made it very vulnerable to attack by explosives; but two months later the heavy winter rains closed it far more effectively than we could have ever done by bringing down a large landslide. This bridge had been well prepared for blowing by the Italians, who had sunk five timber-lined holes 4 feet square and 6 feet deep in the crown of the arches. The partisans had already laid their charges of Italian blasting powder and had filled the holes to the brim with earth and stones. Unluckily the man in charge, who knew nothing of the fine art of destruction or of the use of detonating fuse, had fused each charge separately with safety fuse. This meant that the charges would go off at different times, thus losing much of their effect, or that the explosion of the first might perhaps dislodge or break the fuses of the others before they had acted. It was too late to dig out the holes and connect up with detonating fuse. The anticipated failure occurred next day. Only two of the charges went off, blowing a small hole in the middle of the road and a bit out of one side.

On the morning of 1 October, I watched the long-expected German column drive past. From the monastery spur several miles of the white ribbon of road were in sight before it disappeared round a corner just short of the bridge about to be blown. Headed by motor-cyclists and staff cars, sixty troop-carrying vehicles and two 115 mm. guns crossed the bridge at the bottom of the Cepo valley—where they halted to inspect the three dead men and the ambushed trucks—and parked themselves in a wood two miles beyond. The troops disappeared round the corner on foot and a distant rumble announced the partial blowing of the bridge. Battle was joined. We were merely distant spectators. Only the bursting of shells on the heights across the Dhrino, and the burning of villages high up on both sides of the valley on the second day, told us that the attack was making headway. A small cluster of houses at the foot of our valley was wantonly burnt by men from the vehicle park. Although they were a bare 500 yards from our outposts, the partisans held their fire. It is possible to write calmly enough about burning villages, but when we actually see men at work setting fire to one peaceful, familiar little homestead after another, the rising flames, the roofs falling in, and the labour and loving care of years dissolving irretrievably in a few minutes, it is impossible not to experience a hot wave of dismay, revulsion and hate. To watch fires caused by bombing or shelling is bad enough, but guns and planes seem impersonal and their effects do not rouse the same intense feeling.

Couriers kept arriving at our H.Q. in the monastery at all hours. In the little room in which we ate and slept, a sea of confusion eddied round the stalwart figure of the 'Papa', who, unmoved as a rock, served our meals with the same regularity as before. At night he slept fully clothed, his hat on his head and a handkerchief over his face, oblivious of comings or goings, or the ceaseless clatter of a typewriter.

On the 4th we heard that Kuc and its depot had been abandoned, and from the silence that reigned over the distant Tepeleni gorge we concluded that the Germans had at last broken through. But worse was to come. On the evening of that day a mule train with about 150 men appeared from the direction of Gjinokastre and suddenly halted on the bridge where the road to the monastery turned off. Were they going to bivouac there for the night or were they after our dump? We breathed more freely when they started to move on but, having crossed the bridge, they turned off the road up a narrow valley which would lead them right underneath one of our outposts. Regular troops might have contained themselves, but for irregulars the target was altogether too tempting. It was impossible to send any orders there in time, and a few minutes later the crackle of rifle fire warned us that our precious dump was now in jeopardy. I have never understood what intentions those Germans had, but from the unconcerned way in which they marched into that narrow defile I am sure they had no knowledge of our presence. Had the partisans who opened the ball been in sufficient force, or well-enough armed, to have made a clean job of the ambush, all might have been well. As it was, a few men and mules were hit, the rest promptly scattered in the scrub, and under cover of the gathering dusk began to fight back. Signal lights soared up, and the ripping sound of the fast-firing German machine-gun showed us with what we had to deal. One could not but admire the speed with which they recovered from what must have been a very painful shock.

The battle so unluckily begun continued for two days. In the morning the Germans, who had withdrawn to a position near the bridge, were reinforced from Gjinokastre. On the 6th twelve troop-carriers and two 115 mm. guns arrived from the north. Although the partisans fought well, the ultimate issue was not in doubt. Our two 40 mm. anti-tank guns, to which as a gunner I attached myself, firing from some scrub on the face of the spur, made the main road impassable. A truck which foolishly stopped near the bridge was hit at a range of 3000 yards and set alight. The guns were, of course, soon spotted and neutralised by the fire of a heavy mortar firing from behind cover. One of them received a direct hit. While the fight went on those men who could be spared laboured to clear the monastery and the dump of arms and to hide what they could in the bush. The difficulty of feeding men in the firing-line, 1000 yards or more from the monastery, made a long resistance unlikely. Everything had to be carried by hand and nothing hot could be provided for them.

When the two guns began shelling the monastery and its approaches Badri gave the order for retreat. The dump was set alight and the partisans started to steal away, covered by the fire of a few machine-guns. All tracks converged on the monastery, where the shelling seemed likely to start a panic among tired men unaccustomed to that kind of warfare. Badri and Shefket cursed the fugitives into shame and some kind of order, while the 'Papa', armed with a gigantic umbrella, showed the most soldierly bearing of any and beat into submission anyone who attempted to argue. He, who was shortly to see the monastery to which he was devoted go up in senseless flames, was the most to be pitied; he would, I think, have preferred us all to stand there and die. I was ashamed to look him in the face.

We retreated up the valley towards the barren Kurvalesh hills while the Germans followed slowly, burning every village in sight. Badri's plan was to reorganise before crossing the Dhrino back to Zagori. I was anxious to return to Shepr, so I started out alone that night. Skirting high above the Cepo valley I dropped down into the Dhrino valley in the dark, where I found a house with a light burning. The occupants were, with difficulty, persuaded to open and with more difficulty to give me a guide for the crossing of the river. No doubt they thought I was a German or a Balli.

Thus in October, with winter at hand, the bright prospects of the partisans and their supporters had faded. They had lost most of the recently gained arms and equipment, two of their strongholds had been overrun and burnt, and the burning of ten villages at the beginning of winter had severely shaken the morale of the population upon whose support the partisans depended for food and shelter. In addition, their break with the Balli Kombetar was now almost complete; from criticism, recrimination, and suspicion, they were about to pass to open war. The L.N.C. declared that their plans were betrayed to the enemy by Balli spies, that no Balli had yet fired a shot for the liberation of the country, and that now they must make up their minds to fight the enemy or the L.N.C. But in spite of these setbacks their organisation throughout the south had been growing stronger, and that of the Balli Kombetar weaker. Whether they wished it or no the Balli were forced for their own preservation to proceed from covert to overt co-operation with the Germans.

CHAPTER XI

WINTER

───◆───

During September and October, arms, clothing and boots for the partisans had been arriving at the rate of three or four plane loads a month. The pilots were always able to find the dropping ground in the Zagori valley about two miles from Shepr. It was a heartening sight to see a big four-engined Halifax roar down the valley five or six hundred feet over the signal fires, drop its load, do a tight turn without troubling to gain height, and come back for its second run. As the plane turned the navigation lights on the wings seemed almost to brush the hillside. In my subsequent experience I never met any squadron which approached the standard of that one operating from Derna in the autumn of 1943. One night we had three planes over the target at the same time, their headlights full on to avoid colliding. The valley looked like Croydon on a busy night, and I wondered what the Germans in Gjinokastre thought of it. Between sorties life at Shepr became almost indecently dull and placid. My sergeant and corporal had our establishment well organised and were on excellent terms with the villagers. From a prosperous trader, whose morals were not severe, who had irons in many fires, and whose black-market activities would, I feared, end one day in front of a firing party, we bought amongst other things six mules. They were to carry our equipment when the Germans obliged us to run; in the meantime we used them for carrying wood to the dropping ground and stores away from it. We ate our three good meals a day, ciphered signals, visited neighbouring villages, showed the partisans how to use explosives, and argued more or less amiably with various people who came to see us. The main points on which they desired to be enlightened were, when were the British going to invade the Balkans, why we continued to support the Balli and the Zoggists, and why the Albanian broadcasts of the B.B.C. never denounced these two organisations by name and carefully refrained from naming the L.N.C. For many months all actions in Albania were referred to as having been carried out by 'patriots' which, of course, might mean anyone. To none of these questions, except the first, was it easy to find a convincing answer.

From this comfortable cabbage-like existence I had frequently and gladly to depart on longer journeys, travelling fast, living hard, and always returning with increased zest to the masterpieces of Cesio our cook. The first of these sorties was provoked by the burning out of the condenser of our wireless set. The corporal went off to the nearest mission in Greece for help, while I went to a mission of ours near Valona to send a signal. On this and on subsequent journeys I took with me one partisan, dispensing with the escort which the partisans deemed necessary and liked so much to provide; for to travel with an escort was to double the time taken and to multiply many times the difficulties of food and shelter at the villages on our route. For our safety I relied on speed, and the good sense, native caution and craft of Mehmet my partisan guide. He came from the Korca area, but soon got to know all the tracks and by-paths of our zone perfectly. He was uncannily clever in the dark and could follow the faintest of paths on the blackest of nights. He was intelligent, active, stout-hearted, cheerful, good at driving a bargain, a good mixer, and a good walker. Most Albanians are not good walkers. They are for ever stopping, either to have a chat, a smoke, a drink of water, or a rest. On the limestone mountains of Albania the rain sinks down (leaving the upper parts bone dry) to gush out in innumerable springs near the valley floor. In summer it is quite impossible to get an Albanian past one of these springs. They are great water connoisseurs, and will distinguish between the excellence of one village and another solely by its water. But even between one spring and the next, and usually the distance is not great, you will often hear from the perspiring rear-guard a plaintive cry of 'Avash, Avash'; for which a free translation would be, 'For God's sake, stop'. I say 'perspiring' advisedly because they liked to wear all the clothes they possessed all the time. However hot the day or steep the hill they never shed a garment. While I would be going along coolly and comfortably in nothing but a pair of shorts, they would be wearing two or three sweaters and a pair of thick homespun trousers. No wonder they were thirsty souls. Through his long association with me, during which he complained of loss of weight, Mehmet acquired more sense—in this respect, at least, if not in others—but I don't think I saw him with his shirt off more than once. I believe he thought it indelicate.

We crossed the Chayup pass in the dark, where the Vlachs were preparing for their winter trek to the coast, and where we had a running fight with one of their savage white dogs—our hard-flung stones he just tried to catch, so that Mehmet was reduced to using his Sten, fortunately without fatal results. These dogs are said to be descended from wolves and they seem unable to forget it. We forded the Dhrino, crossed the road, and headed for Cepo. Amongst the black shadows cast by the cypresses, the moonlight played on the blackened shell of the silent monastery. No burly 'Papa' welcomed the wayfarer. The vines were cut down, the bees were gone, and the body of the old mad woman lay buried in the courtyard. The little church stood alone untouched and untended amid the ruins.

Our first halt was at Golem, one of the highest and poorest villages of southern Albania set in the middle of the barren uplands of Kurvalesh. It was as yet unburnt. The inhabitants were Moslem and, until recent times, could look back with pride upon a long and successful record of brigandage. If there were no partisans in a village Mehmet would go to the headman, who either took us in himself or sought out for us the best accommodation. We would leave our boots in the passage outside the living room (this sensible and labour-saving custom is facilitated by the type of shoes Albanians wear), and our host would seat us in the place of honour on sheepskin rugs on each side of the fireplace. The wood fire would be heaped up and a bottle of raki produced, while the women prepared food. Before eating, our host or one of the women would bring basin and ewer and pour water over our hands. Then the low round table was brought in, the bowl of food, and a hunk of bread and a spoon for each man. Everyone except the women squatted down, seized a spoon, bared his right arm, and then devil take the hindmost. To sup with the devil requires a long spoon, but for me it was equally necessary when supping with Albanians. With a short body and not long arms, unable when squatting to tuck my legs neatly under me, I started with a heavy handicap. That I was not holding my own was so apparent that they usually conceded me a small private bowl. When the big bowl was emptied we threw our spoons into it, the bread was swept up, the table carried out, and we went back to our rugs.

> We cleansed our beards of the mutton grease,
> We lay on our mats and were filled with peace.

For simplicity, economy of utensils, labour, and washing up, much can be said for the Albanian way of serving a meal.

From Golem we crossed another pass and dropped down to the Kuc valley where the partisans still had their H.Q. in a farmhouse. In the town itself there was not a single house with a roof—burnt-out trucks, burnt rifles and guns, littered the streets. Passing down the Shushice valley through the woods of Kalarat we met hundreds, or even thousands, of semi-starved Italians who lay about listlessly in improvised shelters. They were ultimately dispersed by the L.N.C. amongst various villages, where they were fed in return for work. In my opinion, for thus maintaining alive, at no small sacrifice to themselves, the men to whom they owed the invasion of their country and the destruction of their homes, the Albanians acquired great merit. Acts of magnanimity amongst nations, especially those of the Balkans, are so rare that this example of returning good for evil deserves remembrance.

At Brataj, fifteen miles south of Valona, we came upon an unfinished motor-road. Brataj was occupied by partisans, but the next two villages were strongholds of the Balli who looked at us with curiosity and suspicion as we passed through. To all enquiries Mehmet's reply that I was a German officer greatly facilitated our passage and threw some light on the changing attitude of that party. We finally ran the mission to earth in a leaky hut on the summit of the high ridge which separated the Shushice valley from the sea. In an area where sympathies were so mixed their position was unenviable; after doing his utmost to work with both parties, according to instructions, the officer concerned eventually elected to champion the cause of the Balli. This had unfortunate results for everybody. He established a sea base in some caves on the rocky coast of the Karabarun peninsula, known to us later as Seaview, where in time a good many tons of arms and ammunition were landed. As in the meantime the Balli had become so flagrantly unfriendly, the distribution of these arms to them was banned; but since they held all the land approaches to Seaview, the arms could not be issued to the L.N.C. So they lay there uselessly until in the end the base was betrayed to the Germans, who stepped in and took the lot.

With the coming of winter weather the supply of arms sent by air became extremely meagre. In November it rained every day and on the 9th of that month the first snow fell. Nevertheless, in accord with the exhortations of the B.B.C. broadcasts to augment the resistance movement, the forces of the L.N.C. steadily grew larger. By December five mobile brigades were in being, and if they were to be maintained increased supplies were essential. We, therefore, made efforts to establish a sea base in territory controlled by partisans.

From their point of view the most suitable place was Grava Bay, just south of Panermo Point. From here there was a track leading inland to Kuc, which could be used for the rapid distribution of stores.

Accordingly, Mehmet and I set out on another long journey, first to Seaview to consult a naval officer who had been sent there to assist with sea sorties, and then to Grava Bay to reconnoitre. As the Dhrino was now in flood we took a different route. After crossing Chayup we traversed the hillside high above the river by a path which led to a big iron bridge near Tepeleni. We stopped at the village of Lekei where we were entertained by the very militant priest of the church, who was one of the many Albanians who had been to America and spoke very fair English. Finding his congregations becoming less, he had exchanged the Bible for a rifle and now marched in the ranks of the partisans.

The bridge above Tepeleni was a fine steel girder structure upon which I should very much have liked to have tried my hand. But it was the only link between Gjinokastre and Kelcyra where there was a large grain market upon which Gjinokastre and many other places depended for food. At that time Kelcyra was in the hands of the Balli. When they banned the export of grain, as they presently did, the people of Gjinokastre experienced a lean time until Kelcyra was finally taken by the partisans in the spring. Avoiding Tepeleni, where there was a garrison, we marched for two days through wild, sparsely inhabited country until we again reached Brataj. There we found the 1st Brigade whose inauguration parade I had watched in August near Korca. A state of war now existed between the Balli and the L.N.C., and the 1st Brigade had been sent there to gain control of the country with an eye to opening the way to the arms and ammunition accumulated at Seaview. The commander of the brigade, Mehmet Schio, an able soldier and an ardent Communist, was not pleased when he heard where we were going. He doubted if we should get through the Balli village of Dukati where we had to go to obtain a guide to Seaview, but at the same time he gave no hint of his own intentions regarding that village. He expressed the greatest disgust at our policy of backing both parties, and gave me a personal message for the officer at Seaview that he, Mehmet Schio, would not be responsible for what happened if the 1st Brigade ever got there.

He himself talked at length but he was far outdone by a young woman on the Brigade staff. Her manners were offhand, her appearance was a 'check to loose behaviour', and she poured out an incessant stream of parrot-like propaganda until after midnight. There was only one bed in the room the brigade staff occupied, and I made no bones about accepting when they offered it to me. The woman slept under it.

At dawn next morning Mehmet and I stole silently away without as much as a 'Goodbye' to avoid reawakening that terrible tongue. We crossed the Lungara range by a narrow pass, whence we caught a glimpse of the Adriatic and the barely discernible Italian coast, and then zigzagged steeply down through a forest of oak and pine to Dukati. Before entering the village Mehmet was careful to remove the red star from his cap. The houses of Dukati straggled along the bank of a deep, dry ravine. In 1930 it had been shattered by an earthquake, but I was not aware of this at the time, and we did not notice any evidence of the disaster in the well-built houses. We were in no mind for close observation for the nature of our reception engrossed our thoughts. The place made little impression on me, and I confess I was surprised when I read how Edward Lear the landscape painter had painted Dukati in words in 1852: 'Shut out as it stood by iron walls of mountain, surrounded by sternest features of savage scenery, rock and chasm, precipice and torrent, a more fearful prospect and more chilling to the very blood I never beheld.'

As a British liaison officer I was politely received, though there were black looks when they heard with whom I was working. The English-speaking Balli leader, dressed in 'plus-fours', gave us lunch in the inn and was perfectly frank about his attitude. The village was in easy reach of the main coast road and neither he nor anyone else there had the slightest intention of doing anything to provoke the Germans. They were willing to help us clandestinely, but to be openly hostile to the Germans, like the L.N.C., was absurd. Their only ambition was to keep themselves alive and their homes unburnt until the war ended, when they naively hoped for the coming of what they called a British 'political' mission to settle their differences with the L.N.C. or 'Communists', as they preferred; and, of course, since the Germans were opposed to Communism, it was only natural if occasionally they gave them a hand against the L.N.C.

After lunch they found us a guide, for they were in close touch with the officer at Seaview, and an escort to see us safely over the coast road. We had then to face a strenuous climb over the 5000 ft. bare limestone ridge which still separated us from the sea. As we reached the crest the sun was sinking behind the far-off southern Apennines. As the leaden pallor of evening crept slowly across the face of the Adriatic, behind us, to the east, the snow-clad summit of Tomorres still glowed opalescent in the dying rays. Five thousand feet below, where the sea broke gently on a rock-bound coast, our guide vaguely indicated the direction of the caves and left us for a shepherd's camp. There was no path, so down over rough coral-like rock we sped in a race against darkness. We found the troglodyte mission, discussed our business, and left early next morning for Brataj.

A disinterested listener in the cave that night might have thought that representatives of the Balli and the L.N.C. in British uniform were telling each other a few home truths. Most liaison officers must have found that after living and fighting with people for some time that they become partisans in the real sense—blind followers of party or cause. The ideal liaison officer, I suppose, would not be subject to this fault; but ideal officers are rare, and no doubt for this reason the views of those in the field were heavily discounted by the dispassionate Olympians at Base. In this account I have tried hard to be objective, but, like Boswell's Mr Edwards who 'tried to be a philosopher but found cheerfulness always breaking in', I have found it difficult to exclude a preference for men who fought on the same side as ourselves.

On top of the ridge next morning we ran into rain and drizzle so thick that we got temporarily separated. Half-way down the other side when we had emerged from this we anxiously scanned the road for signs of movement. There was no traffic, but we were alarmed by sounds of battle apparently from the direction of Dukati. When some frightened villagers whom we met on the road told us that it had been attacked that morning by the 1st Brigade, we struck straight up the hillside in order to skirt it on the south. We came out on a ridge some 1500 ft. above the village and sat down for a bite of bread. Below were groups of armed Balli, and moving along the hills to the east we saw long files of partisans. A light mortar was in action against the village and machine-guns were stuttering. Although we had not exposed ourselves unduly the partisans had spotted us. A shell from a 40 mm. landed on the slopes below and the next round burst on the ridge to our left. We backed hastily away and continued up the reverse slope, where we were at once seen by the Balli who proceeded to spray us with a machine-gun. We were too tired for any more detours so we pushed on recklessly over bare grass slopes, hoping to get within speaking distance of the partisans before they shot us down at long range. Suddenly a shout rang out and we found ourselves covered by a machine-gun and several rifles 100 yards off. In spite of his parched throat and some excusable nervousness Mehmet waxed loud, eloquent and convincing. We were not known to them personally, but they sent us under escort to Mehmet Schio with whom we had a few recriminatory words for not having warned us more explicitly of his intentions. Presumably, as we were going through Dukati, he had thought it better to say nothing. Before we parted I strongly advised him to go himself to Seaview rather than to take his whole brigade there. At present there seemed little chance of this happening. The battle was not going well, and as we sat there in the rain and gathering dusk, eating freshly killed Dukati mutton, we heard the familiar quick burst of a German machine-gun. The garrison at Logara Pass had come to the aid of Dukati.

From Kuc we went down to the coast at Grava Bay. Towards evening, for it was advisable not to advertise our presence, we walked down a rocky valley and emerged on the narrow strip of fertile coastal plain. In a passing snow squall we walked through groves of olives and orange trees, laden with golden fruit, and came out upon the coast road and the sea. After scrambling down two or three hundred feet of rock we found a sandy beach, hidden from view except from the white houses of Borsh, a mile to the south. Although it was almost dark and looked like snowing again, I felt that a report on the beach would not be complete without a bathe. I found it steep-to, with a bottom of small shingle—an ideal place for landing craft.

It was not until May that we received anything at Grava Bay. For the partisans the sea base became synonymous with the Greek Kalends, or pie in the sky. When they grumbled about the little they received by air, I cheered them by glowing pictures of what a sea base would mean once it was working—tons of ammunition, thousands of boots, telephones, wireless sets, printing presses, or anything they fancied. But, in the opinion of the Navy, Grava Bay lay open to the prevailing south wind and accordingly was undeservedly damned. Stores continued to pile up at Seaview and little interest was shown in any other place. In January I did manage to arrange for a three-day stand-by period but, having gone there with a wireless set, the first signal we received was that no boat was available.

Travelling as we usually did without a wireless set and living mostly on maize bread and cheese, I was always in a desperate hurry to get back to Shepr. I was always anxious to know if any sorties had been received, how many we were likely to get the next month, and whether or no there were any signs of our policy of equal treatment for all belligerents, no matter which side they were on, undergoing a change. About this time Base were still asking us for concrete evidence of Balli collaboration with the enemy.

On our return one very unwelcome signal contained news of the wounding and capture of the head of the British mission to Albania, Brigadier Davies, who had only recently arrived with a large staff. After being on the run for several days he was wounded and taken prisoner and the staff dispersed. His senior staff officer, who then became head of the mission, escaped to Abas Kupi, the Zoggist, but he died subsequently of the effects of frostbite contracted while escaping. The loss of Brigadier Davies, an officer of sufficiently high rank to influence policy, who in the short time he was in the country had come to the same conclusions as myself, had a serious and lasting effect.

There was another signal which seemed to contain the seed of trouble—not so much because it introduced a feminine element, but because it threatened to disturb the placid regime of winter at Shepr.

A party of ten American nurses and twenty orderlies who had made a forced landing near Berat were reported on their way to Shepr for evacuation by sea. They had been flying from Sicily to Taranto in a Douglas and found themselves over Yugoslavia where they were shot at. Having run out of petrol over Albania, they had the good fortune to crash-land near Berat on the only flat space for a good many miles around. They reached Shepr in charge of a British officer, the nurses in good heart and looks, the orderlies—big, stalwart men—tired, bedraggled, and depressed. We started them off for Seaview but they failed to get past Dukati where fighting was still in progress.

The next idea was to have them picked up from the airfield at Gjinokastre, where at the moment there were no Germans. They took up a position of readiness in a village a few miles from the airfield, but no sooner had the detailed arrangements for the pick-up been made than some enemy troops arrived in Gjinokastre. However, the Germans might go, and since no aircraft were to be sent until asked for, they waited. I went over to visit them; and much to my surprise, for I knew the Germans were still there, as I was crossing the Lunxheries I saw eighteen Lightnings sweeping down the valley and a Wellington followed by two Douglas's coming in as though to land. When I reached the village I heard what happened. Apparently the officer in charge of the operation in Italy had got tired of keeping two squadrons standing by and had sent a signal that morning to say they were coming. The British officer took his long-suffering party down and lay up near the airfield, but since there were a couple of armoured cars on the main road just across the river, he rightly refused to give the signal for the planes to land, in spite of the hysterical pleading of his flock. A subsequent attempt to get away by sea was successful. Thus after two months or more of painful wandering, for the most part patiently borne, they landed in Italy and were made much of.

CHAPTER XII

THE TIDE TURNS

With the turn of the year the weather became more severe. All the passes and high mountain paths became snow bound so that avoiding action became difficult. Partisan activity was slight, for it was necessary to balance very carefully the value of any action against the consequences which might follow it. Bad as it was to have your village burnt in summer, in winter it was many times worse. On the other hand, the Germans, who were aware of the partisans' difficulties, increased their activities. Having broken up the Headquarter mission they turned their attention to the mission near Korca, where there were also several officers who had come out to join Brigadier Davies.

On 19 January all these arrived at Shepr, having been driven out with the loss of all their kit. Replacements for this were dropped almost the next night. It is pleasant to recall that missions in Albania were very well cared for by Base; almost too well, in fact, for one of the L.N.C. leaders, Tashko, at one time Albanian minister at New York, gave me a severe lecture on our shortcomings, of which one was the undue proportion of mission stores in aircraft loads. At the time I was pressing for ammunition, of which there was always a shortage, and boots for a new 6th Brigade about to be formed, so that the arrival of a plane with nothing but mission stores caused me some embarrassment.

The Permet pass was still open, and on the 24th I walked over it to attend the first parade of this new brigade. I found Radowicke, Badri, and the other leaders there all very preoccupied. German armoured cars had attacked Kelcyra, from which the partisans had momentarily driven the Balli, and troop concentrations were reported from Gjinokastre and Perat on the Greek border south of Permet. Perat, where there was an important and heavily guarded bridge, lies at the junction of the road to Korca and the road to Permet. The ceremony was cancelled and we returned to Shepr to find these ill-tidings confirmed. A mixed force of Germans and Balli had already crossed the frontier at Dhrimades, at the southern end of Zagori, where fighting was in progress; another had left Gjinokastre for Zagori; and the bridge at Lekei was guarded. All pointed to a concerted drive against the partisans and mission in Shepr, and the only escape route left open was that over the Permet bridge to the east, which was already threatened from north and south. The rain which fell steadily throughout the 26th augmented the gloom hanging over Shepr. The villagers, rightly anticipating the worst, busied themselves hiding their valuables, but still found time for casting reproachful looks at us the authors of their impending misery. That contingency for which for so long we had fed six mules having at last arisen, the mules were not available, having gone to Kelcyra to fetch grain. Most of our kit could therefore be written off, but we hid the wireless, batteries, charging engine, and some food, in a nearby nallah. The other officers, who had spent a happy day lavishly re-equipping themselves, now had to relinquish all and set off for Permet, while I rang up Badri on our local telephone to ask what we should do. He advised leaving with all speed as he could not guarantee holding on to Permet for another day. In spite of the weather I was tempted to lie up in the hills until the gathering storm had spent itself, but decided that the wiser course was to stick to the partisans and the other mission.

We left that night in a snowstorm to the sound of machine-gun fire from lower down the Zagori valley. Although we had started late we soon ran into the tail of the long column of fugitives struggling in the deep snowdrift at the top of the pass. Partisans, wounded men, refugees, mules, and donkeys, plodded dejectedly through the snow. The Permet side of the pass is much steeper. The snow on the track had been beaten into ice, so that our pace became a crawl. We fell in behind a stretcher party. It was questionable who most deserved sympathy, the partisan with a broken leg or the sweating bearers striving in inky darkness to keep their footing on that stony ice-bound path. Our torch helped them a little and, thanks to the drive and determination of the Albanian doctor looking after him, the wounded man was got down before dawn.

Except for a small party which remained for observation, Permet was abandoned that day by the partisans, who crossed the Vjose and took up positions in the scrub-covered hills to the east. There they were reinforced by two mountain guns from the 1st Brigade, manned entirely by Italians who had thrown in their lot with the partisans. The Germans mistimed their advance from Kelcyra and Perat so that the trap closed too late. It was not until the morning of 28 January that the smoke of burning villages on both sides of the river near Permet announced its capture. Taking us with them, the L.N.C. staff rather unnecessarily retreated as far as Frasheri. For although desultory fighting took place on the east bank, and a plane came over to bomb some villages, the Germans made no serious attempt to follow us. After three days at Frasheri monastery I was allowed to depart for Shepr, which I did, leaving the partisans to reorganise.

At Permet no one could tell us what had happened at Shepr, but it seemed extravagant to hope that it was unburnt. Since the village is not visible from the pass, our anxiety remained until we were almost there. Only five houses had been burnt and no one had been shot, but an army of Bashi Bazouks could not have plundered and ransacked the place more efficiently. Everything movable had gone, as had all the animals, which were used to carry away the swag. For this, the Balli who followed the Germans like jackals, led by a man called Ismael Golem, were mainly responsible. Other villages had not escaped so lightly. The small town of Sopik at the south end of Zagori had been completely gutted by fire, as had many villages at the north end, around Permet, and on the other side of Lunxheries. At a place called Hormove, thirty-five old men had been shot in reprisal for an ambush carried out some time before, in which a German patrol had been wiped out near the Lekei bridge.

All our mules and kit had gone, but the vital wireless equipment which we had hidden was intact. Many others have remarked how frequently it happens in war that at moments of crisis the signals one receives are entirely irrelevant or quite infuriating, or both. One expects to be maltreated by one's enemies, but now that the L.N.C. had received a knock-down blow, had had a number of their villages burnt, had seen the Balli everywhere revengefully triumphant, we received a rude kick on their behalf from our friends. On the reopening of communication the first signal to come in conveyed the considered opinion that the partisan brigades were expensive to maintain, militarily useless, and politically objectionable.

Thanks to the weather, supplies by air were so infrequent that the possibilities of using Grava Bay were again canvassed. An officer to assist me in running a sea base was landed at Seaview, but the disturbed state of the country prevented our meeting. He was unable to get past Dukati with his wireless equipment, and we were turned back by the presence of Germans in the Kuc area. This was one of our worst journeys. Bands of Balli were moving about freely, so that a village which was safe one day might be occupied by them the next. Golem was in a state of extreme misery. There were three feet of snow on the ground and the few remaining inhabitants were on the border of starvation. Some houses had been burnt and all had been looted. We could get no news of Kuc there, so we crossed a high snow pass to the even more miserable village of Progonat, where, either through fear or changing sympathies, we met with an indifferent reception. We were not thrown out but, on the other hand, no one would take us in. Cold and wet, we tried one house after another until at last we imposed ourselves almost by force on an elderly couple. Mehmet stuck his foot in the door to prevent them shutting it, while behind it man and wife almost came to blows with each other on the question of whether we should be admitted or not.

Unable to get any further towards Kuc, we re-crossed the pass next morning in one of the severest blizzards I have ever encountered. We were accompanied by some young, thinly clad partisans who, I thought, would never get over alive. The gusts on top were so fierce that it was only possible to move in lulls. Poor and desolate though Golem might be, we could always depend on a warm welcome there. They freely burnt their scanty firewood to thaw us out, and offered us their maize bread. But now that food was scarce in consequence of so much having been burnt, we seldom accepted it.

We had one more adventure before we got back. We were ascending a path from the Dhrino to one of the Lunxheries villages in dense mist. We had heard vague rumours of Balli activity in the Lunxheries, so that when we were loudly challenged by a figure with a rifle, vaguely visible through the mist about thirty yards away, we were considerably startled. Both our Marlin automatics were slung and any attempt to use them would have invited a shot. It was a ticklish problem for Mehmet to solve. If they were Balli and he confessed who we were we should get shot, while if they were partisans and he did not say who we were we should likewise be shot. A tense staccato dialogue, which I could not follow, ensued; with Mehmet apparently sparring for time and a clue as to who they might be. The tension gradually relaxed. We walked forward, rather dry-mouthed, to be welcomed by the partisan patrol leader.

A heavy new fall of snow took place in March. Three feet of snow covered the dropping ground, where on several occasions we were nearly caught out by having the wood for the signal fires buried or by it being too sodden to burn when needed. If a sortie was expected we would tramp out there at dusk with sheepskin coats and a supply of tea and 'raki'. As the partisans were mostly poorly clad, we left them behind with instructions to come out if the plane came. As soon as this was heard the fires were blown into a blaze, signals exchanged, and then, if the plane was for us, the pilot started his run. Along with the loads on parachutes there were usually a number of free bundles of great-coats, battle-dress, blankets. The partisans (and we too for that matter) were a bit nervous about these, for they came down unheralded with a most vicious thud. Occasionally a parachute would fail to open and a big iron container weighing a couple of hundred pounds would half bury itself in the ground. One night a container full of mines, which were 'unarmed', but with the detonators for 'arming' them included in a separate box, landed harmlessly a few yards from where we were standing gazing expectantly upwards. When all the loads had been dropped as many as possible were brought in, and then we bedded down in the snow on a parachute and slept till dawn.

At the end of March a more serious attempt to use Grava Bay was made. There were several bodies from other missions waiting to be evacuated, but we also hoped to receive stores. Our large party from Shepr reached Sterre, a village near Borsh, on the 23rd, where we met my officer from Seaview who had at last got through himself, but still had not been able to bring his wireless set. However, a stand-by period from the 24th to 31st had been arranged beforehand. The citadel of Borsh was found to be occupied by Balli, so we moved round to the next valley to the north, where we took up residence in one room of a house in the little village of Khudesi. Fifty local partisans were detailed as escort and beach party.

For seven successive nights we fell in at dusk and walked for two hours down to the seashore where we sat until one the following morning. The partisans picketed the surrounding area, while we took it in turns to sit upon a look-out rock, thirty feet above the water, solemnly flashing a signal with a hand torch at frequent intervals. The weather was cold, but for most of the time conditions were very favourable with good visibility and an almost flat calm. For the first few nights we rather enjoyed sitting there, the Adriatic murmuring gently at our feet, while we watched a thin crescent moon disappearing behind the black hills above and strained our ears for the sound of an approaching boat. We were in a happy state of expectancy—I felt like a smuggler waiting for a cargo.

But happy expectancy cannot be sustained indefinitely and patience is a virtue easily fatigued by exercise. On the march back in the small hours of the morning, with hopes unfulfilled, such happiness quickly evaporated. We had purposely chosen a period of little moon, lights were not permissible on the march, and the boulders which littered the track had the peculiar quality of merging invisibly into the background. As we stumbled sleepily up the hill to Khudesi, which we usually reached as dawn was breaking, only the thought of the jorum of tea we should presently brew sustained our flagging energy. After that was drunk we slept till midday, had a meal, and slept again until it was time to get ready for the next performance.

On the fourth night an incipient carbuncle on my foot became so painful that I had to ride down on a mule. The partisans became more and more discouraged, and increasingly nervous of the possibility that one fine night we should be surprised. It certainly seemed not unlikely that our strange antics had been observed or reported, so no one was sorry when the curtain was rung down on the seventh and last performance. It was none too soon. We left Khudesi on the very appropriate morning of April Fool's Day, pursued by a German patrol from Himara, where curiosity about our doings had at last been aroused. We heard later that a boat came over on the night of 1 April, having been delayed until then by bad weather off the Italian coast. We had at least learnt that it was essential to have wireless with us, and that unless the partisans could occupy Borsh and securely hold a strip of the neighbouring coast, a sea base would have a short and precarious life.

In April, as the snow melted, activity on both sides increased. The Germans and Balli in occupation of Gjinokastre did their utmost by threats and starvation to bring the populace to their way of thinking. Ismael Golem alternately harangued and cut off supplies. 'Renounce the L.N.C.,' he proclaimed, 'urge your sons, brothers, husbands, to come back from the mountains, and all will be well.' Since no grain was being sent now from Kelcyra, we blew the road between it and Tepeleni. We also started laying mines on the road south from Gjinokastre by which the German garrison brought supplies from their base at Jannina. I attended the first mine-laying exploit in the capacity of safety officer and umpire. It was chiefly remarkable for the smallness of the bag and as a demonstration of how unlucky a man must be to get a hit at night. About three in the morning a large ten-ton lorry came along and was duly wrecked, whereupon our machine-gun party, carefully posted in a ruin fifty yards away, opened up. The gun, which was Italian, was on its best behaviour that night. For nearly five minutes by the clock the night was rendered hideous, and then, in a silence that could be felt, three trembling figures emerged unscratched from underneath the lorry—a German N.C.O. and two Balli. The lorry was empty.

In addition to our harassing by night, the R.A.F. were now making the roads unsafe by day. We also projected an attack on Gjinokastre with air support; for the suffering of the people was having an adverse effect on the partisans, many of whose families were there. We calculated that, if attacked, the Balli would withdraw inside the Citadel, a move which could only be prevented by some well-timed bombing. A plan was made and approved, but after repeated postponements we were advised that no bombers were available. The partisans concentrated for the attack were drawn off by a German drive in the Konispol area. By a stroke of luck a Spitfire sweep, happening to coincide with this drive, wrought great havoc amongst the transport—a success which offset our failure to secure the bombers, for the partisans wrongly attributed it to our foresight. Perhaps, like the fly on the wheel, the partisans thought they were responsible for the greater part of the dust raised by the Allied forces in the war effort, but when they heard daily of the thousands of sorties flown in Italy, and saw twenty planes immediately set aside for the evacuation of the American nurses, they felt neglected.

By May most of the snow had gone. Unrestricted freedom of movement, the s*ine qua non* of guerilla warfare, was once more restored. The 5th Brigade, commanded by Shefket Peze, an old friend of mine of Cepo days, having occupied Borsh, seized a strip of the coast from Panormo Point for several miles south, and blew up the road at many points. My assistant, Lieut. Newell, was dispatched to Grava Bay with a wireless set, and the L.N.C. staff was asked to assemble a thousand mules in the neighbourhood. In view of the destitute state of the country this seemed a tall order but, acting with great energy, they succeeded admirably.

Before the landing of stores on a large scale took place, a small craft came over bringing with it my relief. Although I had been ten months in the country I was by no means tired of it, but I was tired of the anomalous position in which liaison officers were placed. The Balli, having been given so much rope, were now out of favour both with ourselves and the Germans, but their place had been taken by Abas Kupi, the Zoggist leader, on whom patience and money, and the services of the senior B.L.O., were now being spent to goad him and his few thousand followers into activity on our side. He might, of course, have re-joined the L.N.C., but that would have suited nobody but them.

On 18 May, having handed over to my successor at Shepr, I said farewell to Radowicke and other leaders. On the 20th I joined Newell and the others who were waiting to be evacuated in a farmhouse not far from the shore. At midnight on the 22nd a great army of men and mules assembled on the beach. In quick response to our signals a light flashed once far out to sea. We waited tensely expectant, until suddenly the open maw of a tank-landing craft loomed out of the dark heading straight for us. As her keel gently took the shingle she looked like some great sea monster coming ashore. Some minutes elapsed before the partisans recovered sufficiently from their astonishment to go on board. Then things moved quickly. An endless stream of excited men leapt up one side of the ramp, rushed to the stern where the loads were stacked, seized one and doubled back down the other side. In thirty minutes thirty tons of stores, neatly packed in forty-pound loads, were ashore, and by dawn the beach was clear. As the last load came off, we bodies embarked. The escorting Italian destroyer which lay off shore was picked up, and together we chugged slowly over the calm water while the hills of Albania faded away between sea and sky.

For my part I returned convinced that our policy of giving moral, financial, and material support to the L.N.C. was just and expedient. Unhappily the goodwill thus earned and deserved was offset by the dislike we incurred for supporting the other two parties. At first all were treated equally, but even after two of the three parties had shown themselves to be useless and untrustworthy, we continued to sustain them morally by sending them missions, by refusing to denounce them by name, and by making only obscure references to the deeds and sacrifices of the L.N.C. The result of this ambiguous policy was that the honesty of our intentions was doubted and that not one of the parties trusted us. In view of our alliance with Russia a plain man could not conceive that it was the taint of Communism which precluded our giving undivided support to the L.N.C. By helping the one party we might offend a large number of Albanians and put them in a difficult position after the war, but having once encouraged the resistance movement we were obliged to befriend those who resisted and no one else. Whether it was over-sensibility or ignorance which moulded our policy I cannot tell. Nevertheless, I was startled by two incidents which came to my notice the day we reached Bari, which seemed to show that if the facts were known they were not understood. At the time I left Albania the L.N.C. were holding an important conference at Permet to state their war aims and to elect a provisional government.* The Albanian broadcast put out by us at the time naturally referred to this, but saw fit to deplore the fact that no representatives from the other two parties had been invited to attend. And on 23 May there appeared in the papers a report of an answer to a question in the House about Albania in which the Deputy Prime Minister stated that 'all parties in Albania were fighting the Germans and that we were endeavouring to bring them together', the first part of which was very wide of the truth.

---

*   This government was accorded recognition by the British Government in November 1945.

The L.N.C. had their faults. For one thing they hoped to form the government of the country after the war. Their declared aim was for a free, democratic, independent Albania, and they were convinced that they alone could realise these aims. This familiar formula has been used elsewhere without too much regard for its meaning, and it remains to be seen how the L.N.C. interpret it. Yet the fact remains that the partisans of the L.N.C. fought, suffered and died for these professed aims and by so doing helped us. The resolution they showed through many months of hardship, danger and disappointment, the will to win, their faith in themselves and in their cause, all seemed to me to establish their claim to leadership and to manifest that in them lay the best hope for Albania's future.

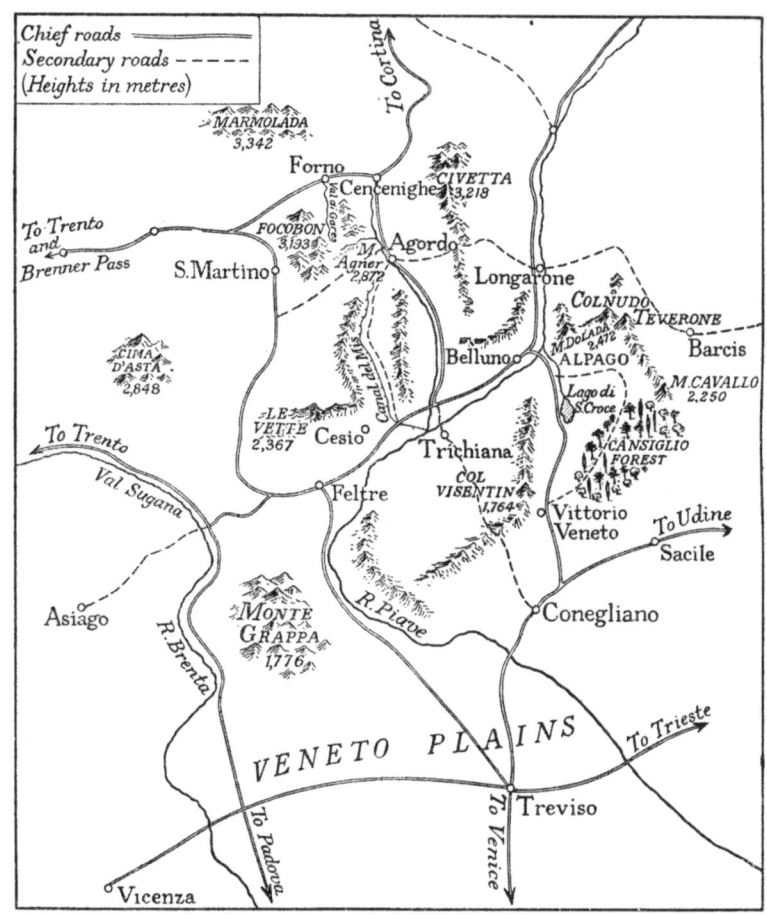

Map 5: Sketch map of northern Italy to illustrate Belluno area; railways and many secondary roads are not shown

CHAPTER XIII

ARRIVAL IN NORTH ITALY

It was my good fortune to spend the winter of 1944–5 in the mountains of north-east Italy, ostensibly with a view to the better prosecution of the partisan war, but in reality with the hope of seeing mountains more satisfying than those of southern Albania. After two abortive attempts we were dropped by parachute ('infiltrated' in official jargon) at the end of August.

Much had to be endured before this happy release took place. To some of us, that summer spent hanging about in southern Italy waiting to be used, seemed very like the previous August when we had suffered a lot of unnecessary anxiety as to whether there would be anything for us to do in Albania when we got there. Now that the Gothic Line had been broken and the Allied armies were at the threshold of the Po Valley, it really seemed hardly worth our while going in for the few remaining weeks, or even days, during which the enemy might yet retain his foothold in Italy. In my own case this impatience could partly be attributed to the call of the mountains; and in Ross, my second, perhaps to the spirit of vandalism innate in many of us, especially in the young—the desire to blow something to bits; for he had not been with partisans before and was probably suffering from a sense of frustration. The other two members of the party, who were Italians, were no doubt anxious to strike a blow for their country.

However, in the last week of August, the operation known as 'Beri-wind' (humorists immediately rechristened us 'Belly-wind') in which we were concerned was definitely 'on'. Besides myself there were three others. Ross, a young gunner captain who, when the war began, was studying medicine at Cambridge; Marini, who might be described as an elderly naval man except that, unlike Gilbert's elderly naval man, he was far from weedy and long but, on the contrary, short and very rotund; having been a wireless operator in Italian submarines for twelve years he was so accustomed to a sedentary life that I had some qualms as to his fitness for the work in hand; and lastly Gatti, the interpreter, who was an ex-officer of Alpini from Trento, with a short but varied career. During the early years of the war he had been, for an Alpini, in the seemingly anomalous position of subaltern in the Italian Camel Corps, somewhere on the southwest border of Tripoli. Having come back to Italy, he was caught by the Germans at the time of the Italian surrender and put in a train bound for Gorizia but, since he was a man of resource, he jumped off and made his way to Rome, where he joined the Allied Army, serving for a time as interpreter with the Long Range Desert Group. He was not long and weedy but emphatically lean, with features so clean-cut as almost to resemble the 'hatchet-faced' men of American detective stories. He spoke excellent English and presumably impeccable Italian.

On a southern Italian airfield at dusk of 26 August our small party, strapped up in Sidcot suits and parachutes, might have been seen moving stiffly towards its appointed plane, a Douglas. We had already concluded a brief and tepid colloquy with the pilot, discussing such matters as our favourite dropping height, whether we preferred going before or after our kit, and signals. As the principal actors in the midnight drama soon to be enacted, we felt the pilot was not as interested in us as he might have been. No doubt he had his own worries, or perhaps he was more accustomed to dropping bombs, which need no consulting, than bodies. We groped our way to the forward end of the plane and subsided uncomfortably on to the piled-up loads. The plane roared down the runway, the lights were turned out, and we settled down in the dark to three hours' gloomy anticipation, chewing hard. At midnight the pilot reported that he was over the target but could see no signals. The moon was three-quarters full and, as we looked down from the door, roads and houses stood out plainly; altogether too many of them, we thought, to be anything like our more secluded target area. As the pilot turned the plane for home, relief at not having to jump was tempered with the thought that it would all have to be done over again.

On the 28th a different plane made the attempt. This time we felt more at home and watched with interest the lights of Trieste appear on the starboard side and those of Venice to port. As I stood idly by the door, peering into the void, I was startled to see several orange-coloured lights wink angrily at us from apparently just outside the door. Then a search-light shot up from below and I realised that the winking lights were bursting flak. Sorrows shared are sorrows halved, so I immediately communicated the intelligence to the others. Marini fortunately failed to understand. He only heard about it when we got back, and suffered such retrospective pangs that he almost refused to try again. Shortly after this the pilot sent word back that we were approaching the target area. Taking advantage of my seniority I had already decided that I should jump first, for I never derived any encouragement from waiting to watch others go before me.

We stumbled back to the door, hitched the 'static lines' of our parachutes to the 'strong bar', put in the safety pin and tested it, turned round and tested it several more times, and finally begged for the assurance of the next man that we were really secured. The four Yugo-Slavs who were responsible for throwing the loads out after we had gone were quite incapable of dispatching bodies. We had to do that ourselves. As I stood in the door, holding hard to either side and glaring fixedly at the red warning light, waiting for it to change to green, time passed unnoticed. I began to wonder if I had gone suddenly colour-blind, incapable of distinguishing green from red, while Ross, in a moment of aberration, suggested I should jump and hope for the best. Fortunately there is a limit to the time for which one can remain in a state of high tension. The spring began to unwind. We began to exchange disparaging remarks about the pilot, who at last sent to tell us that he could not find the target and was going home. Never was word more gratefully received. We had been standing at the door for an hour.

Our third attempt took place on the last day of August. This time there were nine bodies in the plane, another mission having had orders to go. Again I took first place, the leader of the other mission offering to dispatch me. A good dispatcher is most useful. A determined roar of 'Action Stations' pulls everyone together, and a still louder and more determined roar of 'No. 1 Go' compels the first victim, however reluctant, to leap into the void in a more or less correct position. So it was on this occasion. Word came that we were 'running up', but there was no need for me to concentrate so intensely on the warning light. Red turned to green and simultaneously, with a stentorian 'Go' still ringing in my ears, out I went.

There is a verse in that pathetic lament 'Nothing' which, to my mind, aptly expresses the act of stepping out of a plane in mid air:

> Nothing to breathe but air,
> Quick as a flash, 'tis gone.
> Nowhere to fall but off,
> Nowhere to stand but on.

After the first wild and whirling moment, when you sense the grateful tug of the harness, the first emotion is one of satisfaction, not unmingled with surprise, that the thing has actually worked once more. Then you feel you would like to shout with exultation and pride in being such a clever fellow as to float there so delightfully in the moonlight; you wish you could float there for ever. But this pride and exultation does not last. A glance at the smoke of the signal fires below seems to indicate a strong ground wind. You try to remember which way you ought to face, and reach up for the rigging lines to make a turn. The ground seems to be rushing towards you. You realise there is no time to do a turn. Remember at the last minute to keep your feet and knees together, and then—. If all goes well you land like a piece of clumsy thistledown, roll gently on one side, and recapture that feeling of exultation you had when you first became air-borne. But all parachute descents do not end so happily. You may acquire an uncontrollable pendulum motion, or other factors quite beyond control, such as the speed of the wind or the nature of the landing ground, may lead to minor accidents.

So it was on this occasion. I was swinging pendulum-wise and on landing went over like a ninepin, striking a rock with the base of my spine with no ordinary violence—a blow which even the packet of two million paper lire stowed away in the seat of my Sidcot suit failed to mitigate. Ross landed in a tree from which he had to be cut down, Gatti was all right, and Marini sprained his ankle. All of us landed wide of the target. Worse was to follow. Mist and cloud swept over the fires, and though we could still hear the plane circling we could not see it, and no doubt the pilot would be unable to see the target. Accompanied by the reception committee, and feeling some concern about the absence of the other five and more concern about the loss of our kit, we made our way to a nearby hut, where we had hot milk. A few minutes later the missing five walked in to report that the pilot had only had time to drop them before the target was obscured. The plane had now gone home, taking all our stores with it. This was upsetting, but we imagined that another plane would be sent in the course of the next few nights. As luck would have it, four months were to elapse before the next successful 'drop'.

The place where we had landed was the Alto-piano d'Asiago, a broad heavily wooded plateau between the Brenta and upper Adige valleys, overlooking the plains north of Vicenza. Ever since the Italian surrender in September 1943 the bolder spirits of northern Italy, eager to atone for the long years of willing slavery under Fascist rule, and burning to show once and for all where their sympathies lay, had been organising themselves into resistance groups—clandestinely in the cities, towns, and villages of the plains, and more openly in the mountain regions. From east of Udine, where they were in touch with Tito's Slavs of Gorizia, round to the French border in the west, there were ill-armed, inexperienced, but eager and determined bands of men. In the late summer of 1944 hopes ran high. Large stretches of country in the more mountainous areas were completely controlled by partisans, the Allies seemed likely to break into the plains beyond the Po at any moment, and as yet neither Germans nor Fascists had had either the time or the men to devote much attention to the increasing attacks on their communications.

For our part we had already dropped a large number of Italian agents, recruited from our side of the lines, to send back information about the strength of the various groups and to organise the reception of supplies. British liaison officers were now being sent in to act, as their name implies, as a direct link between the partisan leaders and the Allied army, to encourage and train bands in the use of arms, explosives and incendiary devices, to arrange for their supply, and generally to hearten the whole resistance movement and discourage political differences. Organisation and command were the responsibilities of the partisans themselves.

There were already two widely separated British missions in northeast Italy when we arrived to bridge the gap between them, one of them being that of Major Wilkinson who received us. He was unfortunately killed in an ambush in the following March. My mission was allotted to a formation called the Nino Nannetti Division, then operating in a large area stretching from Monte Grappa to Vittorio Veneto in the south, and from Monte Marmolada across to Cortina in the north, that is to say, a large slice of the Dolomites, the foothills to the south of them, and the upper Piave valley.

In view of the shortly expected break-through on the Italian front and the retreat of the Germans it was essential, we thought, for us to make contact with the Nannetti Division as soon as possible. For in these operations the partisans would be required to play an important part by blowing up bridges and roads and generally harassing the retreating enemy. Unfortunately our wireless set had gone back with the plane and, until one was dropped, which we hoped would be in the course of the next night or two, we could be of little use to either the partisans or the Army. Marini, the operator, was unable to walk and I was unable to stand—for an 'actual necessity', as the French put it, I had to crawl away into the forest on hands and knees. We therefore sent Ross and Gatti off on 2 September to find Divisional H.Q., trusting that by the time a set arrived we should be able to follow.

Major Wilkinson and a band of some 200 partisans were living in rough shelters made from parachutes in the middle of a pine forest. The smell of the pines and the air, for we were about 5000 ft. up, set my blood tingling. On 2 September I walked fifty yards, the day after that 300 yards, and on the 4th I managed to reach a hillock half a mile away, from where I could look down to the chequer-board fields and poplars of the Veneto and see to the east the massive rounded hump of Monte Grappa. As our missing stores had not yet arrived, Wilkinson, knowing I was impatient to be off, lent me a spare wireless set and battery, and another Italian operator in place of the injured Marini. This was the last I saw of the elderly naval man. I heard later that some time during the winter he had crawled out of his 'bunker' or foxhole straight into the arms of some waiting Germans. He was said to have proved a first-class operator but quite unable to walk. As I had expected, his twelve years' submarine service had deprived him of the use of his legs. The operator who came in his place deserves a few words of introduction. He rejoiced in the name of Pallino. He was very young, and his service in the Italian Air Force had not only failed to quell his natural exuberance, but had instilled in him a violent dislike of control of any sort.

He was a gifted operator. With the most amateurish aerial, which the experts would view with derision, he would in a few moments make contact with Base several hundred miles away, and pass and receive messages singularly free from corruptions. But his other virtues he hid under a bushel. He was idle, insubordinate, temperamental, mindful of his own comfort, and extremely touchy if any of his shortcomings were pointed out to him. He was like a desert sore, always there, always irritating, and quite incurable. Many times we sighed for Marini. Many times we were on the point of having Pallino shot. But good operators were irreplaceable, and when he was working, pounding out messages with frozen fingers by the light of a guttering candle, we forgave him all; indeed we almost loved him. But when he had finished his schedule and started crooning, probably the 'Internationale', for he was an ardent Communist, murder would again raise its snaky head.

On the night of 5 September Pallino and I set off to join Ross and Gatti. The speed of our journey was a striking tribute to the good organisation of the partisans and to the control which they exercised over the country at that time. Accompanied by a small escort armed with Stens and Berettas (the Italian sub-machine-gun) our truck shot through Asiago in the middle of the night, and early in the morning we were delivered safely to an outlying company of the brigade. The next night they took us to a village overlooking the Brenta valley. Here we met another escort who was responsible for getting us safely over the main road and railway down in the valley, the only place where there was any chance of meeting a German patrol. The clatter we made descending a steep, loose, stony path roused all the dogs in the neighbourhood, but in the valley all was as quiet as the grave. Having crossed the river in a boat we began the long grind up the slopes of Monte Grappa, a journey which engaged all our energies for the rest of the night. Monte Grappa was the scene of fierce fighting in 1917 and 1918. Parts of the summit are as much pitted with shell holes as the most hotly contested ground on the old Western Front.

In an 'albergo' near the summit we found the mission who had dropped with us already installed and holding a conference of partisan leaders. Monte Grappa was in the Nannetti Divisional area, but was occupied by a motley collection of partisans from various formations and of various political hues. The inevitable lack of cohesion probably had a good deal to do with the debacle which took place a fortnight later when the Germans attacked in strength and completely broke them up. Commanding as it did the Brenta and Piave valley routes, Monte Grappa was of great tactical importance, and the Germans saw to it that no partisans remained there.

After another all-night march we joined Ross and Gatti, who were temporarily held up in the village of Cesio in the Piave valley. They were occupying the best villa in the company of one of our Italian agents, a man of infinite resource and sagacity who had fought in the Spanish war. He disdained secrecy, and trusted to forged documents and a good 'cover' story which seemed to enable him to go where he wanted and get what he wanted. Although the owner of the villa, who had the misfortune to be wealthy, was suspected of having Fascist tendencies, the villa was later burnt by the Fascists, presumably because it had harboured the agent and ourselves. To be neutral in civil war is to be damned. One side helps itself at your expense, and the other side either shoots you or burns your house for having helped its opponents.

Several times in the months to come we were to live in the vicinity of Cesio or to pass through it furtively at night, for the personality and energy of one man had made it a focal point of partisan activity. This excellent man, Orestes by name, was always a present help in time of trouble. He was an old soldier of the previous war, a man of decided opinions, in politics a democrat, a loud and indefatigable talker, and withal he was extremely deaf. He ran a small squad of half a dozen local men, whom he called his 'boys', who did odd sabotage jobs. He also helped the regular partisan formations living in the hills by organising their supplies. This type of partisan, who lived peacefully in his village by day and became an active partisan at night or as occasion warranted, belonged to the organisation known as G.A.P. (Gruppo Azione Patriotico). Almost every town and village of northern Italy had its own small G.A.P. squad, and very bold and keen partisans many of them were. Orestes was a builder by trade, and one of the best types of Italian artisans. He had a wife and several children, who were later turned out in the street by the Fascists and their house burnt. Around Cesio, Orestes was something of an oracle. Men hung on his words. With a hideous white-peaked cap on his head, and a thick stubble on his chin, he loved to talk of General Alexander and of what orders he, the General, had sent to Orestes. Every telling point, and there were many, was delivered with a characteristic gesture of smiting the hollow of the right arm with the left hand, and with the exclamation of 'Ostia!'

A cloak of fictitious secrecy hung round us while we were in Cesio, for I think everyone knew what we were. When darkness fell we were taken round to the 'Albergo' to drink with the local patriots, and the priest, who was also a staunch patriot, entertained us to a bottle of wine. With the priest's permission we had already climbed the church tower to obtain a view of the Piave and the villages on the south side through which our route lay. Like most of those in the villages of the Piave, the church had a very lofty tower in which the bells had been hung by no less a man than Orestes himself. Many of these towers are built separate from the parent church. The valley hereabouts is wide, hot, fertile and beautiful; full of vines, apples, pears, peaches, mulberries, walnuts, maize and wheat. One of the severest penalties of our furtive existence was that we seldom saw the charming pastoral scenes of that lovely country by day. Sometimes, like a belated fox making for its earth, we might be surprised by dawn while still on the move, wandering through country lanes under shady chestnuts, through orchards and field paths, by trellised vines, plucking the red grapes still wet with dew.

By 8 September Orestes' arrangements for taking us across the Piave were complete. Flying patrols, supplied by girls on bicycles, were put out along the road as far as the main Feltre-Belluno highway. Towards dusk we piled into a sort of butcher's van. Three of us were concealed in the back, while I with my uniform hidden by an old raincoat sat in front with Orestes. We crossed the highway without incident, and found our escort waiting for us on the bank of the river. Even at that time of year there was a lot of water, but, as it flows in several channels in a wide stony bed, it was just fordable. As we were not allowed to wade we crossed on the shoulders of the escort. By midnight we had reached Trichiana, where we were received in a large country house by an English-speaking Italian lady, known to us subsequently as 'Giuliana', or sometimes as the 'Countess'. She and her two brothers were active patriots, and were always very kind to us.

Here we got bad news. Nannetti H.Q. were then in Cansiglio Forest on the east side of the Vittorio Veneto-Bulluno highway. In this ideal partisan country there were said to be some 3000 men. They were, of course, indifferently armed, had few machine-guns, and little experience. There were in addition three brigades, of perhaps 500 men each, in the country to the west of the highway and to south of the Piave. Couriers from these were now coming in to report the beginning of a big 'rastrallamento' (literally 'combing') against the partisans in Cansiglio. They had had no communication from Divisional H.Q., which had been dispersed, and they were unable to get us across the road even supposing we still wished to go. Conflicting reports continued to come in all day, but the upshot was that we finally decided to join the Gramsci Brigade, then located in the mountains to the north-west of Cesio, and there await news of Divisional H.Q. The local leaders assured us that this was where H.Q. would 'rendezvous' if they had been dispersed. Accordingly we recrossed the Piave that night, passed once more through the sleeping village of Cesio, this time in real secrecy, and next afternoon joined the Gramsci Brigade on Le Vette. Our experiences on Le Vette and the dispersal and flight of the Gramsci Brigade, in which we were willing participants, deserve a chapter to themselves.

CHAPTER XIV

WITH THE GRAMSCI BRIGADE

LE VETTE IS A HIGH GRASSY PLATEAU (*c.* 7000 ft.). To the north it presents a long cliff face of rotten rock, which can only be climbed by one difficult path, while on the other sides there are only four possible lines of approach. The top is a large saucerlike depression divided into two parts by a high grass ridge running between the northern and southern rims. Except for a few boulders it is bare of trees, scrub or of anything that might give cover. At first sight its scant and easily defended approaches would seem to make it an ideal partisan stronghold. They merely give to it a pleasing but entirely false sense of security. The approaches are of necessity the exits, and if these are closed all freedom of manœuvre, the *sine qua non* of partisan warfare, is at an end.

As we plodded slowly up the last steep zigzags of the mule track we were suddenly challenged by an obvious Englishman dressed in the shabby nondescript clothes of a partisan. He proved to be an escaped prisoner-of-war and this was the block-post guarding the main approach to Le Vette. Inside a tin-roofed shed were ten other Englishmen, all escaped prisoners-of-war, who had thrown in their lot with the Gramsci Brigade. They formed a small detachment of their own known by the honourable title of the 'Churchill Company'. Of the many British prisoners who had escaped at the time of the Italian Armistice, some had been recaptured, many were living with Italian families, a few had escaped through Yugo-Slavia, and a few had joined the partisans.

Naturally they were surprised and pleased to see us, and questioned us closely, particularly as to the probable duration of the war, for they were undecided whether they should or whether they should not try to get through to our lines. Our advice was to stay. We argued that even if the expected break-through did not succeed and a German withdrawal did not take place, the battle was almost certain to become more fluid, and escaping through the lines then would be a simpler matter than now.

The block-post was connected by telephone line to Brigade H.Q., about ten minutes' walk away. Our arrival was reported and permission obtained for us to pass through. Suspicious or highly improbable arrivals, such as we were, were always detained at the post until their *bona fides* had been established. Spies and informers abounded, and if discovered met with no mercy. It was astonishing how many there were. They were even found in the ranks of the partisans and no one not personally known could be trusted. The systematic elimination of spies and informers in towns and villages went on all the time, and information was forcibly extracted from them before they were shot.

There were about 300 partisans on Le Vette. A very numerous H.Q. staff was living in a long, stone, tin-roofed cowshed (a 'malga' as it is called) at Pietena. A battalion called Zancanaro lived in another 'malga' in the other half of the basin beyond the ridge; and the Battisti Battalion lay two or three miles to the east guarding the approach on that side. The Nannetti Division itself, its brigades and battalions, were all named after either heroes of the Risorgimento, such as Mazzini, Bixio, Pisacane, Cairoli; or patriots, mostly Communists, who had bitterly opposed Fascism in the twenties, or who had fought and died in the Spanish Civil War on the losing side. Nino Nannetti and Gramsci, for example, were two such patriots. Later on battalions, or even brigades, were named after well-known partisans who had been killed in action or who had been executed in the present struggle.

The Nannetti Division was what was known as a Garibaldi formation. These Garibaldi units were raised and organised in the first place by the Communists who, in Italy, as in Yugoslavia, Albania, and perhaps Greece, were the backbone of the resistance movement. There was, in my opinion, no doubt that the Garibaldi formations were the most effective. They were better organised, better led, and attracted a more ardent and more determined type of recruit than the so-called independent brigades or the brigades sponsored by other political parties. The practice of forming brigades on a political basis was, of course, deplorable. But until someone could be found strong enough to lead and control the whole resistance movement, and until the Communist Party relinquished control of the Garibaldi formations, such a basis was presumably unavoidable. Later all formations, irrespective of political colour, were embodied in the Corpo Volontario Delia Liberta, or C.V.L., under the control of the military branch of the Central Milan Committee of the C.L.N.., or Comitato di Liberazione Nazionale.

Most of the Garibaldi leaders were Communists; some of long standing and of conviction, others more recent converts whose interests were politic rather than political, who had embraced the faith for the sake of peace and quietness and to avoid the barrage of political harangues to which they would otherwise be subject. The rank and file, or garibaldini as they were called, were more mixed. Among them would be found the fanatic, the enthusiast, the lukewarm, the indifferent, and the politically independent, who had become 'garibaldini' merely because they were the most numerous and the best organised. At this time the whole of our area with one small exception was 'Garibaldi'. Later two independent brigades were formed, but they were not of much importance.

The 'garibaldini' liked to wear red scarves, as much presumably on account of the red-shirts of Garibaldi's Thousand as of any Communist association—and when possible a grey long-peaked cap, like a French kepi but softer, with a red star in front. Below that anything was permissible, nay welcome; scraps of German, Italian and British uniforms: the uniforms of Italian policemen, firemen, sailors, customs officials, forest guards, or carabinieri; and, of course, every conceivable kind of civilian rig. Many were ex-Alpini and wore the dashing Alpini hat of their regiments. Alpini beards were always fashionable, until they became too dangerous, as a man with a beard was *ipso facto* a partisan or brigand according to one's point of view. I never saw the clenched fist salute given by the partisans of the mountains, though I believe it was common enough in the plains. A normal salute was used and the invariable greeting on meeting, or on entering a room or leaving, was 'Morte ai Fascisti' (or Fascismo) with the reply 'Liberta ai Popoli'.

Every H.Q. down to that of a battalion had its Political Commissar who was particularly responsible for relations between partisans and the civil population, for the maintenance of morale, and for political instruction. He worked in the closest contact with the Commandant and all orders were invariably signed by both. In the Gramsci Brigade the 'ora politica' was strictly observed. This was a daily set period when the Commander or Commissar addressed the men on questions of discipline, organisation, interior economy, or politics, and when any man could get up and raise any question, not excluding the behaviour of his leaders. Later it fell in abeyance either because of the reduction in numbers or because of the weakening of political interest in the face of the increasingly critical situation of winter. A few Russians, escaped prisoners-of-war, who were on Le Vette with the brigade (one was a Company Commander), took particular care that there were no absentees during the 'ora politica'. They seemed efficient soldiers, these Russians, who took life seriously. There was nothing funny about them except their names—Borlikoff, Orloff, Shuvoff, etc.

Discipline was fairly good but nothing like so rigid as that maintained in similar formations in Albania, where minor thefts, drunkenness, or immorality, were alike punished with death. Discipline in a spontaneously formed, free body of men is a delicate and difficult problem. If the men are highly imbued with a sense of dedication to a sacred cause, then extremely severe rules may be made without much fear of having them broken and without the correspondingly severe penalty having to be enforced; but in the case of a more mixed and less highly principled body, the eyes of those in authority must be frequently shut to all but serious military offences. Much then depends on the strength of personality of the commander. Things were certainly more lax in Italy. Even control of stores received on a dropping ground, an elementary and fundamental matter, was not always satisfactory. I knew of only two instances of partisans being shot, one for drunkenness when out on patrol, and one for repeatedly taking food from civilians by force for his own use. For disobedience or neglect of duty a man might be tied to a tree for a few hours, or in more serious cases dismissed.

Bruno, the Commander of the brigade, was a man of strong personality, respected and liked by his men. He was an ex-officer of artillery but, having served only with anti-aircraft units, he had no experience of infantry tactics or of fighting. His brigade was well organised and well disciplined, and the arms, such as they were, well cared for. They were extremely keen to fight—'Give us arms and ammunition' was the daily burthen of their song. This theme became more insistent as one blank night followed another, and as indications of an impending 'rastrallamento' became stronger. But in spite of our fervid signals, couched in language which became ruder as time went on, nothing came except our signal stores and kit which were eventually dropped at Monte Grappa, where they were either stolen, or lost in the 'rastrallamento'.

That Pietena was not impossible to find was shown when an American plane came over to drop two Italian agents. The ground was most unsuitable for bodies, but having been told to receive them we lit the signal fires. About midnight a Liberator flew over high, circled once, and disappeared. Nothing was seen to drop. However, at dawn a strange and rather haggard figure, wearing a Sidcot suit, appeared and asked if we had seen his companion. Search parties were sent out. They found the unfortunate man suspended head downwards over a cliff. He was not seriously damaged, but we took no credit for that.

Although the partisans were surprised and disgusted at our inability to help, we remained good friends. I think they attributed our failure to incompetence rather than to unwillingness, and in this, of course, they were quite right. The more ardent Communists among them liked to believe that their politics were responsible for this apparently deliberate withholding of arms, and short of a plane-load of Bren guns falling at their feet, or better still on their thick skulls, the theory was difficult to kill no matter how strongly we might protest that so long as they were willing to fight they might be anarchists for all we or our employers cared. In spite of our shortcomings they accepted us as one of themselves. They supplied bedding, for we still had nothing but the clothes we wore, toilet kit, bowl and spoon; they saw that we got our cigarette and tobacco ration, and even supplied a tame Fascist, whom they had not yet shot, to bring our meals from the kitchen, where food for all was cooked in a vast copper cauldron. We fed very well. We began the day with a bowl of ersatz coffee and a roll—the small Italian loaf of about 100 grammes of good coarse wholemeal; at midday a bowl of broth with meat or 'pasta', or sometimes 'pasta schiuta', and another loaf; for supper a bowl of minestrone, that is, thick vegetable soup with beans, another loaf and perhaps a bit of cheese—uncompromisingly Italian but satisfying.

Beyond ciphering and deciphering messages, visiting the battalions, and getting to know the geography of Le Vette, there was nothing much for us to do. On 17 September, taking advantage of the presence of the Commissar of the Pisacane Brigade who was about to return, Gatti and I made a quick trip to Forno, south of Monte Marmolada where this brigade was stationed. It was a journey remarkable for the variety of transport employed, and is worth describing very briefly to show the ease with which one moved about at that time compared with the difficulty we experienced later.

Upon reaching the valley head below the Battisti Battalion post, we took a mule trap to road-head represented by a blown-up bridge. There we embarked in a long, lean, black car driven by a partisan who professed to be a racing motorist. Two beady eyes peering out of a mass of auburn beard and hair were all I could see of his face. In the gathering dusk, without lights or brakes, along narrow winding secondary roads, we careered at something like 40 m.p.h. For a hundred yards or so we had to traverse the main Belluno highway before turning on to another side road, and when we caught sight of the lights of a German truck behind us, the speedometer needle appeared to revolve completely in front of my frightened eyes. Our mad career was happily cut short by the necessity of observing the curfew restrictions imposed at eight o'clock, after which hour no civilian cars were allowed on the road.

We pulled up with two flat tyres to spend the night in a hayloft. A closed van belonging to the TODT organisation was waiting for us next morning. TODT was the civilian labour corps nominally working for the Germans but with the least display of zeal consonant with safety. In delightful contrast with the Grand Prix affair of the previous night, we tooled sedately up the Canal dell Mis, stopping a few miles short of Agordo on the main road, where there was a German garrison. Here the plan was to find the local head of the TODT, a man in league with the partisans, whose presence in the front seat might, they thought, ensure our passing the German block-posts unchallenged; the Commissar, Gatti, and I were to sit in the back presumably with our fingers crossed. Although it would save us a long walk, the plan was not one which I liked. In fact, I was seldom more relieved in my life than when we heard that this useful official could not be found. It was then one o'clock, so hiding the van in a wood we set off on our feet. Agordo, with its streets full of Germans, whom we could see walking about, was successfully avoided, and a pass, the Forcella Cesurette (6000 ft.), crossed. From there I caught a glimpse of a tiny glacier high up on the Pala di S. Martino which gave me a thrill out of all proportion to its size. Eight hours later we limped into Forno. The Commander of the Pisacane Brigade came in next morning to discuss arrangements for dropping grounds, and I handed over a substantial sum of lire as an earnest of our intentions. Tall, lithe, dark and good-looking, with pistols sticking out of every pocket, he looked like a Naples bravo. Carlo was in fact a Neapolitan, which was strange, because there is no love lost between northern and southern Italians; but by his many bold actions he had earned the command of the brigade and the respect of all. One of these actions was a daylight raid on the Belluno gaol where, mainly by bluff, he had released a number of partisans. He later commanded the Belluno G.A.P. and carried out some quiet but effective work with a silent pistol we had got for him. He was an exponent of the 'cloak and dagger' school, wore strikingly different clothes each day, and never slept twice in the same place.

The situation at Pietena when we returned on the 20th was unchanged, except for the weather which was becoming colder. The pond in which we washed wore a film of ice in the morning and on the 28th snow fell all day. Pietena would be untenable during the winter, but Bruno, wishing to hang on as long as possible, proceeded to have the draughty 'malga' well lined with hay. His decision was determined by the lack of arms and by the ever present possibility of their arrival. But it was now becoming a question of which would arrive first, the arms, winter, or the Germans; and the odds were heavily on the last. It was evidently the enemy intention to clear up the whole of the Piave valley. They had already dealt with the Cansiglio area and the Monte Grappa, and on the 29th our turn came. In the meantime we had our first contact with the Nannetti Division in the form of a flying visit from Filippo their Commander. He promised to return in a few days to take us to their new headquarters, but on his way up on the 29th he ran into the Germans, who were attacking us, was shot at, lost all the division's secret files, including the locations and signals of all dropping grounds, and disappears from history.

About five o'clock on the evening of 29 September we were startled by a distant burst of machine-gun fire. The Churchill Company block-post reported that a German patrol had attacked the post and the store in the valley some 2000 ft. below. The store was in flames. The long-expected 'rastrallamento' was evidently about to begin. The commanders of the Zancanaro and Battisti Battalions arrived to attend a council of war, bringing with them news of German movement below their posts. Bruno, who was something of a fire-eater, had only one thought, or plan—to fight to the last man and the last round.

'The camel driver has his thoughts and the camel he has his', was the reflection that crossed my mind on hearing these ominous words. I had heard them before, but never in connection with partisan warfare, for here the loss of ground or positions should mean nothing. The function of the partisans was to remain intact as a fighting force, constituting by their mere existence and by occasional pinpricks, a constant threat, to meet which the enemy must hold in readiness troops which could be more usefully employed elsewhere. The only value of Pietena was as a dropping ground. But it was neither a good one, nor was it the only one, and winter would soon force us to abandon it. As yet nothing had been dropped there and we could give no guarantee that anything would be dropped in the future. We pointed out these objections—but to no purpose. The honour of the Gramsci Brigade was at stake; the rout of the partisans on Monte Grappa must be avenged: sentiments which were received with acclamation by an easily swayed, uninstructed audience. I might have gone on to point out that the best of partisans cannot hope to hold even the strongest position for long against trained troops with mortars, machine-guns, unlimited ammunition, intercommunications, and the power if need be to reinforce; that the ammunition available was 300 rounds per L.M.G. and thirty per rifle; that there was food for only a few days with no hope of getting more; and that partisan morale can best be served by inflicting casualties and suffering none in return.

These warnings went unheeded. Perhaps they lost their force in the interpretation, or perhaps were attributed to our pusillanimity. Indeed Bruno suggested the mission should withdraw that night before it was too late, but this eminently sensible plan was rejected. It was a question of what interpretation would be put upon our action if we agreed. Would they take the common-sense military view that the safety of the mission with its wireless set and all the possibilities of future supplies which this implied, should not be hazarded uselessly, or would they think that we were running away? Not that this should have mattered much to me, for in common with the rest of the British Army I had spent much of the war running away in order to fight again; but it might adversely affect the future by impairing what little influence we had. On Bruno's assurance that he would not only see that the mission got away but that the brigade would also emerge from the crisis intact, we decided to await the event. In face of the fact that the four known exits were already in process of being blocked, his plan for effecting this was not very obvious. We hopefully assumed that there were other routes unknown to us and went to bed.

Developments in the morning were slow. The only news of fighting was from the Zancanaro Battalion on the west, and by noon it was clear that this was where the attack was being pressed, and that on the other approaches the enemy were merely in the nature of 'stops' to prevent the game breaking back. The majority of the Battisti Battalion were brought over to Pietena to reinforce the northern rim and the ridge dividing the basin, on which machine-gun posts had been prepared some time before. Some official visitors from below, who had been caught out by the promptness with which the exits had been blocked, tried to get out by the difficult track down the north face. They came back later with the news that that too was blocked by patrols in the valley below.

There were at least fifty partisans hanging about round the H.Q. 'malga': the H.Q. staff, clerks, cooks, couriers, intendants, and the other idlers who commonly collect round a H.Q., those whom the Army call rather unkindly the 'unemployed men'. There were also stragglers from Battisti who had come down to try to find out what was happening. They were not the only ones seeking enlightenment. News was scarce, and in no very easy frame of mind we kicked our heels in the customarily depressing atmosphere of those left out of battle. Bruno still radiated confidence, but early in the afternoon he went up to the dividing ridge from which there already came sounds of firing. Shortly after this he sent orders to remove everything and everybody to the top of Duodieci, a rocky broken summit on the rim just above the north end of the dividing ridge. Legs of beef, sacks of bread and beans, cooking pots, typewriters, were hoisted on to men's backs and carried away in a manner that one could not help thinking was only half-hearted. Preparations for a last stand on Duodieci at this early stage was surely a counsel of despair and that must mean the battle was not going well.

Leaving Ross and Pallino at Pietena with orders to have our few belongings ready to move, Gatti and I went up to find Bruno. The climb of nearly 500 ft. to the ridge took us about twenty minutes. On our side of it, the lee side, most of the stuff removed from Pietena had been dumped, and only a few of the more obedient were still struggling up the rocky slopes of Duodieci with their loads. The crest of the ridge was under mortar fire. Seizing our opportunity we ran over the top and found Bruno in a covered machine-gun pit on the forward slope very busy with an old French machine-gun which would only fire a couple of rounds at a time before jamming. Through the slit I could see that the Zancanaro 'malga' was already in German hands. Where the mule track crossed the western rim, 2500 yards away, the mortar which was now busy with our position could be seen firing. More Germans were advancing unconcernedly across the basin towards our ridge, while another party of a hundred or more had just begun moving along the crest of the rim towards Duodieci. All partisans had withdrawn to the dividing ridge.

Bruno, with the light of battle in his eyes, paid little attention to my question of what he proposed doing. My suggestion that at this moment he ought not to be fiddling with a machine-gun, and that in any case to fire that ancient and obdurate weapon at men over 2000 yards away was a waste of effort, fell on deaf ears. In the moments he grudgingly spared from his struggle with that miserable piece, we wrangled uselessly while mortar bombs burst more or less harmlessly about the position. Three partisans had so far been wounded. The Germans, I imagine, were unscathed. Most of the partisans in the vicinity, except Bruno, looked decidedly and, I thought, justifiably, scared. At length Bruno agreed to withdraw at dusk and promised to send out orders to that effect. Whether this had been his intention all along I cannot say. Perhaps the speed with which the Germans got to the Zancanaro 'malga' had surprised him, but as we had waited so long it was sensible to wait until dusk before retiring.

We left Bruno with his machine-gun and went back to Pietena to warn the others of the new plan. It was then about 7 p.m., just about sunset. Whether 'our brows, like to a title-leaf, foretold the nature of a tragic volume', or whether it was the few words we exchanged together, I cannot tell. The effect of our arrival, however, was immediately harmful. A lot of shouting broke out amongst the H.Q. company, and some Battisti who had wandered down from their post on the rim, and a 'sauve qui peut' seemed imminent. At the same moment men were seen streaming away along the northern rim from the direction of Duodieci. That was decisive. The time had come for us to fend for ourselves. We picked up a blanket each, put the 6-volt battery on a mule, and Ross shouldered the suitcase containing the wireless set. I went off to see if the Churchill Company had received any orders to retire—for it seemed likely that they would be forgotten in the confusion—while the whole mob straggled off towards the Battisti track. They had not gone far before figures appeared silhouetted against the evening sky on the southern rim. Spurts of flame ran along the ridge and tracer bullets began zipping over the heads of the fugitives or thudding against the rocks. Although the Germans were at least 1500 yards away they made good practice in the failing light, and so frightened the mules that we lost our battery. When it was dark we halted and Bruno came up. He handed over the conduct of the withdrawal, an unenviable task, to his second-in-command, saying that he would wait to see what the Germans did.

The track to Battisti followed the north rim just below the crest, and at about eleven o'clock when we were within about a mile of the Battisti 'malga', a patrol was sent ahead to estimate the chance of passing the block-post unseen, or of attacking it. There was a lot of snow about and for an hour the fugitive mob, for we were little better, sat about on stones waiting dejectedly for the verdict. When it came it was the expected, 'None'. More talk broke out, but this time it was conducted in fearful whispers. The plan favoured by the majority was to try to cross a valley to the south, though it was known that it was picketed by the enemy.

Burdened as we were with a wireless set which we could not afford to lose, I did not fancy the idea of running the gauntlet in this valley, so I suggested to the others an alternative plan of lying low on the north face of Le Vette until the enemy got tired of looking for partisans. We might even find a way down, but at the worst the Germans were not likely to remain up there for more than a couple of days. This plan they agreed to. The Churchill Company, in a body, asked to come with us, and the Italian cook from Pietena, who was a friend of ours, offered to carry the wireless set. This made a party of sixteen (and others would have attached themselves had they been allowed) instead of the four or five I should have preferred. We left the path, shook off some would-be adherents, and struck straight up to the crest, carelessly leaving our tracks in a patch of snow close to the path. As we gained the crest we saw below us the fires of the enemy pickets in the valley the partisans hoped to cross.

We began a descent of the first likely looking gully on the far side, the first few hundred feet of which consisted of steep frozen scree and patches of snow. Soon we were brought to a standstill by the gully falling away abruptly, so we scratched out a platform of sorts and turned in—that is to say, lay down. We had one blanket apiece and no food; moreover, we were 7000 ft. up and it was late September. I entertained a slight hope of being able to force a way down, but a search made next day showed this to be difficult for a small, strong party of climbers and quite impossible for a party such as ours. We were a very weak party for mountaineering, even on Le Vette.

A cautious look over the top of the gully at dawn revealed groups of Germans on the track below evidently engaged in the search for the no doubt numerous Brer Rabbits who, like us, were 'laying low and saying nuffin'. They were three or four hundred yards away, and to my imagination, quickened by a night's fast, they seemed to be discussing the marks we had made in the snow as we left the track. I tiptoed carefully down the gully and warned the others. The first hour of a day of continuous apprehension was the worst. After that it became obvious that the party I had seen was not coming to inspect the north face, but for all that we breathed more freely when dusk fell.

That night the wind rose. By dawn a blizzard was blowing from the north, the one quarter from which we had no protection. It blew all day, but wretched though our situation was, the faint sound of automatic fire, borne to our ears against the gale, persuaded us to stick it out for yet another night.

By the end of the third day we had to move whether or no. No one had eaten for seventy-two hours, some had frozen feet, and all were stiff with cold. The start was not auspicious. Having gone to the top of the gully at dusk to reconnoitre I was recalled by wild cries from below. Since for three days no one had dared to raise his voice above a whisper, it seemed something important must have happened—perhaps they had found some food. In fact, one of the ex-prisoners-of-war had slipped. I found him lying dazed with a severe gash in his head, on a ledge sixty feet below our 'gîte' on the lip of a straight drop of a like distance. His hands were lacerated too, but securing him to the tail of my coat, I eventually dragged him to the top of the gully where the remainder were now waiting. We had lost much time, and what with having frozen feet, and limbs so stiff that for many walking was a matter of difficulty, my plan of finding a safe way out along the crest of the rim had to be abandoned in favour of following the track. With every step we took our confidence increased. We met no one and by daybreak we were lying in a wood staring with longing intensity at a farm below. One of the Englishmen who knew the place went down, the signal for 'all clear' was given, and soon we were enjoying our first meal since lunch on the day of the attack. The Germans had left the day before, having first burnt all the 'malgas' and a few farms in the valley suspected of being sympathetic towards the partisans.

CHAPTER XV

THE NINO NANNETTI DIVISION

ALTHOUGH THEY HAD ESCAPED with comparatively slight loss from the trap into which faulty tactics had led them, the Gramsci Brigade, which was regarded as the best in the division, ceased to exist. It was reorganised in skeleton form during the winter, but it did not become effective as a fighting force until the following spring. The whole division was now in a critical state. A new H.Q. had yet to be organised, the partisans at Cansiglio, Monte Grappa, Pietena, and those on the south side of the Piave, had been dispersed; and the comparative ease with which this disastrous disruption had been brought about had gravely shaken the confidence of the population in the partisans and of the partisans in themselves. Many 'malgas' and houses had been burnt and some partisans hanged. It was said that they had been strung up on meat-hooks inserted under the chin, but so many atrocity stories were in circulation that unless proof in the form of a photograph were available we reserved judgement. For instance, it was strenuously asserted that Gianna, a young and very pretty girl courier, having been caught at Pietena, had met a terrible fate. She had been tied to a wire cable-way used for bringing wood down the mountain and sent hurtling down it like a faggot and had been smashed to pulp at the bottom. Happily, however, in May, after the surrender, Gianna stopped us on the road and we had the satisfaction of giving her a cigarette. But even without the horror stories there was enough killing and burning to lower everyone's morale, and the widely expressed dissatisfaction was directed at the H.Q. and leaders generally because of the obviously faulty tactics employed.

One of the first of the critics to express his views in the most vehement way was our friend Orestes. When we reached the valley we sent for him to give us a picture of the general situation and to find us a hide-out until our next move was decided. With much arm slapping and many 'Ostia's', he inveighed unceasingly against the stupidity which had resulted in the rout of the brigade which he had done so much to help. His contempt for so-called guerilla leaders who allowed their men to sit on top of a mountain until they were surrounded was boundless. He himself was as crafty as a fox in war or politics. In politics his heart might sometimes get the better of his head, but his mature experience would never have allowed this to happen in action. When night fell he took us to a hay-loft on the hill behind Cesio. There were several houses on fire in the valley that night, his own amongst them, which added fresh fuel to his anger.

We remained there for three nights while various partisan leaders from far and wide came in for discussions. One of these was Hugo, the Divisional Commissar, who shortly afterwards resigned. He was a cheerful, pleasant man, with the appearance of a prosperous gentleman farmer, but was in reality, as we were told by one of his non-admirers, a professional revolutionary, having taken a degree in that difficult art in Russia. Like so many of the partisan leaders, he had served a long term of imprisonment in the early days of Fascism. These men who had thus proved their early and rooted antipathy to Fascism had considerable ascendancy over their fellows. Another of them was Boretti, a Bologna Communist, who took Hugo's place for a short time; he had done his twelve years, and his health had suffered for it. There were many Bolognese among the partisans in the Belluno area. They seem to have the same reputation in Italy as Scotsmen have abroad. You may go anywhere in Italy but will always find yourself forestalled by a Bolognese running whatever there may be to run.

Deluca hailed from Bologna, too, and was one of the original organisers of the Nannetti Division. He was a Communist and a successful business man who was said to have done very well in the fur trade. He used his business as his 'cover' when bicycling through northern Italy on partisan affairs, as he continued to do untiringly until the war ended. He always carried with him as corroborative detail a couple of moth-eaten marten skins to give 'artistic verisimilitude to an otherwise bald and unconvincing narrative'. The production of the necessary forged documents to cover those who had to play a double game was an essential and highly successful branch of the C.L.N. organisation. Either the Germans were pretty 'dumb' or skilled forgers were common. Deluca was an able, active and influential man, and the greatest help to the mission and the partisan cause; among his many accomplishments were the ability to skin, dress, and cook anything that walked. His spiced kid, spitted and roasted, was perfection.

The present situation found the Germans very much in the ascendant, with the people increasingly fearful and less sympathetic or even hostile to the partisan movement. The loss of arms and equipment, food dumps, and shelter (through the burning of so many 'malgas'), demanded a new policy of small mobile groups and a period of quiet in which to build up a new organisation and to try to obtain supplies.

As there was by now too much coming and going in our vicinity, we moved very secretly to a small hamlet east of Cesio, where we lay hidden in a farm for a week awaiting the arrival of the new commander of the Nannetti Division. Though we were comfortable the strict confinement was irksome. Ross and I shared a double bed with sheets, but we were not obliged to remain in this all day. The wireless could only be worked with an indoor aerial. One morning the sound of firing in S. Giustina, a village two miles away, alarmed us all so that we packed and moved into a small wood a short distance from the farm. Anxiety turned to fright when a battery of 88 mm. began firing from the road below into the hills above our wood. This activity proved to be a two-day exercise of which the Germans had omitted to give notice to the civilians, either through malice aforethought or through forgetfulness. The nervousness of the civilians at this time was extreme. We slept in the wood to ease the minds of our hosts and in consequence enjoyed two suppers, one from the farm and one from a woman who found us lurking in the wood and who no doubt mistook us for escaping prisoners. It consisted of a magnificent minestrone, cream cheese, peaches, and unfermented grape juice.

At last, Milo, the new Divisional Commander, having arrived, we set out for Cansiglio forest where Divisional H.Q. was again to be set up. Milo was an ex-officer of infantry and a recent convert to Communism. He was an able man, talked well, knew his business, and ultimately made the Nannetti Division one of the best, if not the best, partisan formations in northern Italy.

Travelling as usual by night, we crossed a 300-yard-long bridge over the Cordevole river, fortunately meeting no one, and then gained the south side of the Piave by another bridge. We stopped the day with one of the brigades (Tollot), and next night crossed the Vittorio Veneto-Belluno highway to a small 'malga' on the edge of the Cansiglio forest, above Vittorio Veneto.

We lived with about fifteen men of the H.Q. staff and a floating population of visitors from outlying brigades, civilians, members of the C.L.N. (Committee of National Liberation), couriers from nearby brigades, and from committees and formations as far away as Padova. The courier service was maintained by girls who found it a simple matter to cycle about the country without being stopped or searched. Although it was a risky job, we heard of only one who came to grief. The 'malga' consisted of a hayloft in which all, men and women, slept, and a small kitchen in which we all ate. The room below was the quarters of four cows who stayed with us until they were sent down for the winter. We regretted their going, as much for the loss of their milk as for the absence of the sweet-scented warmth their presence gave to our dormitory above.

Besides the Commissar, Vice-commander, Chief of Staff, clerks, intendant, cook, there were one or two odd-job men such as a guide for the forest and a mule-man who went down daily for supplies. The guide was an unbelievably dirty, shock-headed, uncouth youth who appeared to have only recently given up living in the trees. We called him 'Tarzan' or the 'Animal Man'. He played a mouth organ excruciatingly and was responsible for some classic remarks. Of these perhaps the best was when he was detailed to take down a battery for recharging. The weight rather staggered him, and he wanted to know 'if it weighed so much when discharged, what the devil would it weigh charged?' The mule-man, who did more real work than anyone else, was a cheerful soul with a Rabelaisian wit and a loud laugh which in his case did not 'bespeak the vacant mind'. His excessively sinister appearance earned him the title of 'the Second Murderer'.

Another character not 'on the strength' was the bird-man, who was in appearance rather like the wrens he spent his time catching. The owners of these 'malgas' on the outskirts of the forest eke out the slender income from their cattle by the netting of small birds, mostly wrens and finches, which they sell for the table. The trap was an elaborate affair of a twelve-foot-high, small-meshed net, hung on poles surrounding a circular space of about fifteen yards across. Some twenty live decoy birds in cages were put down and the trapper, armed with a number of throwing sticks, took station in a big camouflaged tower just outside the net. When the decoys had attracted sufficient birds inside the enclosure, the man threw one of his sticks high into the air. The whistling sound it made, not unlike the rush of a stooping hawk, so frightened the birds inside that they flew straight into the net. A day's catch might be anything up to a hundred. In peace-time they are sold in the markets of the plains, but we ate most of those caught by our bird-man. They are either fried or cooked in a thick stew and are eaten whole, bones, head and beak. Helped down with 'polenta' or maize cake, the staple dish in poorer households that cannot afford wheaten bread, they make a crackly, tasty mouthful.

Although the 'malga' was not much more than an hour's march away from the nearest Fascist garrison, H.Q. were absolved from finding its own guards by the presence of partisans in neighbouring 'malgas'. The nearest of these was the so-called 'Tiger's' Battalion which had just come up for a rest after a month of action in the plains. The Tiger himself was a terrific figure with a bronze bushy beard, two automatic pistols, ten bombs, a knife, and a large Alsatian dog. He later increased his bomb load to the round dozen by having a special waistcoat built to his own design. Another battalion (Nievo) of about thirty men lived in a 'malga' up in the forest, about an hour and a half's journey from us, which was at first the site of our dropping ground. During October and November six attempts were made to send us stores, but all failed either because of bad weather or bad navigation. The system used to advise us whether or not to expect a plane was simple and worked well. It consisted in short Italian phrases (known as 'cracks') supplied by us and broadcast by the B.B.C. on the Italian news at 4.30 p.m., 6.30 p.m., 8.30 p.m., and 10.30 p.m. One phrase was 'negative', meaning no plane need be expected, and the other 'positive', which meant we must stand-by. For example, 'Polenta e Grappa' might be the 'negative' and 'il Maggiore senza barba' the 'positive' phrase. Our arrival at this place, to await the coming of planes of which we had been advised, soon became a time-worn jest and was usually the occasion for the consumption of the battalion's reserve supply of 'grappa', a fiery white brandy similar to the raki of Albania or the arak of India which is much in demand in winter, and in summer too, for that matter. There was also a pleasant, sweeter, darker, thicker type made from plums, called Grappa de Pruna, similar to the Slivovitch of Yugo-Slavia; but that was for pleasure, whereas the ordinary grappa was for use—the bread of life, not the cake. What the partisans, or we, would have done without this bottled lightning I hesitate to say. The higher criticism of various marks exercised our minds during many weary hours; in moments of despair or jubilation it was our unfailing solace, and for heat or cold, dryness or thirst, fulness or fasting, it was an unfailing remedy.

On the last day of October Milo, Gatti and I went down to a house on the outskirts of Vittorio Veneto to meet the local Committee of National Liberation. To any civilian we met on the way Gatti and I posed as German prisoners, an easy pretence as there was a general ignorance of foreign uniforms. At an 'albergo' we stopped to confer with the engineer in charge of the electric-power system for the Veneto region, concerning our 'anti-scorch' policy, and the sort of sabotage the partisans might effect without doing irreparable damage to the plant or without inflicting too great hardship on the populace for too long. Towns such as Venice depended entirely on electricity for light and cooking. The little charcoal that was being made was used solely in gas-driven vehicles. As a rule 'albergos' were better avoided. They were the favourite hunting-grounds of Germans who came both for pleasure and for business. The 'business' consisted of the rounding up of young men either as suspects or as recruits to swell the ranks of the TODT organisation, or for work in Germany, or for enlistment in the local Alpine Polizei. Churches on Sundays, or when there were 'festas', were also favourite targets for raids of this type. Being near Vittorio Veneto we were no longer in Germany but in Republican Italy. The Province of Belluno to the north had been annexed to the Reich and was administered and policed by Germans, while Treviso Province, in which we now were, was run by the Fascists, so that Germans were not very numerous. The conditions were much less dangerous for the partisans, who held the Fascists in supreme contempt.

The Committee of six was in conclave when we arrived. It comprised one representative from each of the political parties—from left to right, Communist, Socialist, Action, Christian Democrat, Liberal—and an independent chairman. Shortly after this meeting the chairman was arrested and languished for many months in gaol in Venice. He was a remarkable figure—a professor—with a very soft voice, small beard, and delicate features. Both his legs were paralysed, and he sat with a little machine in front of him rolling and smoking endless cigarettes. The atmosphere of this secret meeting, with the passwords, pistols, and the suave, soft-spoken, paralysed chairman, was the very essence of romantic story; while they deliberated over roast chestnuts and wine my fancy strayed to the sinister forms of Professor Moriarty, Long John Silver, and the paralysed Couthon of the Committee of Public Safety.

At the latter end of October, gales of wind and rain heralded the coming of winter, forcing upon us all the consideration of how best to meet it. Hope of an allied advance was no longer entertained. General Alexander in a broadcast to the partisans had already stressed the wisdom of reducing their numbers, and had urged them to hibernate and husband their resources for the spring campaign, while our H.Q. had warned us, perhaps unnecessarily, that the R.A.F. would only be able to send a few sorties during the coming winter. This, indeed, was a glimpse of the obvious, for we had already been in the field nine weeks without receiving so much as a pair of socks or a spare shirt, and we were to pass yet another eight before this happy event occurred. We became halting disciples of Socrates, striving to accept the master's dictum that to 'want nothing is divine, to want as little as possible is the nearest approach to the divine'.

Early in November Deluca came, bringing with him one of the Regional Committee from Padova, which was the C.V.L. committee responsible for partisan affairs in the whole of the Veneto region. This was Ascanio, a Communist of long standing, who had suffered imprisonment for his beliefs. On leaving Cansiglio on this occasion his assistant was arrested near Belluno and subsequently hanged. This had repercussions, as had most arrests, for the Germans had ways of making their victims talk. Ascanio was himself arrested and remained in daily expectation of death until rescued in the last days of April by the patriots of Padova. He was a man who impressed me with his ability, patience, commonsense and sincerity.

Lying in the hay, the door firmly shut, with rain sweeping incessantly across the little clearing in which the 'malga' lay, the leaders discussed winter plans for the best part of two days. The fortunes of the partisans were at a low ebb. They had received no help from us, their abettors, and now they were faced with the problem of maintaining themselves during the difficult winter months. Warm clothing, food and shelter, were as urgently needed as arms. We were asked to guarantee enough winter clothing for 500 men, but this was, of course, impossible. Before this conference there had been some talk in H.Q. of dispersing or even of retreating to Yugo-Slavia. Ascanio asked us what we proposed to do, and we could only say that we intended to stay as long as there were any partisans with whom to work. He was quick to squash any idea of withdrawal. It was finally decided to reduce numbers to a minimum, to keep only the strongest and trustiest men in the mountains, to build alternative huts in the forest, and to procure as much warm clothing as possible locally. The organisation of Division and Brigades would have to be adapted to present needs and with a view to rapid expansion when weather and the state of the war justified it. In practice this meant that only about sixty men remained in Cansiglio and a similar number west of the highway. North of the Piave, where conditions were more difficult, a new division, known as the Belluno Division, had been formed, comprising Gramsci, Pisacane, and three other brigades. The British officer who had dropped with us, and who had lost all his wireless equipment on Monte Grappa, had since joined me, and I decided that as soon as a second wireless set arrived, Ross and I would go to the Belluno Division, leaving him with the Nannetti. But until a second set was sent nothing could be done.

On 10 November the first snow fell at Cansiglio. Snow had already fallen on the mountains to the north, and in my opinion the draping of the Dolomites in a mantle of snow was a notable improvement. In late summer they seemed to me altogether too stark and ragged to delight for long even such a mountain-starved eye as mine. Snow softened their jagged outlines, toned down the angry colouring, and dispelled the atmosphere of fierce aridity which, in summer, had forced upon me unwelcome comparisons with those terrible bare carcasses of mountains seen along the shores of the Red Sea. But aesthetically pleasing though the snow may have been, from the point of view of a partisan it was everything that was evil. The once friendly mountains turned hostile overnight, shelter became a necessity instead of a luxury, movement became difficult or impossible, and tracks were an open book betraying all who made them.

The snow brought a brief spell of fine, sunny weather. The southern edge of our little glade became a 'belvedere' where we could sit and gaze at the ordered, civilised expanse of plain at our feet, melting in the distance into the lagoons of the Adriatic coast, where the spires of Venice showed like a mirage, partaking of neither sea nor land. Away to the east the snow-covered Julian Alps swept in an unbroken arc to meet the warm brown of the Istrian hills beyond Trieste. Far above, the vapour trails of four-engined bombers stretched out towards Austria in ever-lengthening wedges, while above these the fighters drew graceful curves in faint single strokes. Perhaps a burst of flak or the rumble of bombs would draw everyone with a rush to this vantage point to watch with satisfaction a cloud of smoke ascending from some train attacked by fighter-bombers.

It was on such a morning that our interest in attacks on trains was diverted to the more pressing interest of an attack on ourselves, of which the first intimation was a burst of 20 mm. fire obviously aimed at our positions. Soon we could see the enemy deploying on the slopes 1000 ft. below us, and the men of the Manara Battalion running to occupy their posts on a spur commanding the track. We packed up ready to move, hid the surplus stores, and an excellent bean soup simmering on the fire was prodigally poured away. Then we thought the Manara men had halted the attack, the stores were brought back, and another lunch was prepared. Finally, bullets started whipping over our heads as we lay watching on our belvedere, and we hid everything once more before hurrying away to a higher 'malga'. In the evening we returned to find several 'malgas' burning, but our own intact. Three men had been killed and the leader of the Manara Battalion, a fine partisan, gravely wounded.

Our alternative barracks, hidden high up in the forest, were now ready, but Milo was loath to move into them until compelled. The Manara Battalion, having had its home burnt, had withdrawn, leaving no one between Divisional H.Q. and the enemy. That night snow fell heavily, and next morning there was rain. Milo, having decided to hang on for another day, was still in bed when firing broke out in the direction of the 'Tiger' Battalion. Sacks of bread, beans, macaroni, were hastily hidden in the dripping bushes, and the heavily laden procession set out again in the snow and sleet for the Nievo Battalion 'malga'. We had stopped to rest before crossing the main mule track up to the forest known as the 'Patriarchal track', when a prolonged burst of automatic fire, not 200 yards away, shattered the silence of the forest. We thought it was a Hun patrol on the track which was firing random bursts into the bush, the tactics they usually employed when carrying out a 'rastrallamento' in thick country. A few days later, however, when we were discussing the day's events with the Nievo Battalion, they themselves claimed to have fired the burst at an enemy patrol and to have killed three. When all was quiet we crossed the track and reached the Nievo 'malga' only to find it abandoned. Trudging through a foot and a half of snow had made us so wet that we decided to stay for the night. We had our reserve rations (every man now carried bread, salami, sugar, and pasta for six days), sundry bottles of 'grappa' were found in the pockets of our rucksacks, and we spent a cheery evening.

More snow fell during the night and all paths were obliterated. Led by Tarzan, the procession stole stealthily through the silent forest like a party of mourners going to a wake. A large sooty cauldron dangled from a pole carried by Ross and myself, the Second Murderer carefully balanced on his shoulder a straw-covered 'grey hen' of grappa, while the necks and corks protruding from coat pockets and rucksacks showed that there was still plenty of corn in Egypt. We approached our new home in a roundabout way, very conscious that in our wake we had left damning evidence of the passage of a small army. There were two log cabins about 100 yards apart in the middle of a magnificent straight-growing beech forest. The larger had two tiers of bunks to take about twenty, the other formed the kitchen and mess room. Water came from a pond 300 yards away. This was now snow-covered, but later in the winter was covered with a foot of ice, for we were over 4000 ft. up and Cansiglio Forest is a notoriously cold place. Half a mile to the west and 500 ft. below was the house of the Forest Guard situated on the motor-road leading to the Plain of Cansiglio and to Alpago and Belluno. We worked all afternoon clearing a track to the pond and doing what we could to efface our tracks of the morning.

Some time before I had arranged by signal a meeting with the next mission to the east at a place called Barcis in the Val Cellina. Any escaped prisoners-of-war or forced-landed airmen we collected for evacuation to Yugo-Slavia had to go via Barcis, which was on the other side of the Passo di Cavallo, two days' march away. As, in addition to keeping our appointment, I was anxious to see if the pass was still open, Gatti and I left on 19 November, taking with us all we possessed, for it was unwise to leave anything in case of a 'rastrallamento'. At some higher 'malgas', now occupied by the men of Nievo and Manara, we picked up two guides and began a hard day's work breaking trail in soft snow. The close of the short winter afternoon found us on the other side of the pass, but in some doubt as to the whereabouts of the partisans with whom we were to spend the night. Our shouts and shots met with no response. We dosed the guide and Gatti, who were showing signs of collapse, heavily and unwisely with grappa, and struggled on. Two hours later we made contact. The guide was now helpless and Gatti little better. The first partisan I met was extremely suspicious. He thrust a Sten into my stomach, searched me, and finally took away my pistol; but with these trifling formalities over I was allowed to go to their hut to send out help for the others and to get food and drink ready. When the two stragglers were brought in they had to be carried straight to bed, drunk with exhaustion and grappa.

Next morning, when we were but a short way from the hut, the partisan commander who was guiding us pointed with satisfaction to a patch of blood-stained snow marking the grave of a spy they had shot the day before. By the way he eyed me I think he still inclined to the belief that if everyone had their deserts I should be lying there too. Having introduced ourselves to another battalion of the Osoppo Brigade, living in a charcoal-burner's hut, we left our kit and went down into the Val Cellina to Barcis, where every house but the inn had been burnt. My opposite number did not arrive, and as I had another appointment with an American mission in the contrary direction, we hurried back. All was quiet at the barracks, where we found a welcome addition to the English-speaking community in three American airmen who had been shot down. We made several attempts to send them to Yugo-Slavia for evacuation, but all failed owing either to snow or to enemy activity. When the war ended they were still at Cansiglio, along with some twenty more who had been brought in by the partisans. By then we had a landing strip on the Plain of Cansiglio, and had made arrangements for their removal by air.

On the night of 22 November Ross and I set off with the Commissar of the Division bound for the Tollot Brigade, stationed west of the Vittorio Veneto-Belluno highway, to meet an American officer who had recently dropped there. We hoped that he would be able to make good the needs of the partisans in that area. We crossed the road at midnight about a mile from a German block-post, and addressed ourselves to the steep climb to the high ground west of the road. Hardened though we were to night marches, we again experienced the deadly weariness that attacks one in the small hours. Our vitality required replenishing—mine had nearly all ebbed away—so we called a halt at a house known to the Commissar. The women in Italy never grudged being roused at two or three in the morning to attend to the wants of spent partisans. Here the mother and a laughing comely daughter, who were alone in the house, bustled about, lit a fire, and soon had us sitting comfortably toasting our feet, eating roast chestnuts and drinking red wine. The chestnuts were roasted to such perfection in a sort of warming pan that the skins fell away at a touch, and the wine had the rich earthy tang of the local 'Clintot'. One of the nicest features of the houses in these parts is the fireplaces. This is a six foot by six foot stone dais, about one and a half feet high, surrounded on three sides by a wooden bench. Sometimes it occupies a corner of the room, and sometimes it is built in an alcove projecting from the room. The fuel is faggots of small dry twigs which blaze gloriously, while a huge hanging chimney, with a mouth as big as the dais, takes care of the smoke. From the chimney dangles an iron chain and hook for cooking pots. If a tavern chair be the throne of human felicity, commend me to one of these noble fireplaces with a bottle of wine on the hob and a plate of roast chestnuts by my side.

When we gained the ridge at dawn we were greeted by the sound of firing. Our hearts sank. If there were a 'rastrallamento' in progress our journey here would be in vain. However, at Tollot Brigade H.Q. all was quiet; we were told that the neighbouring Mazzini Brigade was engaged near the San Boldo Pass. Tollot was not inclined to worry about the troubles of others, having enough on hand at the moment with the turning of two large pigs into salami. After witnessing this display of single-minded devotion, it was distressing for us to hear that two days later they were themselves attacked and all the salami captured.

Having seen the American officer, Deluca, and other leaders we returned to Cansiglio. The great question there was how, with the number of men available, twenty or less, we could best ensure our safety. The nearest battalion was two miles further from the road than we were, and this road was used daily by German trucks either going through to Alpago, where there were garrisons, or engaging in the transport of wood. On some days there were as many as twelve of these loading the timber which was being felled a bare quarter mile from our barracks. We made a practice of sending out two standing patrols before dawn. These were relieved every two hours until eleven o'clock, when we considered the danger over for the day. Patrolling was bitterly cold work, especially the dawn patrol; but volunteers for that were never lacking because they were allowed a grappa ration. These patrols covered all the likely lines of approach. Merely by listening we could usually tell what was going on for some miles around, for in the still cold air of the forest sound carried amazingly. On one occasion, during an attack on the Nievo Battalion, we heard the shouted orders of their commander and thought they came from some Fascist patrol about to attack us. We imagined the place reasonably secure against surprise, but early in January, after our mission had left, a party of Germans in snow-suits approached unseen and unheard from an unlikely direction. Had they held their fire they might have captured Nannetti Division H.Q. lock, stock, and barrel, but they opened up at 300 yards range, giving the alarm to everybody and hitting no one. Except for a spare wireless set and some reserve food which were buried, everything was lost and both barracks were burnt. Without doubt this must have been the work of a spy well informed about the locality and the dispositions of the patrols.

Another security measure required everyone to pack and be ready to move by seven o'clock. The enforcement of this wholesome rule demanded more discipline than the partisans possessed. At that hour it was barely light and very cold, and I have seldom met anyone so reluctant to get out of bed, even in milder conditions, as the Divisional

Staff—there might not have been an enemy within 100 miles of them. If at nine o'clock, when I came back from the kitchen, my cry of 'Waky, Waky' met with their unfailing response, 'yet a little sleep, a little slumber, a little folding of the hands to sleep', I immediately lit the stove which smoked abominably. The acrid fumes soon penetrated to the top tier of bunks where Milo and the higher ranks slept, who would seldom hold out for long after that. The mission occupied a modest portion of the lower tier, where we lay cheek by jowl in comparative comfort except for the disturbing presence immediately above of the Second Murderer, who snored. As Mr Bulstrode remarked: 'The society of a grampus delights nobody and offends me.' The presence of so many more or less unwashed bodies in close proximity inevitably occasioned the usual troubles. We longed for a change of clothing.

Patrols, ciphering, chopping wood, fetching water and hay for 'Giulieta' the mule, and visiting the battalions kept us occupied. At night there were often stores and recharged batteries to be brought up from the Forest Guard house, which was used as a sort of entrepôt by us at night and by the Germans during the day. Since our move into the barracks the dropping ground had been changed to the new Nievo Battalion location. Our luck, however, remained the same. On 2 December two planes dropped their loads, including our wireless stores and three months' mail, to a Fascist garrison ten miles from Cansiglio. This tragedy naturally disgusted the partisans. Visitors from the plains described to them with a wealth of loving detail how the Fascists were smoking English cigarettes and eating English chocolate, while they busied themselves stripping and reassembling handsome new Bren guns and Stens for use against the partisans. We were angry and depressed, refusing to believe such a fantastic story until a signal told us it was only too true. But, in spite of this deplorable record of failure, we remained good friends. That we were in the same destitute condition and that we shared equally their guards, patrols, and fatigues, were possibly points in our favour. We could offer no plausible explanation for this unbroken record of failure, for the partisans found it difficult to believe that the R.A.F., in whom they had such confidence, could be so incompetent.

During Christmas week we enjoyed a spell of exceptionally good weather—fine days and clear cold nights. Preparations for Christmas were in full swing, and for our part we hoped to make the partisans the sort of present we had been waiting for for nearly four months—a good load of arms and stores. A few scraggy hares and hens, quantities of wine, brandy, and grappa, were brought up; the wife of the head forester baked prodigious cakes; but no plane was signalled. Christmas Day opened promisingly with a generous tot of 'zabaglione' (a sort of flip made from cognac and egg) for breakfast. For dinner we had a very special *pasticcio di maccheroni, ricotta del Cansiglio, chicken à la Bolognese* (the cook hailed from Bologna), and several hunks of delightfully soggy creamy cake. The usual toasts were drunk and speeches made; and then Ross, Gatti, and the more educated members of the Divisional Staff, excluding, that is, Tarzan, the Second Murderer, and myself, began a long and exciting discussion on 'What is Art?'

All things come to those who know how to wait. On Boxing Day the great event occurred. Two planes were signalled, and off we went at dusk through the deep snow to light the signal fires. When all available partisans, excluding those needed for patrols and guards, were standing by, we had about fifty men to handle the expected five tons of stores. We sat round the fires, as we had done so many times, in a mood of cynical expectancy trying hard to think of something fresh that might go wrong. This time there was no mistake. The leading plane (we heard later the crew was Polish) was over us almost as soon as we heard it. It flew straight on to the target and dropped its load within 200 yards of the fires. The other followed and then we got to work. Some Christmas comforts, including several bottles of inferior whisky which had been scattered promiscuously among the various loads, were soon discovered by the partisans, but in spite of this handicap we had nearly everything hidden by three o'clock. One body, a wireless operator for the other mission, dropped wide of the fires but made a comfortable landing in deep snow. Perhaps he had been priming himself with what Jorrocks called 'jumping powder', or perhaps the men who retrieved him from his snow bed had been administering our whisky as a restorative, but when I first saw him, he too, like a few of the partisans, was not quite sure whether he was in Jericho or Jerusalem.

We slept by the fires until dawn, when the search for missing packages was continued. The patrols reported that all was quiet below. No inquisitive Huns or Fascists from Alpago or Vittorio put in an appearance, though they must have been aware that a 'drop' had taken place. And then, as if to emphasise what none of us had ever doubted, that 'drops' were to be 'like angel's visits few and far between', we recorded another failure two nights later. A plane was signalled. We sat round the fires until midnight, singing songs of expectation and listening to a plane, which may or may not have been ours, circling questingly in the distance, and then trooped sorrowfully home through the snow to bed.

Our mission at last was free to depart for the Belluno Division whom we feared would by now be in despair. We had done little enough for the Nannetti Division, and for the last three months of 1944 they had achieved little themselves except to keep a few enemy troops preoccupied on their account. The insecurity of the partisans' position and our inability to supply their urgent needs had imposed almost complete inactivity. This state is always demoralising, and upsets partisans much more than it does regular troops, who have routine duties and training programmes to keep them up to the mark. Nevertheless, their keenness was undiminished and had withstood the drastic reorganisation, the impact of winter, and much disappointment. In many respects they were stronger. Experience in living and fighting in winter conditions had been gained, and they had learnt how to allow the storm of a 'rastrallamento' to blow itself out more or less harmlessly. We left the Nannetti Division in good heart, fully assured that when better times came the little we had sown would bear good fruit.

CHAPTER XVI

THE BELLUNO DIVISION

❖

I MUST CONFESS THAT WHEN I decided to leave the Nannetti Division to the other mission, I was aware that north of the Piave we should be nearer the Dolomites. Living in a forest in winter has its own particular charm. Perhaps this can be best appreciated when you are one of 'the hunted', for the feeling of security it gives compensates for the absence of sunlight and the monotonous and limited outlook. But after some weeks in Cansiglio the sense of confinement became oppressive, and I greeted a clearing in the forest with the delight that a townsman greets an open space, free from bricks and mortar, in the heart of a town.

Though we left Cansiglio on 29 December we did not establish contact with the Belluno Division until 9 January 1945. The Tollot Brigade, located south of the Piave, was being harried by the Germans, who had posted numerous small garrisons throughout the area. Their communications with the north bank of the river were therefore interrupted. We lived for a week with the Brigade Commander in the company of other birds of passage—a Frenchman, who was subsequently shot, a Yugo-Slav, two Poles, and a Russian. This was no happy band of brothers. The Poles hated the Russian, and, being in opposite political camps, concealed any love they may have had for each other; the Frenchman disliked the Italians and the Italians distrusted him; while the Yugo-Slav despised everyone, including ourselves, except the Russian.

We once more met Deluca, who was now accompanied by a Major Abba, the recently appointed Zone Commander, whose function was to control and co-ordinate the two Garibaldi Divisions and the two or three non-Garibaldi Brigades in the Belluno Zone. They pressed for a mission to be allotted to Zone H.Q., but I thought this was premature as at that time H.Q. consisted of Abba and Deluca, who were living nomadic lives on bicycles, 'travelling', as they said, 'in furs'. Moreover, it was of the first importance that we should join the Belluno Division, who had been so neglected, and supply them with arms before they became disgusted with us.

We finally crossed the Piave on the night of the 7th and marched across country to the foothills west of Belluno where we slept in a cowshed. The presence of thirty cows made blankets superfluous. Our only adventure was when a German cyclist patrol passed close by us. In our anxiety we took it to be a patrol, but it may equally have been some men with late passes returning from the Belluno cinema. A heavy snowfall next day, and the nervousness of the 'padrone' and his family at the dangerous guests secreted in their cowshed, kept us indoors during the day; but at night we moved on to another cowshed near the village of Bolzano where we at last met Franco, the Divisional Commander. Conditions here were very different. The partisans lived for the most part in the villages as civilians, sleeping out in caves and holes. Their activity was confined to the cleaning up of spies and informers, of which there had been a great many. The Belluno G.A.P. under Carlo, formerly Commander of the Pisacane Brigade, was engaged in Belluno itself in eliminating prominent Fascists. Bolzano was only a couple of miles from Belluno where a large garrison and S.S. Headquarters were stationed, but so far it had escaped their attentions, and the people were intensely loyal to the partisans. Though it was desirable to arrange a drop somewhere near Divisional H.Q., we did not think it expedient in view of the close proximity of Belluno. There would be the risk of losing anything dropped, and in the event of a 'rastrallamento' there could be no refuge in the snow-covered mountains. Also, if Bolzano were compromised, the whole divisional organisation would be disrupted. We therefore decided to find a dropping ground near Forno, where sorties could be received in comparative security. There would be obvious difficulties about the subsequent distribution of stores, but Franco thought that might be managed by civilian trucks.

The Fratelli Fenti Brigade, who occupied the Forno area, had to be warned of our intentions. Until they were ready for us we were to live in the strictest seclusion. Accordingly, the same night, our kit was loaded on to a sledge drawn by two oxen and we started for what was called 'the cave'. At the entrance to a narrow valley we left the sledge, shouldered our rucksacks, and began one of the most perilous night walks I have ever indulged in. Along the precipitous valley side a sketchy path, deep in powder snow, pursued its tortuous way, around trees, past jutting boulders, and across frozen gullies. 'He who stands upon a slippery place makes nice of no vile hold to stay him up.' We clutched with bare hands at branches, brambles, and glazed rocks, until our fingers froze and the sweat of fright and effort dripped from our faces. At midnight we reached a high cliff which overhung slightly. Under two of the best overhangs the partisans had rigged up a kitchen and sleeping quarters with the help of Italian bivouac sheets. It was a wild spot. The stream, frozen into silence, lay some 500 ft. below, its opposite bank rising abruptly to the rock and snow of Monte Serva 5000 ft. above. Beyond our bivouac the cliff was split by a frightful chasm whose smooth walls, at their base only a few yards apart, almost met 100 ft. above. By daylight it was a strange place, by night an eerie one; and much more so when we found that it served as an execution ground for spies.

Here, with three partisans, we lived for three weeks like hermits. Sometimes, growing weary, like that profane monk of Algeria, 'we gave a yell and jumped out of our cell'. In other words, we left our camp to spend an evening in the hamlet of Gioz with the family of Burrasco, one of our fellow hermits; but the perilous path, which had always to be traversed at night, was a powerful deterrent to too frequent breaches of security. On those rare occasions then, having reached the road-head, Burrasco would borrow a sledge from the nearest farm and the three of us would pile in, with him in front as pilot. As 'burrasco' is Italian for 'storm', it was a suitable *nom de guerre*, for he was of a vehement, headlong nature, and he urged the willing sledge accordingly. He was an ex-Alpini soldier of dashing appearance and manner, great among women, and great in war, too. Later he was severely wounded in the chest, and when we saw him again in Belluno after the surrender he was but a shadow of his former swashbuckling self. This mile run through the cold night air down the winding smooth-surfaced track to Gioz was, to say the least of it, stimulating. We spent the evening in a small kitchen, usually crowded to capacity with partisans, while Burrasco's mother, a delightful, homely, stout woman, plied us with food and drink. Her younger son, a nice-looking lad, was an active partisan too, but was not known to be one. He was thus able to go into Belluno to buy stores and to arrange for forged documents when needed. Once he went into the hospital there to commiserate with a prominent Fascist who was lying at death's door as the result of a murderous attack by Carlo's amateur assassins.

Pulling the loaded sledge back was less exhilarating, and by the time we had done that and overcome the 'via pericolosa', we were sobriety itself no matter what our condition when we set out.

One other diversion I had was to climb Monte Serva (*c.* 7000 ft.). It took me about seven hours and, although it was not a difficult matter, even in winter, it had the salutary effect of astonishing the natives—even 'The Storm' was impressed. There was a bitter wind on the summit ridge where I had to cut a few steps with an axe borrowed from Burrasco, who thus had a vicarious interest in the climb. Like most easily accessible mountains, Monte Serva had not escaped the enormous wooden cross with which the Italian priest loves to decorate any handy summit.

Our departure was delayed by the necessity of organising escorts and stopping places for the four-night journey to Forno. This was not so simple a matter, because beyond Agordo we had to use the main road. After one false start we set out on 30 January, stopping the first night in a house at the entrance of the Canal del Mis, which was then the H.Q. of the Pisacane Brigade. Their commander was killed the same day by an S.S. patrol on the road near Bolzano. We took with us as divisional representative, Carduci, a very fine type of partisan. We met him first on Pietena, where we admired his activity and liked his ways. He was most unfortunately killed on the last day when attacking an armoured car near Belluno with hand grenades.

The Canal del Mis must be one of the deepest and narrowest rock defiles in the Dolomites. Nevertheless, it is traversed by a motor-road. In some places it is hewn out between the limestone wall and the torrent; in others the rock is tunnelled. The number of excellent roads cutting through the Dolomites in all directions always astonished us. First thoughts would suggest that this was ideal country for partisan warfare; in practice the number of roads was a serious menace. The Dolomites do not run in ranges like the Alps, but are formed of half a dozen isolated groups of mountains separated by deep, narrow, flattish valleys. They are thus extremely accessible—I am not thinking of the tops—and sitting in a car one can almost touch the living rock at their

Dolomite scenery:
S. Martino di Castrozza (1,444 m.), behind the Gruppa delle Pale (circa 2,500 m.)

bases. Though this is literally true for the Canal del Mis, elsewhere, perhaps, it is an exaggeration; but in better-known places than the Mis valley, Agordo or San Martino for example, the great carved, fluted, many-hued rock faces, two or three thousand feet in height, stand so close to and rise so cleanly from the valley that they have not that quality of aloofness that the big mountain ranges possess.

We were fortunate in that we met no patrols in the Mis, for even on foot it is often not easy to get off the road. There was considerable evidence that the Germans were busily engaged in making emplacements and dug-outs for a defensive line. In one of the long rock galleries we passed a concrete-mixing machine which our escort obligingly promised to throw off the road into the river on their way back. At dawn we reached the village of Rivamonte where we stopped in a wooden house of alarming cleanliness, owned by a very active old lady who was a pillar of the local resistance movement. Her wireless set, the only one left in the village, daily attracted a large crowd to listen to the news. After the straw bunks, hay-lofts, cowsheds, and rock shelters which had been our portion for so long, one needed assurance and a certain indifference to the impression left behind to make use of the beds and sheets provided.

From there we descended into the Agordo valley, striking the main highway just above the town where there was a garrison and a flood-lit power station. These places were heavily guarded. At night low-power searchlights swept the vicinity searching for saboteurs. At midnight we stopped at an 'albergo' facing the main road. Instead of merely having 'one for the road' and pushing on as we expected, we were astonished to find that we were to pass the next day there. From an upper window, discreetly curtained, we had the pleasure of watching staff cars, fatigue parties, and civilian lorries pass along the road beneath us. At the sight of these novelties we experienced all the sensations of a 'hick', who, with the straw still in his hair, had just arrived in town, and the rarer pleasures of a spy observing his enemy at close quarters. One or two cars stopped at our inn, and then our pleasure stopped too. We even worked a very successful wireless schedule with an aerial in the loft while the Germans made merry on the floor below.

The final stage to Forno was tricky. We had to follow the main road for six miles to Cencenighe before turning off on to a secondary road.

Here we had to elude a garrison and a searchlight. We started the night badly by meeting a truck unexpectedly—an incident which cost me a piece of the seat of my trousers, which was torn away as we leapt off the road down the revetment. Our entrance to Cencenighe resembled a rehearsal for the 'Dance of the Gnomes' by a nervous and very third-rate caste. In single file we tiptoed over a bridge past a lighted house, while the producer of our ballet, the leader, with muted voice and gestures of terrifying intensity, implored the silence we were only too anxious to give. Having turned the corner of the house we had to plough our way through three feet of soft snow lying on the wooded slope on the outskirts of the town. Whenever the searchlight of the power station turned its inquisitive beam in our direction, which it did frequently, we dropped like one man. Carduci, who wore a very hairy coat and who was of very short stature, would often disappear altogether in the snow, to reappear a moment later looking like a small, angry bear, emerging prematurely from hibernation. An hour or more of this very hard labour brought us, still undiscovered, to the far end of the town where, so deep was the snow, we only found we were walking on the cemetery wall by tumbling off it into the cemetery. Another detour over a high spur was needed to avoid the barracks, and then we more or less fell down a steep slope on to the Forno road. There the usual cowshed was waiting for us, but we only stayed long enough to compose ourselves with grappa before putting the loads on to a sledge and beginning the last stage up the Val di Gares. The Val di Gares is a charming little valley which runs south from Forno for five miles to terminate in an imposing rock cirque below the Altipiano delle Pale di San Martino. Up on the Altipiano are the peaks of the San Martino group, which rise to 10,000 ft. The valley floor is nowhere more than half a mile wide, and both sides rise steeply to seven or eight thousand feet. A more difficult target could hardly be found. In the first place it was not easy to pick up and, secondly, a plane could not come down to obtain the necessary accuracy of aim. If the drop was inaccurate, the amount of snow and the nature of the country would prevent the recovery of the loads. For the dropping ground we chose an open space, clear of pines, about three miles up from Forno, and arranged with Base to use delay-action parachutes. If this were done the plane could fly high enough to clear all the nearby peaks, say seven to eight thousand feet above the floor of the valley, and at the same time ensure that the parachutes did not open until only a few hundred feet above the ground. We had had no experience of these, but it was that or nothing.

While awaiting the event we lived in a little wooden cabin, cunningly built under a rock overhang, 1000 ft. above the valley. Two partisans came up daily from Forno with supplies, using skis up the sleigh track as far as the dropping ground.

Most of the Forno men were good on skis, the Brigade Commander, Della Nera, being very expert. As perhaps was only natural, the men from these high valleys seemed more virile and tougher than any we had yet met. In marching, carrying loads, or digging snow, they were eager and enduring.

The first plane came on the night of 13 February, ten days after our arrival. In order to maintain secrecy we had made no preparations on the dropping ground, so, in the few hours between the warning signal and the expected time of arrival, we had to work hard. Signal fires had to be sited, the holes dug, and several sledge loads of wood brought up. The men worked with a will, shovelling away the snow with their long-handled shovels until they reached the earth three feet below. The wood arrived, small fires were lit, and we settled down to wait in no easy frame of mind. Would the plane find us, hidden away as we were in this deep valley? And would the delay-action parachutes work? These were the questions we repeatedly asked ourselves. At last there came the welcome cry of 'Rumore'. Sure enough it was a plane. The partisans had provided as a signal lamp the giant headlight of a truck. With this young searchlight Pallino got to work, almost beside himself with excitement when he got an answering flick from the plane. Seemingly miles high, it made repeated wide turns until we almost thought he was not going to 'drop'; and then, with the sound of rushing wind, there suddenly appeared floating above the fires a beautiful array of parachutes and containers. It was a first-class shot at a very awkward target. The partisans worked fiercely, up to their waists in snow, and by dawn everything had been sledged down to Forno and hidden. Four nights later two more planes made almost equally successful drops to the great delight of all concerned.

Having thus received fairly substantial quantities of arms and explosives, we were now anxious to get back to the Belluno area to see that they were used to the best advantage. Moreover, as the weather in February had been so extremely fine and warm, the snow was now fast disappearing from the southern slopes, and it seemed probable that by March we should be able to find a dropping ground that was more accessible. Having advised Divisional H.Q. of this we had to wait for ten days while arrangements were being made for our return. During this time I amused myself on the ridge above the hut. With the aid of a pair of snow-shoes I could move fairly freely, and presently I discovered a long gully which proved to be the key to the climbing of Cimon della Stia and the other bumps on the main ridge in spite of the existing snow conditions. This had been swept by an avalanche which had left behind it a bed of hard snow in which I had to kick or cut steps with an axe lent me by Della Nera. So pleasing was this gully and so greatly did it facilitate movement, that I even entertained ideas of climbing the Mulaz or Focobon itself, but after a narrow escape from being taken for a ride on an avalanche my ardour cooled. I was alone on these occasions, for Ross, although young, strong, and in full possession of his faculties, mental and physical, was strangely inappreciative of the mountains which surrounded us. At times this indifference verged on hostility, and only the presence of Huns in the valley could persuade him to forsake it for the mountains. Perhaps his attitude towards climbing might be likened to that of the Johannesburg Jew towards shooting lions. Of him it is related that when asked by some keen big-game shot why he never hunted lions, he replied that he saw no reason to as he had not lost any.

The rapid disappearance of the snow enabled us to return to Rivamonte by the Cesurette Pass (*c.* 5000 ft.) which led into the Val di San Lucano, thereby avoiding the main road. Walking down this valley the mountaineer has eyes for nothing but the magnificent tower of Monte Agner on one side and the gaunt yellowish cliffs of the Pale di San Lucano on the other. As the sun sank behind the pass, an endless variation of colour and form played upon these two mighty bastions. The yellows turned to a warm terra-cotta, to grey, and then to black, as the shadow of some isolated tower, hitherto invisible against the face, was cast upon the parent mass behind. It is one of the beauties of the Dolomites, some compensation for the absence of the glory of glacier and snow, that the rocks reflect with a warmth and richness of their own the most delicate variations of the sky.

At Rivamonte, which we reached on 1 March, we met unexpected difficulties. The Canal del Mis was now constantly patrolled, the passes were not yet open, and the sole means of communication with the Belluno area was the main Agordo road. A bus service was still running from Agordo, by means of which the girl couriers kept us in touch with Divisional H.Q. whom we kept advised of our plans. One of the reasons for this enemy activity was that, on the night of our arrival in Rivamonte, all telegraph and telephone lines in the Zone had been cut by partisans and some thirty miles of wire totally removed.

We spent a week in Rivamonte in strict confinement, for Germans from Agordo visited the village frequently on foraging expeditions. Having been advised that two attempts to send our escort through the Mis valley had failed, we fell to discussing other means of getting down. The suggestion of going by bus or truck dressed as civilians was vetoed 'nemine contradicente'. Because of my beard and the intrinsic slovenliness of a well-worn British battledress, I was assured frequently that if I kept my mouth shut I could pass as an Italian labourer—a wood-cutter. Of Ross I was doubtful. He spoke Italian well, but though no one would suspect him of looking very English, his appearance might arouse curiosity as to what country he did profess to belong. Gatti, who was frequently mistaken for an Englishman by his own countrymen, had fortunately gone on a week's leave to his home in Trento. Pallino had not to be considered because he had already assumed civilian clothes, and had more or less dissociated himself from us except when working his wireless set. It was our opinion that if we were caught wearing uniform, there was only a likelihood of our being shot, whereas if we dressed as civilians there could be no doubt at all as to what would happen. In discussing this hypothetical question the partisans may have thought we were unduly sensitive about our own safety, but Ross and I took the view that it would be a mistake to give the Germans the chance of resolving these doubts for us merely to get to Belluno quickly. The upshot was that they arranged to take us in a wood-truck, concealed under the wood. We sketched out the general idea; the details were left to their undoubted ingenuity.

The first attempt on the night of 3 March failed owing to the big ten-ton lorry stalling on the icy road up to the village. We could have gone down to it, but we should have had to do without the essential shroud of wood which was lying in Rivamonte waiting to be loaded. On the 8th a smaller truck arrived in the village before dark. The civilian driver was extremely nervous on account of the compromising freight he was to carry, for whatever happened to us the Germans would show no mercy to him. At dusk we went to the loaded truck waiting for us outside the village. They had built a lidless, open-ended coffin, big enough to hold two bodies and a few rucksacks. This had been laid upside down on the floor and then covered with two or three tons of wood. When the side of the lorry was let down we were able to insinuate ourselves, head-foremost lying on our backs, into the coffin. The raising of the side was the equivalent, so to speak, of screwing down the lid. Thus we were driven boldly, but at a suitable hearse-like pace, down the Agordo-Belluno highway past several German block-posts. At these the lorry was stopped and the driver's papers inspected, while the beam of a torch shone cursorily over the innocent load of wood. But no one suspected the presence of the nigger, or niggers, in the woodpile. A good example, I think, of 'exfiltration'.

At a point in the Piave valley an escort had been arranged to meet the truck to help us quickly off the road with our loads. When the truck stopped and noises indicated that the side was about to be let down, we, of course, had no notion as to where we were or who was about to exhume the bodies. Someone laid hold of my feet and dragged me out, and Ross followed in a cascade of rucksacks and Marlin automatics. A figure, which I now recognised as the driver, told us in Italian to 'scran', and off the lorry went. The headlights of several cars coming along the road not far away explained the driver's haste to be gone. With a muttered word of thanks and a handshake we followed his example, staggering away with the loads to the cover of a nearby cemetery. Coffins and everything associated with them seemed unavoidable that night. We were at the rendezvous all right, but though we waited and whistled cautiously for some time no one came. We gave it up and pushed on alone to Bolzano where we were challenged and nearly shot by our impulsive friend 'Thunderstorm'.

THE BELLUNO DIVISION

With winter now behind and the expectation of great events not far ahead, the partisans were more confident. Divisional H.Q. was now living in a small farmhouse up the hill above Gioz. A new policy of 'bunkers'—or 'boonkers' as the Italians called them—had been instituted on a hint from Regional Command. This consisted of a system of cleverly concealed dug-outs, individual or collective, in which everyone slept or went to ground in the event of a 'rastrallamento'. It was a dodge which had been worked very successfully during the difficult winter months on the plains. The one we dug at H.Q. was a good example. In front of the farmhouse was a small terraced field, with a dry stone supporting wall about six foot high. A hole twelve foot by twelve foot by six foot deep was dug in the field near the terrace wall, the inside was lined with boards, and a timber roof added, leaving about 4 foot headroom inside. On top of this the earth was replaced, the field was levelled, and potatoes planted. A small passage-way was made in the dry wall, so built that by replacing two or three big stones at the entrance the wall appeared unbroken. Every night we moved ourselves and our belongings into this, being careful to leave no trace in the farmhouse of our occupation. We were thereupon sealed in by the son of the old man who lived in the farm, and unsealed the next morning by the same hand if all was quiet. While we were there the perfection of the deception was never put to the test. Personally I should have been afraid of a dog scenting us and starting to scratch up the potato field.

The day we returned, the Chief of Staff of the division, a young ex-officer of Alpini who rejoiced in the *nom de guerre* 'Radiosa Aurora'— Shining Dawn—had brought off a highly successful coup, in the shape of a booby-trap, with some of the explosive devices we had got for them. On the Belluno rifle range he had erected two targets representing Hitler, with the adjuration 'Shoot Straight', and had decorated the butts with 'black' propaganda which had been sent us. One target was harmless, under the other he placed a few pounds of explosive and a pressure switch. The party which visited the range next morning for firing practice happened to be a large one with several officers and N.C.O.'s. Such, apparently, was the indignation of the officers, that instead of ordering the men to pull down the offending targets they did it themselves—with fatal consequences. Four officers and N.C.O.'s were killed and many injured. However, the German officers of the

Belluno S.S. were notorious for ruthlessness. Ten prisoners from the gaol, partisans and political suspects, were promptly taken up to the rifle range and hanged there on trees. Four more were hanged in the public square of Belluno a few days later as a reprisal for the shooting of a prominent Fascist by the Belluno G.A.P. At or about this time a total of thirty partisans were thus executed in the Belluno area.

A large proportion of the arms and explosives had been brought down from Forno in safety by the same simple expedient of concealing them under loads of wood. Nevertheless, much more was needed if the plans made for blocking all the roads in the Zone were to be effective, and if the Belluno Division were to be armed to the same extent as Nannetti. Since we left Cansiglio, the ball having been set rolling, planes came frequently. The Nannetti Division had had about forty consignments and was better off for automatic weapons than British or German troops. In view of the urgency, and of the fact that owing to the disappearance of the snow, movement was becoming possible, we decided to arrange for 'drops' near Bolzano, and also further down the Piave valley where our old friends of the Gramsci Brigade were again coming to life.

Meantime Abba and Deluca came to see us and once more raised the question of a mission for Zone H.Q. which was now established and functioning at Alpago, about midway between the two divisions. After some discussion I decided to go myself, leaving Ross to look after the Belluno Division. Since he could talk Italian fairly fluently I could take Gatti with a clear conscience. Another wireless operator was needed, so we arranged for one to be dropped at Cansiglio to which there was now almost a daily, or rather nightly, service of planes.

Much as I liked Abba and Deluca, and confident as I was in their judgement, and in the advisability of having a mission with Zone H.Q. which would have an important part to play when the Allies reached the Piave or when the Germans attempted to withdraw, I was loath to leave the division—the more so as we now had some arms and explosives to use. Though to a less degree, it is the same with partisans as it is in the army, the higher the formation the more it loses touch with realities—a loss which no amount of visiting can replace. However true it may be that a looker-on sees most of the game, I have not yet outgrown the preference for being in the thick of it rather than being relegated to

THE BELLUNO DIVISION

a seat in the grandstand, which is how the headquarters of a formation appears to me. The unreality and disparity of war as experienced at a remote headquarters and in a fighting unit must fill anyone there with a sense of uneasiness, and may well sicken one who grudges the pleasures and wishes to share the pains of the men who have to march and fight. In war personal preference is seldom consulted, but no doubt most of those who have the invidious and onerous task of directing a battle or organising victory would prefer a post of less responsibility, more fellowship, and more danger.

CHAPTER XVII

AT ZONE H.Q.—
THE LIBERATION OF BELLUNO

◆

Our new Italian operator was reported as ready to drop by 22 March. That night Gatti and I walked over to Alpago, escorted by some of Carlo's boys of the Belluno G.A.P. They were likely-looking lads and beguiled the journey with stories of their 'gangster' exploits in the streets of Belluno. Italians are excellent raconteurs, telling a story in the way that children love to have them told with a minute attention to detail and a wealth of appropriate gesture and sound effects. Gangster life and stories of 'rastrallamenti' lend themselves to this graphic method of description—no rifle is fired without the corresponding 'pom', no automatic comes into play without a prolonged 'b-r-r-r-r', while the hand grenades explode with a violence almost as alarming as the real thing. Most of them are natural orators, masters of debate, or at the least accomplished talkers, who can express as much with their hands as with their mouths, demolishing an opponent or charming their listeners with a perfectly timed wave of the arm or shrug of the shoulders.

We forded the Piave a mile above Belluno, the town which we had so often seen but never entered, the town whose liberation would be for the partisans the sign and seal of their final triumph. It had already borne with fortitude the Austrian occupation of 1917 and 1918, and was now suffering with undaunted hope and indomitable spirit a longer and more terrifying ordeal.

At a time of year when one would expect to find rivers in flood, I was surprised that on this occasion the Piave was not more than a foot deep. The reason was that the long dam at Soverzene was closed and most of the water was flowing down the five miles of canal to the Lago di San Croce, where there are the largest hydro-electric installations in Italy. The fall of 1050 ft. is distributed over five power stations with a total horse-power capacity of 300,000. It was assumed that the Germans before leaving Italy would do their utmost to wreck all power stations. One of the main tasks of the partisans, in conjunction with the officials of the Electric Companies, was to prevent this; but when it came to the point the Germans had neither the time nor the will to attempt any destruction anywhere.

We found Zone H.Q. established in a small farmhouse at the southern extremity of the Alpago district. This is an extensive area of rich, hilly farmland north of the Cansiglio forest and east of the San Croce lake. On the east and north it is hemmed in by an unbroken mountain wall beginning at Monte Cavallo, above the pass of that name, and ending with Monte Dolada which dominates the Piave valley at the point where it makes its right-angled bend north. The peaks on this long chain rise to seven or eight thousand feet, but are not true Dolomites. Our cottage was grandly situated 3000 ft. up, overlooking all the villages of Alpago. A stream which had its source on the slopes of Col Nudo (*c.* 8000 ft.) ran immediately below us, and on the far side its steep banks merged quickly into the steeper cliffs of Teverone, a more graceful but slightly lower peak than Col Nudo. To our north only a narrow belt of silver birch separated us from the long 7000 ft. ridge of Monte Dolada.

We had intended going straight on to Cansiglio to pick up the new operator, but we were held up for two days by reports of a 'rastrallamento' there. Meanwhile we made the acquaintance of the Zone H.Q. staff. In addition to Abba and Deluca there was Sergio, the Chief of Staff, an ex-Colonel of Alpini artillery; Rudi, who was one of the first, if not the first, to organise the resistance movement in Belluno where he was a bank manager; he was by politics a Socialist, was well known and respected, and formed an invaluable link between partisan H.Q. and the Committee of Liberation. He was nominated for and later elected as the first post-war Mayor of Belluno. There was also Toni, a clerk from Rudi's bank; Azeglio, a solicitor from Venice who acted as Intelligence Officer, and finally Attilio Tissi who worked mainly with the Committee of Liberation which met almost daily in the nearby village of Plois. He was a celebrated Italian rock-climber who gave his name to the 'Via Tissi', an excessively difficult route on Monte Agner. His most famous climb was on Civetta. This was what the Italians call a 'sesto grado', a climb of the most extreme severity (or 'the limit of human possibility'), entailing possibly fifteen hours of climbing on a 3000 ft. rock face with a liberal use of 'pitons' to overcome the overhangs which seem essential features of a 'sesto grado'.

On the night of the 25th, accompanied by Abba, we walked to Nannetti Division H.Q. which had now returned to its original locality on the edge of the forest above Vittorio Veneto. When we arrived it was actually down below in the plain, living in some perfectly concealed 'bunkers' near a village, while a 'rastrallamento' was in progress near the old dropping ground. This was but a half-hearted affair, for Nannetti were now very strong. A short time before they had ambushed and wiped out a party of seventy of the Black Brigade of the Fascist Republican Army. These men had just arrived from Venice, and were sent up the Cansiglio motor-road under the mistaken impression that the partisans were no longer a force to be reckoned with. Twenty were killed in the first volley, the rest captured and subsequently shot. This may seem cruel, but there was really no alternative. The guarding and the feeding of prisoners were extremely difficult, but, in spite of this, Zone H.Q. had set up a prisoner-of-war cage for a limited number. They actually succeeded in exchanging a few German prisoners for partisans, but there was no market for Fascists.

It was interesting to see all our old friends again, particularly in the happier conditions that now prevailed—vastly increased numbers with adequate arms and equipment, and, above all, no more snow. Most of them wore battle-dress and all were of high morale. Three separate dropping grounds were in use, the road leading to Cansiglio was mined, and a landing strip for evacuating airmen who had made forced landings was being prepared on the Cansiglio plain. Small actions against the roads and railways in the plains were carried out almost nightly.

It was not until a few nights later that our new wireless operator, Nicola, arrived. He was more amenable to discipline than Pallino, but not in the same class as a wireless operator. He frequently failed to make contact, and the deciphering of his messages, filling in the blanks and adjusting the corrupt parts of the text, was a fine exercise in imaginative writing. Fortunately traffic was not heavy and what there was was less important than when we were with division,

Two partisans in Belluno, 2 May 1945

Belluno Zone H.Q. Left to right:
Deluca (Commissar), Abba (Commander),
Sergio (Chief of Staff)

when we had sorties to worry about. But even 'top priority' signals, which at first sight are of stupendous gravity and urgency, will in time answer themselves.

The staff of Zone H.Q. was fully occupied. In addition to maintaining close liaison with the civil side of the movement through the C.L.N., and the general supervision of affairs in the Zone, they dealt with higher appointments, discipline, and the boundaries of brigade areas. These last were sometimes troublesome, because there were now three independent brigades directly under command of Zone who had to be kept in step with the Garibaldi formations. Political jealousies were a fruitful source of headaches for Zone H.Q. For example, a good but over-zealous battalion commander of one of the independent brigades caught and hanged a woman spy out of hand, whereupon the Communist party, professing to be grievously shocked at such brutality, demanded the offender's instant trial as a war criminal. The Intelligence branch at H.Q., as well as collating information received from the two divisions, had its own agents, one of whom was a sergeant-major in the S.S. at Belluno. Contact was maintained with divisions by a daily courier service of girls on bicycles, and less frequently with Regional Command at Padova which also sent round its own inspector once a month. Funds were received from the Central Committee at Milan through Padova and re-allocated to divisions and independent brigades. For the two divisions only general directives were issued and the plans co-ordinated. Each division had already made and submitted its own plan of action in the case of an enemy withdrawal or collapse. Zone H.Q. had no partisans for its own protection, but relied on early warnings of impending trouble and fleetness of foot. A very elaborate 'bunker' was under construction and had just been finished when the war ended.

My duties, therefore, partook of the nature of those of a *Maître d'Hotel*, who has to be on view but who seldom does anything so vulgar as work. As a matter of fact even this was not always necessary, so I went methodically to work climbing all the peaks within striking distance. In addition to those already mentioned there were Capel Grande, Monte Messer, and Monte Venal, all about 8000 ft. None were real Dolomites, yet in late March, when still carrying much snow in good condition, they afforded a lot of fun. Each could be climbed in the course of a long morning, and from most of them our H.Q. cottage could be seen, an advantage in the case of an alarm. Teverone was the most attractive. On the south-west face, which got little sun, there was the better part of 2000 ft. of snow for kicking or step-cutting, and on the rocky summit ridge there were two easy but pleasing pitches that one took *à cheval*.

These jaunts were of necessity solitary. For although the partisans lived among the mountains, sang beautiful songs about them, and liked hearing themselves called mountaineers (with or without the usual epithet 'hardy'), they would nevertheless have been dumbfounded at the thought of climbing one. Tissi was too busy, and in any case these could not be of much interest to one of 'sesto grado' calibre. On an Easter Monday expedition to Col Nudo, however, I had company.

As usual I started out alone. The Zone Commander Abba, lying on his back in the sun, unblushingly declared he was too busy; Gatti, with praiseworthy frankness, thought it was too far—admittedly there were 5000 ft. to climb. At this time of year there was no grass or hay on the higher slopes, and I was therefore surprised to see two people on a converging track obviously bound for the mountain. Before reaching the snow, I saw above me two others inspecting me through a pair of field-glasses. When I reached them I found they were carrying small rucksacks, a liberal assortment of hand grenades, a Sten, and a Mauser rifle. Knowing that the partisans were allergic to mountains I wondered who they were. Had total war been declared on the chamois? Was it the Easter Meet of the Alpago Alpine Club? Or had they merely come up to cool their heads in the snow after the festivity of Easter Sunday? For, as Michael Finsbury remarked of another solemn occasion, the Italian 'festa' is 'serious business and requires a great deal of drink'. But whatever might be their errand, clothed as I was in nothing but a pair of trousers and carrying nothing more dangerous than an ice-axe, the advantage and the first move lay with them.

The very few Italian words I have are seldom understood by those to whom they are addressed, nevertheless we exchanged the usual question. They claimed to be partisans, but I left them to guess what I was and uncommonly hard they must have found it. It was necessary to be cautious. Spies were still common, and the Germans had recently

Outside the Prefettura Belluno, 2 May 1945: Sergio, Chief of Staff of Belluno Zone, and author

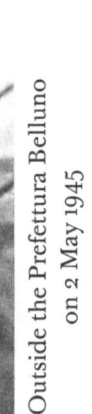

Outside the Prefettura Belluno on 2 May 1945

begun experiments with gangs of what were called 'contrabanditi', namely Germans or Fascists going about in small parties disguised as partisans. This was not, by the way, a difficult disguise to assume. Whiskers, an Alpini beard, or at any rate some hair on the face, and a total lack of uniformity of dress, were the prime essentials. Trust no one was, therefore, the watchword: 'I am suspect, thou art suspect, he is suspect.'

They were bound for the Valbona pass which led into the Barcis valley to the east. My route to Col Nudo actually traversed the pass, which is a high one, but when I started they moved off in the direction of another and lower col. The veteran of the party had been represented to me as a guide, and though their route did not look promising, I assumed that they knew what they were about.

From the pass some 1200 ft. of snow led almost directly to the summit. In spite of the hot sun the snow remained in good enough condition to climb without using the snow-shoes I had brought. 'Fatiguing but repaying' was how Baedeker might have described it. To the north was the tangled forest of Dolomite peaks, rejoicing gloriously in the bright colouring of a spring day and the scanty remnants of their winter mantle; to the south lay the green and peaceful plains, with the merest hint of the Adriatic beyond. Some fighter-bombers roaring up the Piave valley struck a note of discord. On leaving the summit I found the snow in excellent condition for a sitting glissade. I must have come down that 1200 ft. to the pass in less than a minute. In parentheses, and for the benefit of the serious student of military equipment, I may remark that the battle-dress made in America withstood this sort of fair wear and tear better than the British makes, which by 1945 were little more than shoddy.

As I slowed up just above the pass I heard voices. There on an opposing pinnacle above the pass, to which there was obviously no descent, I beheld the four travellers wistfully regarding the haven where they would be. To tell them they were on the wrong road was merely another glimpse of the obvious, but no sooner had I begun to impart this piece of gratuitous information than they turned and fled. I too went down.

A few days later I heard their story at second hand, for they were, in fact, partisans from a neighbouring village. They had set out on their lawful occasions to cross the Valbona Pass, as they had said, but my appearance (I mean my appearance on the scene) had so staggered them that in order to part company as quickly as possible they were driven from their course and to the attempt of a very forlorn hope. The panic which had seized them had evidently had a shattering effect on the guide's judgement; but whether they had taken me for an S.S. Obersturmführer or merely a late survival of the now almost extinct Abominable Snowman Dolomiticus, I was unable to discover.

The final Allied offensive opened slowly. The Germans contested every inch of ground and no spectacular advance was made in the opening phases. It had always been my opinion that if the Germans stood and fought where they were, with the bridgeless Po behind them, and were beaten, they would never be able to get away. They were short of transport and petrol, and they no longer had sufficient troops to keep their lines of retreat open in the face of attack by partisans. This view was a great solace to Zone H.Q. who ruefully contemplated the Piave valley becoming a battlefield with themselves in an uncomfortable position in the German front line.

The Germans did not crack until the third week of April when an American column breaking through raced ahead to capture Verona, the vital communication centre for the Brenner route. We heard of this on the night of the 26th on the Italian news broadcast at 10.30 p.m., whereupon Zone H.Q. sent orders to the two divisions to start blocking the roads in their areas. The following morning we moved to a small village called Arsie, from where we had good observation over the two main highways—one from Vittorio Veneto crossing the Piave at the bridge of Ponte Nelli Alpi and then going northwards up the Piave valley, and the other route from Belluno which joined the first beyond the bridge. It was unlucky that the break-through coincided with a break in the weather, which from now until the end remained wet and misty.

On the first day we counted some fifty vehicles on the road, which was patrolled by an armoured car, but by the 29th all traffic from Vittorio Veneto had ceased. In front of the Nannetti Division was a vast accumulation of transport which had been halted south of the town and which was now under attack from the partisans and from the few fighter-bombers able to fly. Traffic was still passing northwards from

Belluno. One source of this flow was the Piave valley route south of Feltre, which a Brigade of Nannetti in whose area it was had failed to block. In their eagerness to reach the town whose liberation meant so much to them, there was a tendency among the partisans north and south of the river to attack the Germans in and around Belluno instead of concentrating on the traffic on the road.

By the 30th all small garrisons south of the Piave had withdrawn or surrendered, but Belluno was full of Germans, who still controlled the road on the north bank. Our H.Q. had now moved down to an inn close to the main road, only about half a mile from the Ponte Nelli Alpi bridge, and Abba and Deluca were in contact with the German General in Belluno, trying to persuade him to surrender. The rest of us were just sitting down to some food when a report came in that some Germans were preparing to blow the bridge. The bridge was of no use to the Germans, the road having been blocked long since beyond Vittorio, but it was of great value to the 8th Army, a small column of which was already at Treviso. Gatti and I, with a partisan, hurried off to the bridge to find all quiet. The only signs of life were a few Italian refugees returning from Austria. At this point the Piave flows through a narrow rock gorge bridged by a single steel and concrete arch supporting the roadway below. Underneath the roadway, close to the water, was a small footbridge for inspection purposes which was reached by some twenty stone steps cut in the rock of the north bank of the gorge. Wishing to make quite sure that no demolition charges had been laid we crossed the bridge. I climbed over a little iron gate and began descending the steps in order to have a good look at the abutments. I had got about half-way down when a machine-gun opened up from the south side with vindictive accuracy. Bullets flattened themselves on the steps and the acrid smell of stone dust filled the air. To run up the steps, fall over the gate, and lie down behind the wall bordering the road, was a matter of seconds. Gatti and the partisan were already behind the wall, the latter, with his hat hoisted on his rifle, shouting at the top of his voice. We only needed a German truck to come down from the Belluno road to see what was happening to complete the tableau. At last the gentleman with the machine-gun, assuming that we were all dead or suspecting that he had been too hasty, took his finger off the trigger. Gatti and I prudently remained prone, but the partisan bravely stood up and continued addressing his remarks to a hedgerow about 300 yards from the bridge. The machine-gun crew then stood up and the commander came down to survey the damage. He was full of apologies when he found out who we were, but I could only compliment him on his good shooting and his vigilance.

The same afternoon, 30 April, we got in touch with Vittorio Veneto by telephone. A column consisting of one squadron of the 27th Lancers and a motorised company of the Rifle Brigade had just arrived. I suggested that they should move up that night to block the Belluno-Longarone road along which traffic was still escaping. This was now the only road on which traffic was moving northwards, and even this was blocked beyond Longarone. The reply was indefinite as the colonel commanding the column was at Treviso and would have to be consulted before action could be taken.

We waited by the roadside until midnight when, as no column had come, Deluca took me to Vittorio on a captured German motor-bike. The major in command of the column said he had now got orders to establish a road-block north of Ponte Nelli Alpi and would start at 05.30.

By then Deluca had discarded the motor-bike in favour of a small car (he was an energetic 'snapper-up of unconsidered trifles') and in this we went on ahead of the column as far as the bridge, where we met Abba. He had just returned from another meeting with the Germans in Belluno, who were apparently in no mind for surrendering to the partisans, but who, he thought, would readily surrender to the British. The column arrived and Deluca and I in our tiny Fiat took a less prominent place behind the very large armoured car leading the column. At the 'T' junction where the Vittorio road met the road from Belluno, we ran head-on into a long stream of German transport coming from Belluno. The armoured car opened fire with its Browning and the Germans leapt out of their trucks, not knowing whether to put up their hands or to run. Most of them ran, while the armoured car continued to spray the road and the neighbouring fields, and to pick off individual trucks with its 2 pr. They got such satisfaction out of it that they found it hard to stop, but after a few thousand rounds had been fired silence reigned once more and the badly frightened Germans began to crawl out of the ditches like beetles after a thunderstorm.

Belluno Piazza and the Palace of the Prefettura

Belluno Prefettura on right

Marshalling the prisoners and collecting their arms was a difficult job for such a small force. The infantry, who were in the rear of the column, were a long time in arriving, and as far as one could see the enemy transport stretched in an almost unbroken line back to Belluno about three miles away. The vehicles, motor and horse-drawn, were loaded to the axle with men, food and loot. A gigantic petrol bowser was full, not of petrol, but of cigarettes.

Most of the Germans cringed, making no bones about handing over their pistols and automatics, and begging to be allowed to take their personal kit out of the trucks. The back seats of our car and of Abba's were already piled high with Luger pistols. But further along the road we ran into trouble. At a small crossroads where there were a few houses, the leading armoured car stopped. I had heard a single shot, which might have been from a pistol, but I thought no more of it. An 88 mm. gun had been abandoned in the middle of the road, and I busied myself getting some civilians to help to push it off the road. This done I climbed up on to the armoured car for a word with the squadron leader, and was shocked to find him sitting dead in his seat, killed instantaneously with a bullet through the heart. There were a lot of German officers about, some of whom turned truculent, refusing to give up their pistols to the partisans. I suspected the shot may have been fired by one of these from inside a house when the squadron leader was standing up in his turret.

Another armoured car came up to take the lead and off we went again, Deluca and I smoking quite good German cigars. We were now not more than two miles from Belluno. Half a mile further on, as we were approaching another lot of transport, a hand grenade was thrown at the leading car and heavy firing broke out. Deluca and I leapt out of our car and made a dive for the roadside, where, cigar in hand, we lay like the centipede 'distracted in a ditch considering how to run'. Meanwhile, those in the armoured car, not liking the look of things, decided to retire. They backed on to our little Fiat, mauled it, and then went off down the road with it wrapped drunkenly round their rear towing hook. Deprived of our transport, alone in an unfriendly world, Deluca and I turned tail and legged it down the ditch back to the houses where there was the 88 mm.; the Germans meanwhile, having manned a 20 mm. Breda in the middle of the road, fired indiscriminately in all directions. There were several abandoned cars about. We managed to start one and so escaped down the road to where the armoured cars had halted. The affair now took on the proportions of a battle. The Germans advanced and remanned the 88 mm., which we had foolishly neglected to destroy, and so forced the armoured cars to retire still further. The Rifle Brigade took up a defensive position covering the 'T' junction, and a battery of 25 prs., which had arrived from Vittorio, went into action south of the river. The Colonel commanding the column was also now on the spot and made his H.Q. at the inn by the 'T' junction where a portentous array of vehicles soon assembled—armoured cars, White Scout cars, jeeps, and Bren carriers. As luck would have it, this was the first fine day. The R.A.F. were out in force and had already put in some good work on the enemy transport near Belluno, from which several columns of black smoke were now ascending. It was painfully obvious that in the confused situation the concentration at the 'T' junction was the sort of target that would not be given the benefit of any doubt, and sure enough, in spite of recognition strips and coloured smoke signals, it was presently attacked. One man was killed, two or three wounded, and six of the precious vehicles set on fire.

In the afternoon the Germans developed an infantry attack to open the road. There was an excellent observation post for our guns from the roof of the 'albergo' where the H.Q. were located, and the attack petered out under the accurate artillery fire of the Essex Yeomanry battery. The Germans then sent in a flag of truce. That night 4000 of them surrendered, and by eleven o'clock next morning, 2 May, the stubborn remnant in Belluno had laid down their arms.

That morning three of us went on another of Deluca's motorcycles into Belluno, for so long the goal of our ambition. I should like to report that we were wrenched from the cycle by an enthusiastic crowd, borne shoulder-high to the Piazza del Duomo, and there crowned with laurel wreathes to the prolonged and deafening 'Viva's' of the assembled multitude. We were too soon for that. The streets were nearly empty, most of the people wisely remaining indoors until the situation cleared. The few we met smiled happily. In the Piazza some partisans were proudly guarding an ever-growing mob of bewildered Germans, and in the Prefettura, a beautiful fifteenth-century building with arcaded windows from which hung an enormous Italian flag, the Committee of Liberation, the newly elected Prefect, the head of the Administration (our friend Tissi), and Rudi the new Mayor, were already making headway against a sea of troubles.

There we shall leave them. The rejoicing came later when the citizens of Belluno showed in full measure their pride in their partisans and their gratitude to us. But before that happy day there was a miserable interregnum of weeks of weary waiting until the tens of thousands of Germans, who had been trapped by the partisans in the Belluno Zone, and had laid down their arms, were at last deprived of them; when the camps of armed and slightly arrogant 'Tedeschi' with their looted Italian vehicles, horses, and food, were broken up; and when the partisans had attended their last parade.

It is only justice to the partisans that a considered opinion of their worth should be given, for in a few liberated countries, and to a lesser degree in Italy, the misguided actions of some have tarnished the reputation of the whole resistance movement. It is, I imagine, generally agreed that the speed and totality of the German collapse in Italy was in no small measure due to the partisans. In the last week of the war they occupied Milan, Genoa, Turin and other towns without waiting for the arrival of the Allies. They blocked all the roads to the northeast so that tens of thousands of Germans struggling to escape to Austria had to surrender where they stood. Had they done nothing else, the time, the trouble and the lives given by the Allies to augment the resistance movement were amply repaid. But this was not all. For eighteen months the movement had been a running sore in the side of the Germans and Fascists, and in addition had sent out invaluable intelligence, sustained many thousands of our prisoners, and helped hundreds of airmen to escape.

Owing mainly to the excellent Italian road system the occupying and holding of large tracts of country as was done in Yugoslavia, and to a certain extent in Albania, was never possible. The partisans themselves were slow to discover this; not in fact until after September 1944 when the Germans found the partisans just where they wanted them—in large concentrations—and were able to do with them pretty much as they pleased, did they alter their tactics. Militarily the faults of the partisans were due to lack of experience and not of the will to fight—experience of any kind of fighting was lacking in most cases, and few of the leaders, only some of whom had been in the army, had experience of guerrilla warfare. In September they were thinking in terms of fixed positions instead of hit-and-run tactics; nor did they realise that in fulfilling that mistaken role the lack of training, the lack of any weapons other than personal arms or of any means of communication other than runner, and their isolation which inevitably exposed them to encirclement, all precluded a successful defence.

The quality of brigades and battalions was very uneven. Naturally in an irregular, improvised army, without training or tradition, nearly everything depends on individual leaders. In some units the care of weapons was excellent, in others bad. Some men were brave to the point of recklessness, others the reverse. They were often unduly elated or correspondingly depressed. Like our own men, but with more excuse and more opportunity, they believed every rumour. They grossly exaggerated their own losses and those of the enemy, especially the latter. No 'rastrallamento' was ever carried out by less than several thousand Germans who invariably incurred losses which ran into hundreds. Many of the leaders even were subject to this fault and would unthinkingly pass on unlikely or obviously untrue reports.

But when I recall these trivial faults, by no means peculiar to them, I recall too the conditions in which they served which were peculiar to them alone. An Italian who became a partisan had to suffer greater hardships and run greater risks than those incurred by regular troops. Capture almost invariably meant death, with the probability of being tortured first and hanged afterwards. If they were badly wounded their chances of getting away were slim, while for those who did get away medical care was rough and ready. A successful action usually meant reprisals during which friends or relatives might be shot, hanged, or at the best imprisoned, their houses and villages burnt. Food was monotonous, clothing was insufficient, boots bad, cleanliness nearly impossible. They could have no pay, leave, amusements or mail from home; the only newspapers they saw were Fascist; there were no canteens, cigarettes and tobacco were either scanty or unobtainable. There was no organised training or even sufficient work to counteract the long weeks of waiting and inactivity. In short, everything that makes life tolerable for the regular soldier, that sustains his morale in quiet times and in battle gives him a reasonable chance of survival, was absent from the life of the partisan. Nor was this all. There were no periods of rest for the partisans. They lived under the constant strain of surprise, betrayal or attack; the G.A.P. who lived in villages never dared to sleep in houses. And most serious of all, perhaps, were the political fears and jealousies, existing even in their own formations, and the suspicion that for them the end of the war might only be the beginning of fresh political strife.

It is with all this in mind that the partisans must be judged. With no Garibaldi to inspire them with his dauntless and unquenchable spirit the men of northern Italy took the course that he would have taken on the terms he himself had offered to their forebears: 'I offer neither pay, nor quarters, nor provisions: I offer hunger, thirst, forced marches, battles, and death.' Such were the terms on which they served. That they held together indissolubly during the hard winter months, and were able and willing to give of their best when the time came, is some measure of their determination, self-sacrifice, patriotism, and of their rekindled ardour for the cause of freedom.

H. W. TILMAN

The Collected Edition

For the first time since their original appearance, all fifteen books by H. W. Tilman are being published as single volumes, with all their original photographs, maps and charts. Forewords and afterwords by those who knew him, or who can bring their own experience and knowledge to bear, complement his own understated writing to give us a fuller picture of the man and his achievements. A sixteenth volume is the 1980 biography by J. R. L. Anderson, *High Mountains and Cold Seas*. The books will appear in pairs, one each from his climbing and sailing eras, in order of original publication, at quarterly intervals from September 2015:

Sep 2015	Snow on the Equator
	Mischief in Patagonia
Dec 2015	The Ascent of Nanda Devi
	Mischief Among the Penguins
Mar 2016	When Men and Mountains Meet
	Mischief in Greenland
Jun 2016	Mount Everest 1938
	Mostly Mischief
Sep 2016	Two Mountains and a River
	Mischief Goes South
Dec 2016	China to Chitral
	In Mischief's Wake
Mar 2017	Nepal Himalaya
	Ice With Everything
Jun 2017	Triumph and Tribulation
	High Mountains and Cold Seas

www.tilmanbooks.com